Edmond O'Brien

Edmond O'Brien
Everyman of Film Noir

DEREK SCULTHORPE

McFarland & Company, Inc., Publishers
Jefferson, North Carolina

Also by Derek Sculthorpe
and from McFarland

*Claire Trevor: The Life and Films
of the Queen of Noir* (2018)

*Brian Donlevy, the Good Bad Guy:
A Bio-Filmography* (2017)

Van Heflin: A Life in Film (2016)

Frontispiece: Publicity still of O'Brien at home, 1947 (Universal).

ISBN (print) 978-1-4766-7443-8
ISBN (ebook) 978-1-4766-3379-4

Library of Congress cataloguing data are available

British Library cataloguing data are available

© 2018 Derek Sculthorpe. All rights reserved

No part of this book may be reproduced or transmitted in any form or by any means, electronic or mechanical, including photocopying or recording, or by any information storage and retrieval system, without permission in writing from the publisher.

The front cover image is of Edmond O'Brien in *D.O.A.*, 1950 (United Artists Corp./Photofest)

Printed in the United States of America

*McFarland & Company, Inc., Publishers
Box 611, Jefferson, North Carolina 28640
www.mcfarlandpub.com*

Acknowledgments

Grateful thanks to Tommy Ivo. Thanks also to Patrice M. Kane, Jocelyn at the Columbia University Archives and Bill W. Santin. And thanks as always to my family for their constant support and encouragement.

Table of Contents

Acknowledgments v
Introduction 1
1. Tiger 3
2. Broadway to Hollywood 8
3. A Star of Tomorrow 16
4. *Winged Victory* 24
5. Radio Intermission 29
6. Postwar Noir 35
7. For the Love of Olga 42
8. "I want to report a murder." 50
9. *711 Ocean Drive* 59
10. *Between Midnight and Dawn* 65
11. An Easterner Goes West 70
12. Broadway Interlude 83
13. Turning Points 86
14. Working with Ida 93
15. O'Brien the Director 102
16. An Oscar for Oscar 109
17. Family Man 115
18. Television: The Early Days 122
19. After Oscar 128

Table of Contents

20. Johnny and Sam   140
21. New Directions   148
22. A Last Hurrah   161
23. The 1970s   169

Epilogue   176

Appendix: Edmond O'Brien's Credits Across All Media   179

Chapter Notes   203

Bibliography   222

Index   227

Introduction

> I always wanted to be somebody else. Not just one person, but a lot of people.—Steven H. Scheuer, "Edmond O'Brien Wanted to Act," *Citizen Reporter,* Ossining, New York, February 15, 1960, 9

Edmond O'Brien, one of the most admired actors of his time, had a versatility matched by few. He had an ability to capture the postwar anxiety and sense of powerlessness of the ordinary individual in a series of movies that have become iconic. In noir films, he was often the victim of circumstances, most memorably in *D.O.A.* which began with him reporting his own murder. He suffered agonies in films such as *The Hitch-Hiker* and as the protagonist of George Orwell's *1984.* He even suffered as a sweating press agent in Joseph L. Mankiewicz's bitter Cinderella tale *The Barefoot Contessa,* and was rewarded with a much-deserved Academy Award. The typical O'Brien role in noir cast him as a desperate man who is trapped by circumstances, or by his own nature, in a situation which is beyond his control and from which there is no escape.

But noir was only one part of his repertoire: He could be effective in comedies, westerns, science fiction, fantasies, war films and his beloved Shakespeare. His long and highly successful radio and television career should not be overlooked. In addition, it is often forgotten that he was a stage actor of some reputation before he cast his lot with Hollywood. The verse of the immortal Bard retained a special resonance for him and it was a perpetual joy for him to act in his plays on stage with some of the great Shakespearean players of his time including Laurence Olivier and John Gielgud. O'Brien even recorded an album of romantic poems which revealed a far less familiar side of him.

His career followed a similar trajectory to other actors of his generation. After beginning on stage, he gravitated to Hollywood in its glory days and stayed to see its decline and the rise of television. In his early years he proved adept at light romantic roles but in the postwar period he became associated with noirs. Usually his noir characters were embittered, unhappy individuals who were cynical and world-weary. Often, they reflected his own Irish-American background with names like Reardon, Conroy and Muldoon. They might easily be on the right or the wrong side of the law or hovering ambiguously in between. He also showed a natural penchant for comedy, although sometimes of the most mordant kind, and humor informed his work. His character studies were never all one thing: They were not all bad and not all good, but they were human. Even an out-and-out rotten apple like Barney Nolan in *Shield for Murder* could have been a force for good if he had not been overwhelmed by the greed in his own nature. O'Brien invested all his character studies with honesty and, like a mirror to life, showed the failings of ordinary human beings, beset by weaknesses and frailties, trying to live as best they can.

This is the first book dedicated to O'Brien and I feel that this tribute is long overdue. My aim is to shine a light on his overlooked contribution to film and the art of acting. I hope this work will aid the wider cause of cinema studies and prove useful for those interested in the Golden Age of Hollywood and the mid–twentieth century history of entertainment. I was able to see all his films, a fair proportion of his television work and hear many of his radio programs. Most of his films are readily available, as I indicate in the filmography. About a third of his radio broadcasts are extant but the survival rate of his 1950s television plays is not good. I would like to bring attention to the extensive annotated appendix, which provides detailed information of his known credits across all media. I took great pains to ensure the accuracy of this and hope it will provide the major point of reference for all fans of the actor. He might never have been a star but he was an intelligent and instinctive actor who conveyed the hopes and fears of Everyman and as such, the best of his work should last.

❖❖ 1 ❖❖

Tiger

> Maybe it's because it's a kind of dog-eat-dog existence, involving the survival of the fittest—but whatever it is, the New York child seems to have a quicker, spryer, more alert mind than the country kid. He cuts through the deadwood of an issue and gets to the meat. He thinks fast and is impatient with slowness.
>
> —Mel Heimer, "My New York," Peekskill, New York, *Evening Star,* March 20, 1953, 15

Edmond Joseph O'Brien was born on September 10, 1915, in Manhattan, the youngest of seven children of James Alfred O'Brien and Agnes Bridget (nee Baldwin). James had been born in Waterford in the south of Ireland in 1873, the son of James O'Brien and Winifred nee Cunningham.[1] Edmond's grandfather James was a farm laborer who had previously lived in the United States from about 1860. The whole family resettled there permanently from 1888 onwards. The name O'Brien has a long and rich history stretching back to Brian Boru in the tenth century, when he was proclaimed King of All Ireland. His descendants ruled as kings of Munster and later kings of Thomond.[2] The name is chiefly associated with counties Clare, Waterford, Tipperary and Limerick.[3]

Edmond's mother Bridget Agnes Baldwin married James O'Brien on November 23, 1898, in Manhattan.[4] Like her husband, she had been born in County Waterford; Edmond said that they were both from the same village, Tallow (pronounced "Talla").[5] She arrived in the U.S. with her family around 1890 at the age of 16. Her parents, Michael Baldwin and Mary Anne Tobin, married in Fermoy, Cork, in 1871.[6] Coincidentally, both Baldwin and Tobin are of Norman origin; Tobin is the Irish version of St. Aubyn, and is most prevalent in Kilkenny and Tipperary.[7]

In New York, Michael Baldwin worked as an office clerk. Like many

Irishmen he prized education and all his children attended college; two of his daughters became teachers and his son Francis W. Baldwin was a physician who had a private practice. At one time he was also the medical director of St. Vincent's Hospital, one of the oldest hospitals in the city. Agnes' cousin the Rev. Dr. Richard H. Tobin was rector of the Church of the Assumption in Peekskill, New York. In his will he left his chalice and some books to James O'Brien.

James O'Brien was a wholesale butcher by trade. Edmond did not remember him and so naturally spoke of him infrequently. He once joked, "My father used to go back to Ireland every year, come home to New York and have another O'Brien, and then make another visit to Ireland."[8] The eldest of the siblings was James F. (born 1900); then followed Winifred C. (1902), Agnes Mary (1904), Katherine G. (1906), Kathleen Marjorie (1912), Liam Francis (1913) and Edmond.[9] Their father died on February 8, 1919, at the age of 46 when the family was living in the Bronx. Edmond later recalled: "I was born in the Bronx and the family moved to Manhattan, where we lived at 114th Street, in Washington Heights, and 96th Street and Central Park West."[10] The indomitable Agnes O'Brien kept her family together and raised the children alone. It was said that she retained "a lot of the old country humor and wisdom."[11] She proved remarkably hardy and lived to be 94.

The O'Briens were a close-knit family, especially so after the early death of the father. The family all pitched in and little Eddie did his bit: He was a delivery boy, bank messenger, sold books, made sandwiches, carried washing for a Chinese laundry, anything to swell the family kitty.[12] Growing up, Eddie was closest to his brother Liam, who was only a couple of years older, and his sister Marjorie. His elder sister Agnes was a schoolteacher, another sister worked in a bank and the eldest son was a telephone engineer. Two of their unmarried aunts, Elizabeth and Mary Baldwin, were teachers; Elizabeth taught in a public school and Mary was an art teacher in a High School. Elizabeth took an interest in her nieces and nephews; she encouraged young Eddie in his ambitions and could be said to have first piqued his interest in the stage when she took him to see Broadway shows.

Like others in the neighborhood, Eddie spent much of his childhood playing in the streets. Improvised sports were the order of the day. He played stickball, using a broom handle and a high bouncing rubber ball. He later reminisced, "You were pretty good if you could hit it over the 6th Avenue El. My brother Liam hit it there." He always loved baseball and vividly remembered the day he got his first pair of spikes. "We played baseball in Central Park," he recalled. "Our team was named the Emeralds, and it was composed of many nationalities. They were a good bunch of boys."[13] Eddie and Liam later named one of their production companies Emerald Productions; another was named Tiger, Eddie's childhood nickname.

At one time, the family lived on 113th Street opposite the famous magician Harry Houdini. Edmond was fascinated with magic like many a ten-year-old boy, and Houdini taught him a few basic tricks and gave him some useful tips. Before long the budding entertainer was giving magic shows at settlement houses and in the basement of the family home, charging the local kids ten cents apiece to see him as "Neirbo the Great." Neirbo was O'Brien spelled backwards. "Nobody ever asked for their money back," he recalled, "for the very sound reason that the O'Briens were very handy with their fists and were not partial to parting with an easy penny." Edmond once asked the great magician if he could really make people disappear. "It's this way," he replied, "If you ever want to be an actor. If you ever give a bad performance, Houdini will make you disappear forever."[14] Edmond obviously took his words to heart because he never gave a bad performance.

Life was sometimes tough for Eddie and his immediate siblings, but the family always appreciated the value of education. Like his brothers, Eddie attended St. Thomas Parochial School on West 118th Street.[15] Liam progressed to Fordham University and Manhattan College. Marjorie also went to Fordham; she showed early promise as a singer and studied under Millo Picco of the Metropolitan Opera. She made her singing debut in 1945 but gave up that career when she married.[16]

Eddie's love of being somebody else manifested itself early: "When I was a delivery boy, I learned that I could get a big tip if I faked a limp or a speech impediment," he recollected. "I guess that was the beginning of my professional career."[17] As a boy of ten, he knew that he wanted to be an actor and never desired to be anything else.[18]

In 1932, the family spent the summer in Westport, Connecticut. This was fortuitous for the teenage Eddie, who joined a semi-professional fringe group at the Westchester Playhouse. Writer Lawrence Langner saw him in a production there and offered him a part in a tryout for his play *Lady Godiva* starring Violet Heming. It was a minor role: He helped bring the lady's bathtub on stage. Even so, he managed to make an entrance when he staggered on, then stumbled over and fell into the bath, much to the amusement of his entire family who were in the audience.[19] It was just as well the lady wasn't in it at the time.

He recalled his impetus to act: "I suppose I wanted to show off or something. In school, if I had to make a speech and didn't know it very well, I'd do impersonations instead. I went to Fordham, but after a month I decided there was no use kidding myself any longer. My wanting to act always ruined my efforts towards good scholarship."[20] He studied English literature during his brief career at Fordham.[21] (The University has no record of him at all.[22])

Eddie had "a short try at banking" as a clerk; during high school, he briefly worked as a runner for the First National Bank.[23] For a month, he was a counterman at Chock Full o' Nuts at 50th and Broadway.[24] He then managed to win a scholarship to the Neighborhood Playhouse School of the Theater on 46th Street. For his audition, he gave a recital from *Hamlet*. Many other famous names passed through the school, including Betty Garrett, who was there the same year as Richard Conte. Garrett recalled, "Lorne Greene and Edmond O'Brien were in the class ahead of us. Everybody was just so interested and committed, so determined to have careers in the theater, that the atmosphere was infectious."[25] In 1935, O'Brien was among those in the first class taught by famed "method" teacher Sandy Meisner at the school. At that time, Margaret Webster taught Shakespeare and there were classes for all shades of drama. It was a two-year course and the hours were nine a.m. until six p.m. True to form, Edmond put in extra time in order to study Shakespeare further. "At night, I was with the Columbia Laboratory Players, graduate students," he recalled. "They did some of the best Shakespeare until Gielgud."[26] Edmond took part in numerous productions with the Columbia Players at Morningside Heights, where he appeared as Horatio in *Hamlet* and played the title role in *Othello* at the age of 18.[27]

In his second year at the Neighborhood Playhouse, he was given the lead in J.M. Barrie's perennial Edwardian favorite *The Admirable Crichton*.[28] He played a wide variety of roles during his student days including such comedies as *I'll Leave It to You* by Noël Coward. Other works included the eighteenth century play *A Trip to Scarborough* by Richard Brinsley Sheridan and Shakespeare's *The Tempest*. Critics sometimes found fault with the lack of technical know-how among the group but commended them for their enthusiastic and innovative approach to the classics. For instance, they gave a modern dress version of Oscar Wilde's *Lady Windermere's Fan*, in which O'Brien played Lord Windermere.[29]

Young Edmond was in his element. He had found the profession he loved and once remarked that he "read a play a day then," just for fun.[30]

The young students were all keen to learn by experience and earn a few dollars in the process. "Once an Italian group played Broadway," he recalled, "and they sent over to us for actors to fill in as extras at $2 a performance. The play was about Christopher Columbus' discovery of America. Well, we were such eager beavers that we forgot it was an Italian-language play. We loused everything up." In the big scene where they came in sight of land, someone said "Oh boy, that's land ahead," and "the Italian audience howled."[31]

❖❖ 2 ❖❖

Broadway to Hollywood

> For sheer acting fun, to enjoy yourself, the theater is the place.—Gene Handsaker "Sights and Sounds from Hollywood," *The Leader Republican,* Gloversville and Johnstown, New York, April 14, 1951, 4

Edmond spent his summers working in stock companies in Roxbury, Massachusetts, and Yonkers, New York.[1] At Yonkers, in the summer of 1936, he played a short season with a group under the management of Elizabeth Miele at the Urban Playhouse, Waverly Terrace Auditorium.[2] The repertory included the comedies *Meet the Wife* and *Best Years,* described as a domestic tragedy.[3] The 20-year-old O'Brien tended to be well down the cast list, but he made a showing in the popular old mystery melodrama *The Bat.* In that he played a bank clerk and fiancé of the leading lady, and he is accused of absconding with bank money. A local reviewer noted that he "added to the success of the play."[4]

In September 1936, O'Brien celebrated his twenty-first birthday with his first Broadway role. The production was Robert Turney's Greek drama *Daughters of Atreus,* the female lead was Eleanora Mendelssohn, and featured among the cast was Maria Ouspenskaya, a Russian actress who co-founded the School of Dramatic Art in New York. She later became a familiar movie character actress who popped up in several horror films. The play itself was not judged a hit; one of the leading Broadway critics felt that the cavernous 44th Street Theater was a poor choice of venue and said the production was "botched."[5] O'Brien played a minor role as Pylades, who "night after night tried unsuccessfully to dissuade Orestes from committing matricide."[6] Despite the small size of the role, the director Guthrie McClintic nevertheless noticed O'Brien in *Daughters of Atreus* and cast him as the second gravedigger and Marcellus in his version of *Hamlet.* It was a notable production in which John Gielgud played Hamlet, to great acclaim; it was his first Broadway success. *Hamlet* was O'Brien's favorite Shakespearean play. "I practically knew the part before rehearsals," he commented, "for Shakespeare had been my diet for a long time."[7] He considered the Bard fundamental to an actor: "I sincerely believe that a comprehensive study of Shakespeare is the best basic training for not only an acting career, but for every other profession in which use of the voice is required."[8]

He spent his summers back at the Westchester Playhouse in Connecticut and made a big impact as a suspicious gardener in Dorothy L. Sayers' murder-mystery *Busman's Honeymoon* in 1937. The locals were still talking about his portrayal a year later.[9]

In September 1937, O'Brien was cast in a minor role in Maxwell Anderson's comedy *The Star Wagon* at the Empire Theater. The young actor was quite in awe of its iconic star Lillian Gish and relished the experience of working with her. "You could sense the love in the audience from the start," he recalled. "Lillian Gish was very professional. I never saw her offstage. I only saw her at the theater. She was always on time, and line perfect, which was a lesson for all of us. She knew our names and she always said good night to us, as we were leaving. I know this might seem an odd thing to say, a star to remember the names of the minor players. I always thought she was royalty."[10] Burgess Meredith had the dominating role in the play and Russell Collins stood out in the cast. It was, according to many viewers, "beautifully staged and acted" but contained "nothing much that is either new or startling."[11]

Orson Welles gave O'Brien his biggest break: "He let me play Marc Antony when I was 22 years old," recalled Edmond.[12] It was an act of faith he never forgot. Although Welles was only four months older than Edmond, he was already a well-established figure in the theater (an actor, innovator and facilitator) after having entered the Gate Theater in Dublin at age 16 and grandly announced himself as a Broadway star. The stage manager didn't believe him but was struck by his bravado and the audition he gave. Welles was a force of nature who impressed many in the same way. His work with the Mercury Theater brought him acclaim and controversy in equal measure, and he thrived upon it. His modern dress version of *Julius Caesar* was praised for its boldness by many—but by no means all—critics. Some drew parallels with the rise of Hitler. Welles' inventive use of light and mastery of stage technique was remarked upon by one observer who wrote; "The stage effects were done entirely by means of shadows and cones of light, dark figures move incessantly across the scene making one conscious that the fate of millions is in the hands of a few. It is a truly exciting experience." Another reviewer hailed the play as "at once the most novel and outstanding box office hit of the current New York theater season."[13]

O'Brien received good reviews for his interpretation of the role, although many emphasized his youth. One reviewer commented; "Edmond O'Brien, a young actor, almost too young for Marc Antony, nevertheless exhibits moments of real passion."[14] One of the finest critics of the era, Harold V. Cohen, understood the significance of Welles' vision and especially appreciated O'Brien's contribution: "The Marc Antony of Edmond O'Brien is full in stature and rich of tongue, and the oration at the bier of Caesar has seldom if ever been delivered so stirringly. It must have moved even the ghosts of all the Marc Antonys to rousing cheers."[15]

O'Brien's success in the *Julius Caesar* road tour did not bring him instant success. Back in New York, he still had to do the rounds of agents' offices looking for work, which could be frustrating and demoralizing. Once, when waiting for an audition, he leafed through a copy of Ben Hecht's short story "Actor's Blood" and noticed a derogatory reference to a character who was acting "like a road company Marc Antony." "What a blow that was to me," O'Brien quipped, "the greatest road company Marc Antony of all time."[16]

O'Brien once spent three days waiting in an outer office to see producer Jed Harris. When he finally got in, Harris was standing at the window feeding the pigeons. He turned to O'Brien as he entered and said, "You're just the man I need. Go down to the corner and get me a loaf of stale bread to feed the birds."[17]

In 1938, O'Brien played Healy in a road tour of the historical play *Parnell*, which gave him his first shot at directing. He also appeared in the religious drama *Family Portrait*, a retelling of the story of Jesus transposed to a pastoral American setting. He directed a cross-country tour of Irwin Shaw's powerful *Bury the Dead* which ended at the Royal Alexandra Theater, Toronto, Canada.[18] On his return to America, he played the title role in a special production of Ferenc Molnar's *Liliom* in Washington, D.C. It was all vital experience.

In the summer of 1938, he returned to Westchester where he played leading roles in such plays as the college drama *Fool's Hill*.[19] He appeared in most productions that summer season. He played opposite the young Swedish actress Uta Hagen in *Susannah and the Elders*, a satire of the Utopian communities that grew up in rural America in the early nineteenth century. O'Brien played one of the more rational characters, which a local critic remarked he "personified very effectively."[20] He featured in

The Inner Light, a compelling drama set in a Budapest asylum for the blind. An observer noted; "An exceptionally vivid characterization is given by Edmond O'Brien as a youth who has newly gone blind and is unable to reconcile himself to life."[21]

He was next offered the role of Prince Hal in Maurice Evans' production of *Henry IV, Part I,* which marked O'Brien's return to Broadway. Eddie was a bundle of nerves during rehearsals and was finding it difficult to come to grips with the role. He was so anxious that he sought solace in the peace and quiet of St. Patrick's Cathedral, which he found helped to put everything into perspective for him.[22] His faith often helped him in times of trouble. His notices were among the best he had so far received. *Variety* noted that he was excellent in support.[23] Another critic said that he made "something attractive of Prince Hal."[24] One reviewer commented, "Often Edmond O'Brien has the glow a Prince Hal should: plasticity, color, quick casualness, feeling."[25] The play proved so popular at the St. James Theater that the initial three-week run was extended by a full seven weeks. At that point, to acknowledge the valuable contribution of O'Brien as Hal and Wesley Addy as Hotspur, both actors' names were added in lights on the theater's marquee.[26] Young Edmond was so excited to see his name in lights that, as he recalled, "I dashed to a telephone to tell my family, then walked into the theater and gave the worst performance of my life."[27] Leading critic John Mason Brown roundly praised Evans' production and especially his portrayal of Falstaff; he described O'Brien as "engaging."[28] Most critics were impressed with the company's achievement in doing full justice to one of Shakespeare's finest plays, written at arguably the height of his powers in 1598. Richard Lockridge of *The New York Sun* wrote, "Nowhere along Broadway will you find anything more vivid and alive, or anything directed with a surer touch or acted more superlatively." Lockridge described Prince Hal, who later becomes Henry V, as being "as much at home with his sword on the battlefield as drinking with Sir John in the Boar's Head." He felt that the scenes between Hal and his father were the most moving.[29]

As a result of his portrayal in *Henry IV,* Eddie caught the attention of Hollywood scouts and was offered several film roles, which he declined. An MGM producer tried to tempt him with the offer of a long-term contract without the customary need for a screen test. He turned it down because he said he wished to get another two years' experience on stage before making any films.[30] However, several months later when he was about to begin a summer season with Evans' company at the Masonic Theater in Long Island, O'Brien received an offer from RKO to play

Gringoire the poet in *The Hunchback of Notre Dame* (1939).[31] This time he accepted. The director was the renowned William Dieterle, who had made his name with a string of historical epics. The elaborate set of fifteenth century Paris was created from a contemporary wood engraving on a 15-acre site in the San Fernando Valley.[32] The film was made between August and October 1939, as Europe plunged into war. As has often been noted, 1939 was one of the most notable years in cinema history. The film was instantly recognized as a bona fide horror classic to rival those of

O'Brien as Gringoire with Maureen O'Hara as Esmeralda in a publicity still for the classic horror *The Hunchback of Notre Dame* (1939), O'Brien's film debut.

2. Broadway to Hollywood

Universal. It was made with a vision and bravura that seemed endemic in Hollywood at that time, employing thousands of extras for the crowd scenes. The sheer scale of its ambition was impressive. Charles Laughton was superlative as Quasimodo, with Maureen O'Hara ideal as Esmeralda and a uniformly fine supporting cast, especially Sir Cedric Hardwicke as the evil Frollo. O'Brien's role as Gringoire was less prominent but he made the most of it. He was handsome and lively, entering fully into the fifteenth century spirit. One reviewer wrote that he "could play [the poet] Francois Villon, which is praise indeed."[33] A distinguished New York critic remarked, "The Gringoire of Edmond O'Brien is a colorful and appealing figure,"[34] The screen newcomer was also a hit on the West Coast: Edwin Schallert of *The Los Angeles Times* declared, "Exceptionally interesting and alive is Edmond O'Brien from the Eastern stage. He looks to be a screen discovery."[35]

The film was remarkable for its vivid depiction of the iniquities of its medieval setting—the stark contrasts between rich and poor, beauty and ugliness both physical and moral, and between the best and worst of human nature. The brutality was off-putting to many critics at the time of its release, but now, Dieterle's version is generally viewed as the finest of the many attempts to capture the essence of Victor Hugo's novel. The lively score of Alfred Newman added greatly to the atmosphere and was Oscar-nominated. It cost $1.8m to bring the story to the screen, and because of such outlay it made only $100,000 profit.[36] O'Brien enjoyed working on the movie and marveled at Laughton's portrayal of the hunchback. On a personal level, he said that he found Laughton kind and helpful.[37]

While the film was being made, Edmond was caught speeding by a couple of motorcycle cops. He was still wearing his medieval Gringoire costume and couldn't quite explain why he was driving Orson Welles' car without a license. However, once Edmond showed them the scrapbook of his cuttings he was taking to the studio to show a publicity man, they let him off with a warning.[38]

The net result of his impressive appearance in *The Hunchback of Notre Dame* was the offer of an RKO term contract, which he accepted.[39] This allowed him some leeway to resume his theatrical career because it gave him several months free from film commitments. Flushed with success, he returned to the Broadway stage. His next big production was John Van Druten's *Leave Her to Heaven*. This starred Ruth Chatterton in a much-heralded return to the Great White Way as a young woman unhappily married to a rich but much older man; she takes a younger lover, namely her chauffeur (O'Brien). The lover proves to be the jealous type with tragic consequences all around. The play drew praise from most critics. One wrote that O'Brien "plays the young chauffeur with vigor."[40] But another noted, "Edmond O'Brien, acting very vigorously, held it together up to the halfway point but the occasionally inadequate lines provided unintentionally comic anticlimaxes, then the audience got distracted and started to giggle."[41] Overall, most reviewers agreed that both Chatterton and O'Brien "gave magnificent performances."[42] The play was set in London and the genteel coastal resort of Westcliff-on-Sea in Sussex. The English-born Van Druten was a prolific playwright and achieved perhaps his greatest fame with *I Remember Mama,* which was made into a highly popular film. His other works included *I Am a Camera,* which formed the basis of two films; one had the same title, the other was *Cabaret* (1971). *Leave Her to Heaven* was not among his greatest successes; it was dismissed as "a fragile and sometimes silly drama," and closed after less than a fortnight.[43]

George Cukor suggested the idea for a production of *Romeo and Juliet* starring the couple of the moment, Laurence Olivier and Vivien Leigh. It seemed as though it couldn't miss. They had just eloped and Vivien was the toast of America after her success in the role of Scarlett O'Hara in David O. Selznick's *Gone with the Wind* (1939). Olivier's lavish *Romeo and Juliet* had 21 scenes and an impressive revolving stage. It also had a fine cast including such stalwarts as Dame May Whitty. Despite all the promise, the play was mauled by the critics. Olivier came in for the brunt of the opprobrium; he was accused at the least of giving a muted performance. O'Brien understood why: "He thought it should be Viv's show."[44] None of the cast was spared, and even O'Brien as a "mercurial Mercutio" was dismissed as "a mere coxcomb with a ham walk."[45] In the opinion of one reviewer, he made a complete hash of the famous Queen Mab speech: "To hear Mr. O'Brien recite it, you would never know that it was a thing of imagination, humor and beauty."[46] Another opined, "The role of Mercutio has long been regarded as foolproof, but Edmond O'Brien rushes through it and knocks it into a cocked hat."[47]

Among the cast was a young Cornel Wilde, who played Tybalt. He later recalled that the old stage actors—O'Brien included—never made eye contact during their scenes. Wilde said they would look at his forehead, through his hair or over his shoulder, which, unsurprisingly, he found off-putting. Not everyone agreed with the prevailing negative reception. When the play ran at the Geary Theater, San Francisco, a local critic wrote glowingly of the presentation as a modern and emotional experience. He singled out one of the younger members of the cast for special praise; "Mercutio, as played by Edmond O'Brien, is the equal of both principals," he wrote, "and his death scene is one of the best pieces of acting I've ever seen."[48] Nonetheless, the ill-fated production lasted only 35 performances and closed on June 8, 1940, to the relief of all concerned.[49]

3

A Star of Tomorrow

> Hollywood and Broadway don't mix. You can do one or other, but not both simultaneously.—"Film Contract Forbids Plays," *The Philadelphia Inquirer*, August 22, 1943, 11

After his disappointment over the reception of *Romeo and Juliet*, O'Brien responded to some of the film offers he was receiving. Studios had been impressed by his film debut and the handsome young actor was now in demand. By August 1941, he was named as a runner-up in the "Stars of Tomorrow" annual poll for the *Motion Picture Daily*, not for the first or last time.[1] As early as February 1940, he was given an honorable mention as one of the young actors most likely to win greatest fame in the coming year by no less a group than the U.S. Critics.[2] By then he had only completed one film, so his achievement was all the more impressive.

Described by one noted reviewer as "a merry, unpretentious gambol," RKO's *A Girl, a Guy and a Gob* (1941) marked O'Brien's second screen appearance.[3] He played a bashful shipping office manager, Stephen Herrick, engaged to a snobbish society girl. He blossoms when he comes in contact with stenographer Dot (Lucille Ball), her eccentric family and her fast-talking sailor fiancé Coffee Cup (George Murphy). The film, produced by Harold Lloyd, displayed much of the zaniness for which the silent screen comedian was fondly remembered. It was Lloyd who first spotted O'Brien on the RKO lot and arranged for him to be tested for the role of Herrick. Lloyd was so impressed with the young actor that he talked the studio bosses into giving him a long-term contract.[4] Lloyd kept a close eye on the production and even reportedly "gave many tips" to O'Brien and Ball.[5] In the scene when a woman tries to vamp O'Brien in a club by dropping her handkerchief, Lloyd showed him how to pick up the handkerchief, flick it back to her and keep moving. He did this by using a tiny nail in his shoe.⁶ It was a great piece of quick observational humor which O'Brien did expertly. "If he had broken his stride it wouldn't have been funny," observed Lloyd, who said he had first used the gag in *Welcome Danger* (1929).⁷

Lucille Ball was a fine comedienne and also a good actress. There were some delightful exchanges between them and O'Brien displayed a fine sense of comedy timing, tending to underplay in comparison to many of the near-burlesque performances among the supporting cast. He was endearingly gauche. Some of the best scenes were at the theater when he was continually goaded into asserting himself by his society girlfriend and her haughty mother. The scene where he absent-mindedly looks through his pockets for his theater tickets with the assistance of bystander Irving Bacon proved that O'Brien was a natural comic actor. In some quarters, he was "hailed as a real comedy find" and even compared to a young Lloyd.⁸ He made a hit with most female reviewers including one who wrote, "There is a new actor, handsome Edmond O'Brien with eyes like Franchot

Poster for *A Girl, a Guy and a Gob* (1941), in which O'Brien displayed his penchant for comedy. The film set the template for the kind of light romantic roles he was given in his early career at RKO.

Tone and the possessor of a beautiful speaking voice."[9] O'Brien's salary was $11,500 for the film, about $1000 less than Lucille Ball.[10] It was far more than he was ever likely to earn working in the theater. The leading actors took part in several promotional appearances supervised by producer Lloyd. They appeared on the stage of the Golden Gate Theater and Lloyd made a speech. Afterwards, a Navy recruiting officer appealed for volunteers.[11]

O'Brien was among a handful of young RKO players who were identified at that early stage by Market Research as "most likely to become big ticket sellers" in the coming years.[12] Market Research was a tool then in its infancy but which was later taken up by the leading studios. Hence, his wide-ranging ability was soon recognized and he was touted for a variety of leading roles. He was lined up as a possible replacement for Richard Carlson in the musical comedy *No, No, Nanette* (1940), but Carlson played the part.[13] In addition, O'Brien was considered for the juvenile leads in the romantic light comedies *Mr. and Mrs. Smith* and *Father Takes a Wife*, as well as the social drama *Kitty Foyle*,[14] but he wasn't cast in any of them. He was announced for a role in the war film *Bombardier* (1943) with Randolph Scott but did not appear in it.[15]

Made in 1940 and released the following year, *Parachute Battalion* (1941) was a typical wartime recruiting drama for one of the branches of the services. This was a familiar story of raw recruits from different backgrounds who gel into a fighting force. The scenario had the two leads (O'Brien and Robert Preston) fighting for the same girl (Nancy Kelly). Harry Carey was excellent in support as Kelly's master sergeant father, tough but kindly of course. O'Brien, as the colonel's son with doubts about his own ability, did well despite his youth and the confines of the role; his intensity was noticeable even at this stage of his career when he was not widely known. Some scenes were shot at Fort Benning, Georgia, with help from the personnel of the 501st Parachute Battalion. At one stage, Lucille Ball was slated to play the female lead. O'Brien made several personal appearances at the time of the film's premiere at the Fox Theater, Atlanta, for the 500 men and officers of the 501st. He was also on hand to sign autographs.[16] This followed a parade through the city and a fly-past to the Shrine Mosque by Navy planes from Camp Gorden. In the evening, there was a battalion ball at the municipal auditorium.[17] O'Brien also turned up unannounced midweek at a Variety Club in Atlanta. The wives and sweethearts of the club's members rallied round and held a luncheon in his honor. One of the trade papers reported, "O'Brien made a hit with all present with his charming and unaffected personality."[18]

3. *A Star of Tomorrow* 19

Publicity still of Edmond with his co-star Nancy Kelly from *Parachute Battalion* (1941). In real life the two were married in February, 1941, and divorced in December of the same year.

In real life, O'Brien married his leading lady Kelly, a former child actress. They had first become aware of each other when she was only 15 and they had chaperoned and daytime meetings for some time. They lost contact for a while, during which time she met Irving Cummings, Jr., son of a film director.[19] When she was 18, she and Cummings eloped with the intention of marrying in Las Vegas, but halfway there they got cold feet and decided to ask their respective parents' advice. Naturally, both sets of parents urged caution and advised them to wait a year.[20] During that year, Kelly and O'Brien became reacquainted when they worked on a radio show together. From then on, they were seldom apart and the pattern was set for their relationship. Kelly said,

We fought about everything. Both Eddie and I were in Broadway plays and we saw each other every free moment—between acts, between rehearsals, between meals. We were so in love that we became intensely jealous of each other, and that would start another royal squabble. Usually we'd end up vowing never to see each other again, then two hours later we'd make up, convinced that we couldn't live without each other.[21]

They fell out again and hadn't been speaking to each other for a couple of weeks when they met for dinner and give it another try.[22] On February 19, 1941, they eloped to Yuma, Arizona; they were married at the Church of the Immaculate Conception by the Rev. Arturo Vallve.[23] Edmond was 25 and Nancy was 19. She later said she only agreed to the marriage "to please him."[24]

The marriage ran into trouble almost immediately, and a month later she went home to her mother. They got back together briefly but parted again. "We agreed to separate," she commented; "As far as I know, it's permanent." He too accepted the inevitable. "Things just didn't work out," he remarked. "I still love Nancy but I doubt we can ever patch things up now.

Deanna Durbin and O'Brien in a publicity still for *The Amazing Mrs. Holliday* (1943). Despite a somewhat troubled production, the film was a delight and showed that O'Brien had a gift for comedy.

She moved out last Friday."[25] She filed for divorce in June but they reconciled and a month later the action was dismissed.[26] They frequently quarreled and their marriage was described as volatile. Their final reconciliation ended on Christmas Eve 1941, and she filed for divorce again on the grounds of cruelty. She said that at that time, he "induced her to return to him with promises of 'kindness' but that he broke his pledges." She maintained that he refused to provide her with the "good, solid, substantial home" she craved and instead insisted that they live in hotels. In court this accusation was corroborated by her father.[27]

She was not specific in her charge of cruelty but among other complaints she said that her husband was "continually late for dinner."[28] She asked for "a reasonable share" of his salary and placed his earnings at $4500 a month.[29] Edmond strongly denied her accusations of cruelty and said that she had no legal right to claim alimony because of a previous property settlement which they had both signed. She later waived her right and the suit was uncontested.[30]

On screen, O'Brien was next announced to join Charles Coburn and Dorothy Comingore in the comedy *Unexpected Uncle*, (1941), but was replaced by James Craig.[31] The great French director Julien Duvivier worked at RKO during the war and wanted O'Brien to co-star with Lucille Ball and Charles Laughton in a film version of Ferenc Molnar's *The Play's the Thing*. This was variously retitled *Through the Thin Wall* and *Three Rogues*, but the movie was never actually made.[32] O'Brien was lined up to play a reporter in a planned screen version of Pulan Banks' novel *There Goes Lona Henry*. Banks had enjoyed his greatest success the previous year with the film adaptation of his novel *The Great Lie* (1941) starring Bette Davis. Ginger Rogers was sought to star as Lona, but that project was also abandoned.[33]

O'Brien's next film was the undemanding comedy *Obliging Young Lady* (1942). This was a pleasant-enough time-passer of the kind that proved popular in wartime. Designed as a vehicle for child actress Joan Carroll, it centered on the attempts of Linda (Ruth Warrick), a lawyer's secretary, to shield the child of divorcing socialite parents by taking her to a resort. O'Brien played an aspiring novelist with eyes for Linda; the great comedienne Eve Arden appeared as a reporter. There were the expected misunderstandings but the cast made it a breezy and engaging comedy. Warrick ended up with badly bruised legs because she was on the receiving end of many of the knockabout gags played on her by O'Brien and Carroll. Warrick had her revenge: During one scene on a river bank, she grabbed O'Brien by the feet and tossed him into the water. This was not in the script so the look of surprise on his face as he emerged from the depths was, apparently, real.[34] The film proved to be a hit. A Georgia theater manager reported that the feature "kept the whole house in a continuous laugh."[35] The three leads were due to be teamed again in *Angel Face*. This eventually became *Petticoat Larceny* (1943), but O'Brien had joined the Army Air Force by then and his role went to Walter Reed.[36]

Next came *Powder Town* (1942), a loud comedy about an absent-minded inventor (O'Brien) and a group of foreign agents who try to steal his idea about a new kind of explosive. Victor McLaglen in full bruiser mode played O'Brien's bodyguard. It was a boisterous comedy without any laughs; O'Brien later said it was his least favorite of all his films. "When I read the story, I told the studio it was no good," he commented. "I left for New York. They wrote and said the script had been re-written so I returned and found all they did was re-type the script."[37] The film was one of the last by director Rowland V. Lee, whose heyday was the 1930s when he directed popular historical adventures such as *The Count of Monte Cristo* (1934) and *Tower of London* (1939) as well as the chiller *Son of Frankenstein* (1939).

Altogether more suitable for O'Brien was *The Amazing Mrs. Holliday* (1943), an engaging wartime propaganda film starring Deanna Durbin as a teacher who escapes from China with nine child refugees. She makes her way to San Francisco where she pretends to be the widow of a commodore in order to let the children have somewhere to stay. O'Brien plays the commodore's grandson with an air of wide-eyed wonder, displaying a charm that matched the situation perfectly. He is so captivated by Durbin that he even gets in on the act at one stage and joins in a chorus of "Mighty Lak a Rose" while shaving. There was great support from the impish Barry Fitzgerald and, with the redoubtable Harry Davenport on hand as the commodore and Arthur Treacher as a butler, the sheer enchantment of the whole thing was complete.

The film was conceived as a sequel of kinds to Durbin's early hit *Three Smart Girls* (1936). Jean Renoir was first assigned as director but after 47 days he was reportedly some ten weeks behind schedule and decided to leave the project. Producer Bruce Manning replaced him at the request of Durbin. "I wasn't good at this genre," recalled Renoir, "and so it was better for the film to be shot by people more familiar with it than I was." The studio saw Durbin's films as money in the bank and didn't want any tampering with a successful formula. "Even a smile, a wink, was discussed by ten people around a green rug," observed Renoir. "It was difficult for me to work with such seriousness."[38] Nonetheless, there was great rapport

The Amazing Mrs. Holliday (1943) was an engaging Deanna Durbin musical with a fine cast of character players. O'Brien played the romantic lead to effect opposite Durbin. With Harry Davenport (*right*).

on set between the actors, and O'Brien enjoyed immensely working with the old pros who taught him a few tricks of the trade. It was such a cozy film, a million miles from the kind of movie with which he would later be associated, but he seemed as enchanted by it and by Durbin as her many fans. It was O'Brien's last completed film before his war service.

❖❖ 4 ❖❖

Winged Victory

> There is no question that Mr. Hart captured much of the gallantry and pathos of youth rushing towards dangerous adventures with surface enthusiasm and inner dread.
> —Bosley Crowther, quoted in *Halliwell's Film Guide* (London: Guild Publishing, 1983), 902

After his breakup with Nancy, handsome Edmond was one of Hollywood's most eligible young divorcees and unsurprisingly he had many dates. In the spring of 1942, he met the beautiful French actress Michele Morgan, who spent a lot of time with him on the set while he was making *The Amazing Mrs. Holliday*.[1] He described her as "the only girl with a spiritual quality I've met in Hollywood."[2] She married actor William Marshall in September of the same year.[3] O'Brien had dates with many others including socialite Marie Machris,[4] actress-singer Carol Bruce[5] and singer Gertrude Niesen.[6] He was regularly spotted at the usual haunts such as Mocambo's with, among others, Martha O'Driscoll,[7] Ann Miller,[8] Anne Shirley,[9] Claire Trevor[10] and Betty Hutton.[11] At the time he was drafted into the services, he was reportedly going out with Ann Sheridan.[12] During his service, he was said to be smitten with a film extra, Clare Manett.[13]

During the war, O'Brien joined the Army Air Force and started his basic training at the Technical School based at Center No. 9 at Miami Beach, Florida, in January 1943. Here he proved a hit and was soon given the nickname "Jeep" O'Brien. There followed several weeks of combat training, including the expected cross-country runs, assault courses, calisthenics, rifle and tommy-gun training, mess duty, spud-peeling and dishwashing. "It's almost as strenuous as my part in *Parachute Battalion*," he joked.[14] However, he always kept one eye on his acting career. He had begun to make his reputation in Hollywood and many of his films were showing at that time. While in Miami, he took part in a number of radio broadcasts on behalf of the air service on the local WKAT network.[15] He also featured in several episodes of the community program *War Town.*

His first ambition was to become a flyer, after which he set his sights on becoming a gunner. He worked as a radio operator at the Radio and Mechanical School in Chicago. At Truax Field, Wisconsin, he was chosen for officer training, eventually reaching the rank of sergeant. He spent several weeks doing pre-flight training as a gunner but failed to pass his medical and was unable to serve overseas.[16] He claimed that his eye trouble started during his war service: "I suffered hemorrhages in both eyes in World War II," he later said, "I was injured in a plane crash."[17] Whether true or not, he had four eye examinations and was deemed unfit for advancement and sent back to radio operation. It was the first sign of problems with his eyes and he was understandably upset. "I came back to barracks and was pretty low," he said. "And there was an order for me to proceed to New York to try out for this show."[18]

The show was *Winged Victory* and led to great things. Written and directed by Moss Hart, it was described as a "mélange of music, comedy and sentiment" and featured 300 performers drawn from the Air Force.[19] One reviewer described it as "stirring and moving ... a most human play."[20] Among the cast were many young actors who became household names in the following decades, including Karl Malden, Gary Merrill, Lee J. Cobb, Don Taylor and George Reeves. One of them, Barry Nelson, remembered; "It was quite a cast. We were chosen from thousands of Air Force men who tried out for it. The selection was limited to those who had been in show business, since there had to be some starting point."[21] The show spent six months in New York with the personnel billeted together in a hotel that was practically commandeered by the Air Force.

O'Brien played an Everyman, Private Irving Miller from Brooklyn, a married man with a small child. It was a character he admired because he was down-to-earth and his interpretation drew him great praise. His portrait drew the seal of approval from the *Brooklyn Daily Eagle* drama critic, who wrote that O'Brien "makes the winged guy from Brooklyn one of the most moving characterizations that has been seen hereabouts in a long time. O'Brien's Irving is somebody who will make you chuckle with a lump in your throat. This corner is glad that Moss Hart credited him to Brooklyn."[22]

One of the stars of the show was Mario Lanza, with whom O'Brien struck up an immediate friendship. They spent much of their spare time together, and Lanza often visited O'Brien's mother's home in Scarsdale. "I found him so kind to me, my wife, my mother," recalled O'Brien. "He sang 'Danny Boy' for my mother and I didn't ask him to. He said, 'I've got a surprise for your mother,' and Mario with that incredible voice.... If he liked you, the warmth flooded all over the place."[23]

After six months on Broadway, the show toured the country for eight or nine months, visiting air bases nationwide. Despite O'Brien's love of the stage, repetition killed spontaneity. "In the theater," he observed, "after about the fourth week, it becomes a job. The dew is off the rose. The sheer monotony starts to get irritating." Fifteen months with the same show was unsurprisingly boring to the young and restless O'Brien: "If ever I was sick of anything, it was that," he remarked with feeling. When the show's producer-director Hart watched the show after a five-week gap, he was horrified to see what O'Brien had done to the role. Hart said he had made the character into a buffoon. "It's lucky Hart wasn't away a year," quipped O'Brien. "I'd have been playing the part out in the street by then."[24]

During the run of the *Winged Victory* stage show, Edmond went out with several actresses including Betty Garrett, Lois Andrews and heiress Doris Duke, whom he met in New York.[25] When the show reached Philadelphia, Bonita Granville was sweet on him.[26] He later had dates with Jane Nigh and Louise Allbritton.[27]

The 1944 film of *Winged Victory* tapped into the prevailing patriotic mood and proved lucrative for 20th Century–Fox, earning a million dollars at the box office. It was not profitable for the actors who were reportedly paid only one percent of the amount of their previous salary.[28] Most of the cast of the stage show recreated their roles. It was a typical scenario of the era which dealt with the lives and experiences of young recruits to the air service. Viewed today, it does not stand out from all the other films of the same kind. At over two hours in length, the big screen version obviously lost much of the warmth and immediacy of the stage show. There was an attempt to open it out, but the scenes of aircraft and those on the parade ground were too familiar by this stage of the war to hold any surprises. Nonetheless, the film should be appreciated for its effect at the time when it was warmly welcomed across the United States. It summed up the experience of those who fought in the war, embodied many of the values for which they fought, and was of untold benefit to the families of those who were serving. Theater managers were of one accord: According to one in rural Vermont, "Our patrons loved it. Every mother in town who had lost a son in aviation was here to see it and they were so proud."[29] Another in Buffalo echoed the same sentiment: "All in all, a rich emotional experience, and a picture that must be recorded as a triumph."[30] A standout in the cast, O'Brien had one of the main roles, which he invested with

O'Brien was one of the stars of the popular stage show *Winged Victory* (1943–45). He reprised his role in the successful film version made by Twentieth Century–Fox and released in 1944; its poster is pictured.

life and which brought him to the attention of a wide audience. It was also the first time he ever worked for director George Cukor. Cukor asked him about the inspiration for his characterization during filming: "The army deserves the credit," answered O'Brien. "You see, I never lived in Brooklyn but the reason I know this character so well is that I have patterned him after the Brooklyn G.I. Joes I've met in the service."[31]

After the film premiered, the stage show continued for some time; in fact, it was still running after VJ Day. O'Brien did not receive his Army Air Force discharge until December 1945. At one point during the *Winged Victory* stage run, he got into a fight with a fellow cast member. Reports did not say who the fight was with or what it was about, but he received a serious eye injury for which he had to be hospitalized. The eye became infected and it was feared at one stage that he would lose it, but his sight was saved.[32]

❖❖ 5 ❖❖

Radio Intermission

> I'm not hard-boiled except in the studio. My wife would hit me over the head if I tried it.—Erskine Johnson, "In Hollywood: Edmond O'Brien Only Tough in Studio Scenes," *San Bernardino Sun,* December 2, 1950, 4

O'Brien enjoyed a solid radio career lasting about 20 years, from the mid–1930s. He had the ideal voice for the medium and made several memorable appearances, especially a two-and-a-half-year stint as insurance investigator Johnny Dollar in the early 1950s, an enjoyable extension of his noir screen persona.

He made his debut on the medium in the mid–1930s, shuttling between stage work in Connecticut and the CBS studios in New York. He had steady employment in such landmark current affairs series as *The March of Time.* The early days with the *Mercury Theater of the Air* were sometimes ad hoc affairs in which he was called on to play all kinds of roles at short notice. It was stated in a number of his obituaries that he was involved in Orson Welles' infamous "War of the Worlds" broadcast in 1938, and also in some episodes of *The Shadow.* The technology was rudimentary but the performers inventive: "We had no recording or tape," O'Brien recalled. "Did a first show for the West Coast and redid it three hours later for the East Coast. Orson, Martin Gabel and I could do each other's voices. We ate in the basement of CBS. They'd come and grab me, saying Orson ... hasn't shown up and I'd take the script cold and read his part on the air."[1] It was valuable experience and he enjoyed working on those shows but joked that he grew tired of playing drug addicts; "I played so many dope fiends on Orson's radio program, they nicknamed me 'Marijuana,'" he quipped.[2] For all his impressive work on the New York stage, it was actually his radio work which was said to have led to his film debut. Only hours after hearing him on the air, RKO studio executives had him signed and he was on his way to Hollywood.[3]

He played a wide variety of radio parts, including the role of Mortimer in a landmark version of Christopher Marlowe's *Edward II* and John Wilkes Booth in the *Radio Guild Drama* production of Walter Hackett's "The Most Tragic Brutus."[4] He was effective in the unusual and thought-provoking plays of Arch Oboler. In "Crazytown," he played a cowardly bomber captain who wakes to a nightmare world in which he is forced to face the consequences of his actions. He portrayed a man who discovers the dangers of immortality in "Immortal Gentleman." The now-lost episode "The Word" told the story of a young couple who, after a tour of the Empire State Building, discover they are the last people alive on Earth. O'Brien displayed a natural skill of mimicry which saw him imitate public figures of the day, including Adolf Hitler on the *Fight for Freedom* broadcasts. He obviously put a lot into his impression because he once lost his voice imitating der Führer at the time he was working on the film *Powder Town*.[5]

During the war when he was training in Miami Beach, he recorded some dramas commissioned by the Army Air Force and transmitted over the local station WKAT.[6] One of the most interesting of these was an adaptation of Patrick Hamilton's play *Rope*, later made into a famous Hitchcock film.[7] Later in the war, Edmond was a semi-regular on the community-based program *War Town*.[8]

He was effective in several episodes of the highly regarded series *Suspense* including the complex mystery tale "The Blind Spot" and the atmospheric "Muddy Track." There were the expected radio versions of his film hits including *The Killers* and *711 Ocean Drive*. He also had some opportunities to play movie roles that had gone to others, and essayed two of Humphrey Bogart's most memorable parts: Fred C. Dobbs in *The Treasure of the Sierra Madre* with Walter Brennan, and Frank McCloud in *Key Largo*. This latter marked his one and only appearance alongside Edward G. Robinson and Claire Trevor, a great triumvirate of noir.

One of his greatest radio successes was *Yours Truly, Johnny Dollar*, which began life in 1949 on CBS. Dick Powell played the role in the audition show but left to do other projects. The part then went to Charles Russell, who quit after about a year. It was an ideal vehicle for O'Brien and played to his strengths. Dollar was a freelance investigator; "the man with the action-packed expense account." He often employed unorthodox methods but had his own code of honor. The well-written half-hour episodes had all the expected noir elements: shady characters in intriguing situations, plenty of hard-boiled dialogue and lots of alluring dames both good and bad. The wheezy organ accompaniment provided a suitably mysterious ambience. O'Brien made the most of the mordant humor under-

5. Radio Intermission

Yours Truly, Johnny Dollar followed the adventures of a freelance insurance investigator. O'Brien essayed the role for two years from 1950; it proved to be his longest-running and arguably most successful radio series. Above: the cover of a cassette release of two episodes.

lying the scripts. "What do you call a dead husband?" asks a nubile recent widow emerging from a swimming pool in a skimpy costume. "Unlucky, I guess," quips Dollar. The show attracted many familiar actors from the noir genre including Raymond Burr, Ed Begley and Ted de Corsia, who all worked prolifically on radio. O'Brien was well-liked in the role, and explained the appeal of the character: "Johnny's an insurance investigator but we make him human. He makes mistakes. He's not always brilliant and infallible."[9] He enjoyed working on the show but at the same time admitted that he soon got bored playing the same character all the time. Nonetheless, at one stage he tried to generate interest in a television version of the program.[10] The show was popular among his fellow actors; he once joked; "Take George Jessel. He's nuts about the show. He even calls himself Georgie Half-Buck."[11] In a sign of its wider popularity, the series even had a cactus named the "Johnny Dollar" in its honor at the California International Flower Show which O'Brien was happy to accept.

O'Brien stayed with the franchise for 103 episodes, from February 1950 to September 1952, his longest stint on one series in any medium.[12] After he left, John Lund took over. After Lund there were another four actors, including Bob Bailey who played the role for five years. The series disappeared from the network for a year in the mid–1950s, but then it continued until 1962, sustaining its popularity even after the decline of radio generally. Of the estimated 886 shows made, about 720 still exist, including most of the O'Brien episodes.[13] The first attempt at a television pilot, made in 1949, proved unsuccessful.[14] On several occasions, O'Brien came close to making a deal for a TV series. In a 1952 interview he commented, "[Gil] Doud has made each script so that it may easily be transferred to the medium with a minimum of effort. Whether I play the part when the transition comes is another question."[15] Ultimately, he decided against it because he would not have had control over the production: "[There's] no percentage in doing someone else's series," he averred; "that's why I turned down the offer."[16] In the event, it was another decade before CBS made a second television pilot under the title *Johnny Dollar*; it was never shown.[17]

Edmond sometimes appeared with his wife on radio, for instance in plays such as *Blind Alley,* the story of an ex-serviceman and the psychological difficulties of adjusting to life after his experiences. They also guested together on talk shows. He even hoped to net a comedy husband-and-wife detective series with his wife Olga, but nothing came of the idea.[18] He recorded an audition show for *Night Beat,* but the role of the reporter went to Frank Lovejoy.

O'Brien appeared in some intriguing radio plays. He was compelling in the leading role in an adaptation of H.G. Wells' classic short story "The Country of the Blind" for the popular series *Escape.* He was heard regularly on *The Lux Radio Theater* during its ten-year life (1945–55) and on *Mutual Family Theater* over a similar period (1948–57). The *Family The-*

ater had a religious basis and was a broadcasting extension of the Family Rosary Crusade, whose motto was "The family that prays together stays together." One of the stories, "Stopwatch Finale," was written by a priest and concerned a man waiting to be executed at the Riverton "Death House."[19] O'Brien showed remarkable intensity as an agent with a conscience in "Act of Contrition," the tale of an ambitious Pittsburgh girl who will stop at nothing to reach the top as a movie actress. He displayed his natural versatility playing such diverse roles as Robin Hood, Volpone and Richard Dix. His special ability with narration was apparent in Thackeray's "The History of Henry Esmond, Esq." for the NBC University Theater. In "The Star," Ida Lupino played a faded Hollywood actress who seeks to make a return to the screen in ingénue roles. He played the young man who befriends her in a story with distinct echoes of *Sunset Blvd.*[20]

O'Brien had mixed feelings about working on radio. Although he thought it could be fun, he felt it was dissatisfying for the actor. He especially disliked recording transcribed shows which required long timed pauses in which to insert music and effects afterwards. He felt radio lacked spontaneity. "It's the most static of the mediums," he observed. "But working in all of them keeps you on your toes. One technique helps another."[21] An example of this was in his early days when a radio actor gave him some words of advice when he was playing a private investigator questioning a suspect: "Just remember to really *ask* the question." This was something he always remembered on the many occasions when he had to interrogate someone. He also observed how the experts such as Lloyd Nolan did it on screen.[22]

Some of O'Brien's radio broadcasts were later released on record, such as the patriotic recitation "I Am an American," first heard on *The Standard Hour* on September 12, 1953. This was based on a national prize-winning essay, "I Speak for Democracy," written by 15-year-old schoolgirl Betsy Evans from Akron, Ohio. Her words were "developed and adapted" by Adrian Michealis and given a choral-orchestral setting by conductor Carmen Dragon.[23] O'Brien's rendition was later featured on the RCA School Broadcast compilation *Hail, America!* His was the only spoken contribution to the album, which was composed of familiar songs including "The Star-Spangled Banner" and "Battle Hymn of the Republic." He had made an earlier recording of poetry readings for Mercury Records, first released in 1946 as a set of 10" records by the Decca label. *My Beloved* was an enchanting collection of Romantic and twentieth century poets. He displayed a natural facility with love lyrics and once again, his gift for characterization came to the fore. The titles included Elizabeth Barrett

Browning's "How Do I Love Thee," three sonnets by Rupert Brooke, and Edgar Allan Poe's "Annabel Lee." There was some harp accompaniment linking the tracks. The album version was first released in 1950 and was reissued on CD and as a digital download by NAXOS in 2013. For many years his recording was used for diction courses in schools.[24]

He made other recordings, notably *The Red Badge of Courage* by Stephen Crane which was released on Caedmon Records in 1957, with striking cover art by Matthew Liebowitz. This famous Civil War tale was brought to vivid life by O'Brien in his inimitable style. *Billboard* praised his "highly dramatic reading" and further commented that he "brings intensity to the narrative portions and successfully impersonates the varied characters in the dialogue."[25] Several episodes of *Yours Truly, Johnny Dollar* were also released on LP and cassette in the 1970s. Many of O'Brien's recordings are collectibles. They are available digitally from numerous sources online.[26]

❖❖ 6 ❖❖

Postwar Noir

> After the war I came back out here and they had a lot of new guys I didn't know. Nobody knew quite how to use me or gave a damn.
> —O'Brien interview by Earl Wilson, "It Happened Last Night: Clothes Make the Man—and Stars, in Hollywood," *New York Post,* January 13, 1950, 17

With the end of the war, O'Brien was still not widely known in Hollywood, but all that was soon to change with a series of striking movies that have since entered the collective consciousness.

By then he had turned his back on Broadway; his experience in the stage show *Winged Victory* decided him, at least for the short term. In 1943, he signed a contract with Universal in which he stipulated that he would not be able to make any appearances in plays on Broadway. "I was spending so much time riding between New York and Hollywood that the Pullman porters called me by my first name," he quipped. "And I couldn't settle down to one job or the other. Now, with that clause in my contract I'm going to stick to Hollywood because I have to."[1]

At the time he had joined the Army Air Force, several noted his absence from the screen. One was the critic Herbert V. Cohen, who lamented, "The movies have never realized young Edmond O'Brien's possibilities. When I saw him at the Nixon a few years ago as Marc Antony in the no. 2 company of Orson Welles' *Julius Caesar*—O'Brien was only twenty-one then too—I thought he was the finest young acting prospect around at that time."[2] Cohen was one of the foremost critics of the era, although he has seldom been given his due because he didn't work in New York or Los Angeles but wrote for a Pittsburgh newspaper for most of his career. He had a way with words, an independent mind and wrote with great wit and insight. However, O'Brien had been noticed and he was suggested for a number of parts. Lynn Riggs' *Domino Parlor* was originally planned as a starring vehicle for O'Brien by independent producer Marshall Grant. After being deliberated for a couple of years, the project never came to anything.[3] Edmond's first big break came when he landed a key role in director Robert Siodmak's *The Killers* (1946). This was O'Brien's first venture into noir territory and defined his postwar career.

"I wasn't working," he recalled. "One day, Ann Sheridan said, 'Why don't you drop around and see Mark Hellinger?'" He went to Hellinger's office, wearing casual clothes instead of the regulation smart suit. "I put my feet on his desk and somehow got he got the idea I could play the part of the quiet cop in *The Killers*. That did it—it was a great picture and I've been working since."[4]

The Killers took its premise from a short story by Ernest Hemingway, O'Brien's favorite writer.[5] The film version began with the murder of Swede (Burt Lancaster). O'Brien played Reardon, an insurance investigator and the driving force of the narrative; he seeks to learn why a man loses the will to live. Ava Gardner was striking as the ultimate *femme fatale*, and there was sterling work from Sam Levene and a host of familiar faces. Siodmak displayed some deft touches and the script by Anthony Veiller was almost a noir work of art. The diner scene in which Charles McGraw and William Conrad first appear was so full of menace that it sounded like the inspiration for a Harold Pinter play. The cinematography of Elwood Bredell was a key element of the film's success. English-born Bredell worked on *The Amazing Mrs. Holliday* and among his other credits were horror movies such as *The Mummy's Hand* (1940) and the noir *The Unsuspected* (1947). There as a real sense of purpose among all the personnel working on the film, as Gardner recollected: "One thing I especially liked about filming *The Killers* was that Burt and Eddie and the rest of us were in the early stages of our careers, fresh kids enjoying life."[6]

For O'Brien, everything seemed to click into place on that picture, as he observed: "Siodmak and Hellinger gave us a feeling of being part of something important and a sense of what we could do with a scene that gave us extraordinary confidence."[7] The clever use of flashbacks was a notable aspect which gave the film a depth of texture. Events seen from the points of view of different characters at different times gave a more rounded view of the story as Reardon tries to fit together the pieces like a jigsaw puzzle. Despite all the passion, danger and high drama, the noir universe immediately dismisses Reardon's achievement at solving the crime. At the end, his boss informs him that all he has achieved is a saving of a tenth of a cent on each insurance premium.

6. Postwar Noir

O'Brien impressed as an insurance investigator in the terrific noir *The Killers* (1946), which set the tone for his post-war roles.

Hemingway's own reaction to the film was positive; he was used to being disappointed by screen adaptations of his work. According to one witness, "Hemingway watched *The Killers* with a full bottle of gin in front of him. When the movie ended he smiled, held up the still-sealed bottle and said, 'Didn't need it.'"[8] Six cities were chosen for special screenings and previews of the film. Hellinger, Lancaster and O'Brien made visits to Chicago, Pittsburgh, Cincinnati, New York, Detroit and Philadelphia.[9] In addition, there were visits to 14 smaller towns. At a luncheon held at Cincinnati Netherlands Plaza Hotel, Hellinger and O'Brien were guests of honor. Hellinger played a practical joke on O'Brien: When O'Brien arrived at the hotel, he was greeted outside by the sight of a pretty girl holding a sign saying "Welcome, O'Brien." When he got closer, she turned the sign around; it read "Cincinnati loves you, Pat!"[10]

While making the film, he enjoyed a convivial evening with Ava Gardner at Ciro's. After the joint had closed, "night waiters were surprised to see them sitting on the floor as Johnny Desmond and his Orchestra crooned loved songs."[11]

O'Brien was next due to play the other man in *Ivy* (1947) starring Joan Fontaine. However, his role in this unusual Edwardian noir went to Herbert Marshall.[12] O'Brien and Yvonne de Carlo were wanted by producer Joan Harrison for *The Knave of Diamonds,* a proposed film version of the mystery novel by Percy Marks. However, the project did not get past the planning stage. O'Brien hoped to get a really big break and desperately wanted a role in his studio's version of Arthur Miller's *All My Sons* (1948) but lost out to Burt Lancaster.[13] Instead, Edmond's next was *The Web* (1947), a good noir in which he portrayed a lawyer serving as a bodyguard for a wealthy industrialist (Vincent Price) who says his life is threatened. Things go wrong and O'Brien finds himself in an increasingly difficult situation. This superior movie benefited from an incisive screenplay by William Bowers and Bertram Millhauser. The beautiful Ella Raines was suitably ambivalent as the femme in the middle. William Bendix, who underplayed nicely, was coolly laconic as the police inspector and made

Lobby card for *The Web* (1947), a cleverly written noir which starred O'Brien (left and center) as a hapless lawyer who falls for Ella Raines (right). And who could blame him?

great use of the dry humor of the script. "Thanks for nothing!" exclaims a frustrated O'Brien after meeting Bendix for lunch in a bid to try and clear himself; "Any time," says Bendix cheerfully; "Any time at all!" Especially good in support was John Abbott as Price's wary aide.

O'Brien played a rather hapless character who blunders into situations without thinking—a dangerous thing to do in a noir! As Bendix observes, "You know, Regan, for a lawyer, you're none too smart." However, the downright naivety of Regan made the character relatable and endearing. The director of photography was Irving Glassberg, elevated from second cameraman for the occasion. There was some inventive camerawork on show, including a camera at floor level in such a position that Price, Raines, Bendix and O'Brien could all walk around and still be in camera range. Thus, all their reactions could be recorded at the same time.[14] This was the first of three films O'Brien made for director Michael Gordon. The others were *Another Part of the Forest* (1948) and *An Act of Murder* (1948). Gordon made some interesting but often overlooked pictures including *The Secret of Convict Lake* (1951) which might easily be termed a western noir. Blacklisted during the McCarthy years, he was unable to work for much of the 1950s. He returned with a run of Doris Day comedies such as *Move Over, Darling* (1963).

Theater managers labeled *The Web* a sleeper and a crowd pleaser. Notices were generally good and the actors given equal merit. Some reviewers singled O'Brien out for praise, and one of the leading trade papers noted that he "steals top acting honors."[15]

A Double Life (1947) starred Ronald Colman as aging stage actor Anthony John, who is encouraged by his agent to play Othello in Shakespeare's great tragedy. The play is a great success and runs for a year, but the emotional intensity this requires night after night takes a great toll on his psyche. The Moor's dark jealousy begins to infect his thinking and he starts behaving erratically. He begins to suspect his ex-wife of having an affair with press agent Bill (O'Brien). He attempts to kill Bill and his anger leads to tragic consequences. He seems unaware of what he is doing most of the time; the line between what is real and imagined is blurred. *A Double Life* was different from most of the others in the noir genre, and gave Colman the perfect vehicle for his talents. Curiously, the stage, and Shakespeare's plays in particular, were not used elsewhere as the basis for any other works in the cannon. This is surprising considering the darkness of his tragedies with their timeless themes of jealousy, passion, vengeance and honor. O'Brien did fine work as the press agent and Shelley Winters was notable in a good cast as an unfortunate waitress. The film was

Press agent Bill Friend (O'Brien, left) is on the receiving end of Anthony John's (Ronald Colman's) jealousy in George Cukor's unusual noir *A Double Life* (1947).

expertly directed by George Cukor, who made a wide variety of often witty and perceptive films. Alongside popular comedies such as *Born Yesterday* (1950), he also made thrillers including *Gaslight* (1944) and another notable noir, *A Woman's Face* (1941). The *Motion Picture Herald* wrote that *A Double Life* was "at once a character study, a literary work ... a melodrama [and] distinguished entertainment."[16] The story was unusual and the script cleverly handled by Ruth Gordon and Garson Kanin. The film was nominated for a number of Academy Awards, including Best Director and Best Original Screenplay. Colman deservedly won as Best Actor and Miklos Rosza for his excellent score. The luminous cinematography of the prodigious Milton Krasner was, curiously, not nominated.

It was a prestigious production and even though O'Brien had a less prominent role, he was noticed; one of the trade papers critics wrote that he "impresses in the few scenes in which he appears."[17] In one memorable scene, he was almost strangled by the jealous Anthony (Colman). O'Brien admired Colman greatly and found him to be down-to-earth with a fine sense of humor.

O'Brien even appeared in an advertisement for Jergens hand cream in one of the earliest tie-ups between films and product placement. The advert showed a romantic still of Edmond and Signe Hasso with the legend "Women ... as Edmond O'Brien sees them." The caption underneath let it be known that he was "riled by rough hands in a woman" and recommended Jergens Lotion as the best remedy.[18]

❖❖ 7 ❖❖

For the Love of Olga

> Researching a character is the province of the writer. An actor is the emotional instrument who interprets the words of the writer.
> —Charles L. Turner, "*The Long, Hot Summer* to Emphasize Single Episode," *Albany New York Sunday Times-Union,* August 22, 1965, H3

O'Brien had a wide public appeal in the postwar years, and among other accolades he was named the most magnetic star of 1947 by the 3000 members of the Young Women's League of America. It was a special boost to his ego to be voted the most magnetic male by the Young Women's League, which he found amusing. The spokeswoman for the League, Shirley Connolly declared, "All women adore ruggedness. Edmond O'Brien's magnetic appearance and personality most fully stir women's imaginative impulses."[1] Runners-up included opera singer Ezio Pinza and Southern Methodist University football player Doak Walker. The top five on the list were invited to a special dinner in their honor at the Town House in Los Angeles.

In the same year he was acclaimed as one of the Stars of Tomorrow—for the second time—in the annual *Motion Picture Herald* poll, voted for by exhibitors, critics and the public.[2] Competition was at its height in that period with a great many up-and-coming young players. In addition, he was also voted one of the idols of the Boys Clubs of America, on a list headed by General Douglas MacArthur.[3]

He was lined up for the co-starring role in *Black Bart* (1948), but that was assigned to Jeffrey Lynn instead.[4] There were five leading male roles in *Rogues' Regiment* (1948), one of which was first announced for O'Brien, but after numerous changes of personnel, he dropped out of the running.[5]

Another Part of the Forest (1948) was an effective period melodrama

7. For the Love of Olga   43

based on Lillian Hellman's prequel to her acclaimed play *The Little Foxes*. Set in post–Civil War Bolden, Alabama, the story focused on the Hubbard family, presided over with autocratic pride by patriarch Marcus (Fredric March). O'Brien played the eldest son, Ben, who desperately wants to strike out on his own but is constantly thwarted by his father and his own weak nature. Dan Duryea was the younger son, Oscar. Duryea appeared in both this film and the 1941 film version of *The Little Foxes*, but playing a different character. Ann Blyth was the scheming Regina who grows up to be *The Little Foxes*' Bette Davis. Although the earlier film was superlative, it is a shame that it has overshadowed *Another Part of the Forest* so completely. It was the kind of absorbing, well-acted drama that achieved its aims but could never generate the popularity of a contemporary crime drama either then or now. Asked to name some favorites among his films, O'Brien remarked, "I liked the one that didn't make a dollar at the box office—*Another Part of the Forest*... because instead of just getting up and

A prequel to *The Little Foxes* (1941), *Another Part of the Forest* (1948) was a well-made period drama with a fine cast. Left to right: Ann Blyth, O'Brien, Fredric March and Florence Eldridge.

doing dialogue, I had whole scenes to play. It was an actor's picture."[6] (He expressed an interest in emulating the example of March and taking time off from making movies in order to return to the stage at regular intervals.) O'Brien had some problems during filming and one day became frustrated because he could not get the lines. "I blew up on my lines time and time again," he revealed. "Everybody angered me. The usual hangers-on annoyed me. Everything went wrong. I'm so tired of these routines, tired of the people."[7] There were always such days for a perfectionist actor. He received excellent reviews for his portrayal.

After the success of *The Amazing Mrs. Holliday* five years previously, O'Brien was teamed again with the delightful Deanna Durbin in *For the Love of Mary* (1948). This time she was Miss Peppertree, a White House switchboard operator who has an attack of hiccups and is helped out by the president, after which he begins to play matchmaker. In time Miss Peppertree's romantic life becomes so intertwined with politics that it takes several justices of the Supreme Court, the State Department and

O'Brien (*right*) appeared for a second time with Deanna Durbin in *For the Love of Mary* (1948). Don Taylor (*standing*) played a rival for Durbin's affections.

the U.S Navy to sort it out. As usual, this harmlessly silly film was really engineered to provide Durbin with the chance to sing a number of songs, including the sentimental ballads "On Moonlight Bay" and "I'll Take You Home, Kathleen." She also sang "Figaro" from *The Barber of Seville*. O'Brien played one of her three suitors, a Navy lieutenant, and handled the assignment well, looking decidedly dashing in his uniform. Despite the presence of old reliables such as Harry Davenport and Ray Collins, the scenario was too overfamiliar by now to engender much enthusiasm, but it was engaging and a good time-passer for a rainy afternoon. It turned out to be Durbin's final film.

O'Brien next had the starring role in *Fighter Squadron* (1948), a routine World War II adventure directed by Raoul Walsh. There were lots of action sequences and scenes of aerial combat which incorporated unseen footage from the William Wyler-John Sturges documentary *Thunderbolt!* (1947).[8] O'Brien played the maverick fighter ace Major Ed Hardin, to whom control of the squadron is assigned against his wishes. He stood out in the cast, his naturalness and sheer believability before the camera instantly noticeable. The film was a plane-spotter's paradise but rather tiresome for non-war movie fans, involving much repetitive action and a lot of personnel riding to and fro in Jeeps. The use of color tended to heighten the feeling of artificiality, as did the unconvincing "English" background and stock characters. The comedy subplot involving a womanizing sergeant was heavy-handed and seemed to come from an entirely unrelated film. The music of Max Steiner was one of the best things about it. Some of the scenes were filmed at the Oscoda Air Base in Michigan, and Lake Huron doubled for the English Channel. The Army gave full cooperation and soldiers were drafted to play Germans.[9] The locals were shown rushes of the day's filming.[10] The scene where O'Brien jumps from a burning aircraft was filmed partially on location and in the studio where a 35-foot-high platform was constructed and a special boom camera was used.[11] Cast member Walter Reed suffered a broken leg during a wrestling scene involving O'Brien and Robert Stack.[12] The film marked the screen debut of Rock Hudson, who required 38 takes for his one line.[13] While working on the film, O'Brien was sent the unusual gift of a zither from a local fan, and said he would try to learn how to play it.[14]

In a similar vein to *Fighter Squadron*, the dull *Task Force* (1949), a Gary Cooper vehicle concerned with the importance of aircraft carriers in wartime, utilized a lot of newsreel footage. O'Brien was heard but not seen; his was the voice on the radio announcing the Japanese attack on Pearl Harbor. A potentially far more interesting project was *These Many*

Years, based on the war memoirs of Vince Evans, commanding officer of the Memphis Belle. Edmond's brother Liam intended to collaborate with Evans on the screenplay for Warner Bros. but the idea was not followed through.[15]

Since returning from war service, O'Brien's name had been linked with a number of girls, but none of them seemed to be serious. In August 1946, he was reportedly the "secret thrill" of socialite Mollie Netcher.[16] He later had dates with Peggy Knudsen, showgirl Mike Mauree and actress Helena Carter.[17] He sometimes went out with those who were not professional actresses such as Jane Roberts.[18] He also went on dates with, among others, Audrey Totter and Joan Caulfield.[19]

When he met Olga Mercedes San Juan, it was love at first sight. He first became aware of her when his brother Liam went on a date with her. Edmond met Olga properly about a year later when they were seated opposite each other at a Paramount studio luncheon given in honor of President Elpidio Quirino of the Philippines.[20] Olga was a lovely, petite 21-year-old actress of Puerto Rican descent who had been born in Flatbush. When she was three, the family moved back to Puerto Rico, hence she learned to speak perfect Spanish. When she was six, they returned to Flatbush, later moving to uptown Manhattan.[21] She had been dancing since before she could remember and from an early age she effectively supported her family, including her grandmother. "By the age of 14," she recollected, "I worked at the Astor with a band, then formed my own band to play there and from there we went to the Copacabana."[22] In fact, she started so young that she was underage and still supposed to be attending school. One day one of her teachers happened to be in the audience and rec-

Actress-singer-dancer Olga San Juan (1927–2009), who became Edmond's second wife in September 1948.

ognized her. She threatened to tell the authorities but Olga pleaded and cajoled and the teacher finally relented—under the promise that she would attend school in Hollywood.[23] In the movie capitol, Olga enjoyed a short but successful film career as a singer and dancer beginning in 1943. Dubbed "the Puerto Rican Pepperpot," she had a vivacious screen personality along the lines of the great Brazilian singer Carmen Miranda. Olga was seen in B-movie musicals and in support of such actresses as Ava Gardner in *One Touch of Venus* (1948) and Betty Grable in *The Beautiful Blonde from Bashful Bend* (1949). Despite outward appearances, Olga was shy. "I've been shy all my life," she admitted. "My mother always traveled with me. She's really an old-fashioned Spanish mama. She didn't pay any attention to show business, just watched over me."[24]

At first, Olga gave Edmond the runaround. "What do I have to do to get your number?" he asked. "Call Paramount or keep trying," she answered.[25] He kept trying. On their first date, he quoted Shakespeare to her. "She thought it a bit corny but she liked it."[26] She said she was first attracted to him because "he was kind and thoughtful and because he had a real love for his family."[27] They went steady for a while and when he proposed, she told him he had to ask the permission of her mother and grandmother first. This caused confusion all around, because their English was no better than his Spanish, but in the end, Mother and Grandmother got the gist of what he was trying to say and were only too happy to welcome him into the family. On September 26, 1948, Eddie and Olga were married at the Santa Barbara county courthouse by justice of the peace William M. Quinn. They honeymooned briefly in the area.[28]

Edmond often liked to surprise Olga with unusual gifts. Just after making *Fighter Squadron,* he bought three gardenia bushes from Java. Forty-eight hours after planting them, they all died because the roots were eaten by gophers.[29]

The engrossing drama *An Act of Murder* (1948) broached the thorny subject of euthanasia in its last quarter. Judge Cooke (Fredric March) has a reputation for handing down long sentences, but seems to be a different man in his private life. Crusading lawyer David Douglas (O'Brien) is opposed to Cooke's whole approach, believing that justice should have some heart in it. He is in love with Cooke's daughter (Geraldine Brooks), much to Papa's chagrin. Cooke's wife (Florence Eldridge) is worried about recurring headaches and spells of paralysis in her arm. She consults a family friend who is a doctor; he runs a lot of tests on her unbeknownst to her husband. The results indicate she has a terminal illness; the doctor makes the decision to tell her husband but not her. When the Cookes go on a second honeymoon, the car crashes on the way home, and Cooke, wracked with guilt, believes he has killed his wife and wishes to be put on trial for her murder. Against his wishes, O'Brien is appointed his defense attorney. The tale was well-acted by all, particularly March and the often-unsung Florence Eldridge (March's real-life wife). O'Brien was effective as always as a character who comes and goes in the story and comes to the fore at the end when he defends his future father-in-law. The film was based on *The Mills of God* by Ernst Lothar, who wrote the screenplay with two others.

Widely commended for daring to talk about a deeply controversial subject, the film was a nominee at the 1949 Cannes Film Festival, one of only two American films nominated that year (the other was *Act of Violence*). The cast was uniformly praised, and O'Brien drew the attention of many critics as a fine dramatic actor; one wrote that he was "forceful and

O'Brien made an impression as a crusading lawyer in the thought-provoking drama *An Act of Murder* (1948), which broached the thorny subject of euthanasia. Geraldine Brooks co-starred.

earnest," and concluded that he "should never again be wasted by his studio on trivia."[30] Edmond and Geraldine Brooks got along well when they discovered a mutual love of Shakespeare; "We're both Shakespeare addicts," she disclosed. "When we had time between scenes, we'd get together and read scenes from *Romeo and Juliet, Macbeth, Hamlet*—oh, all his plays. It's such *fun* to find someone who enjoys reading plays as I do."[31]

❖❖ 8 ❖❖

"I want to report a murder."

> I got tired of asking for good parts. Anything that happened to me was despite the bosses, not because of them. I never became anything at the box office until I got out on my own.
> —Joseph Finnigan, "Free-Lancing Pays Off for Edmond O'Brien," *Schenectady Gazette*, November 19, 1964, 36

From 1949, O'Brien went freelance, and in the following five years found some of his best and most iconic roles. These were his finest years and culminated with a much-deserved Academy Award in the middle of the decade.

In May 1948, O'Brien signed a term contract with Warner Brothers.[1] His first assignment with his new studio was *Backfire*, which was not released for two years. Originally known as *Somewhere in the City*, it was an intriguing, atmospheric mystery drama with O'Brien as Steve Connolly and Gordon MacRae as Bob Corey, one-time Army buddies who always dreamed of running a ranch together after the war. Bob has severe spinal injuries that requires a lengthy stay in hospital, and Steve becomes restless and disappears. One Christmas Eve, a mysterious female (Viveca Lindfors) visits a heavily sedated Bob and tells him that Steve is in great peril. On his recovery, Bob finds Steve is accused of murder and sets out to discover the truth. Despite the occasionally muddled screenplay, this was a good, well-acted film. The opening scenes were shot at the Birmingham Veterans Hospital. Other locations included the Biltmore and Fremont hotels and City Hall.[2] The use of flashbacks worked in context. Dane Clark stood out and there was excellent support from a fine cast including Virginia Mayo as the nurse and Ed Begley as the police chief. O'Brien was natural as always but, if anything, he just wasn't in it enough. Owing to the flashback device, he weaved in and out of the screenplay, which made his role dis-

8. *"I want to report a murder."* 51

O'Brien did well in *Backfire* (1950), a rather convoluted noir made by Warner Bros. just to employ six idle actors. Seen with him in this publicity still is Viveca Lindfors.

satisfying. A contemporary critic perceptively remarked, "Of the supporting cast, Edmond O'Brien plays crisply and engagingly enough for a much better film."[3] *Backfire* was not well-received, and has often been overlooked in the genre. It was directly inspired by the war and the difficulties of adjusting from war to peace. The protagonists all knew each other in the Army and each go completely different ways thereafter. Steve finds it hard to make his way in the postwar world and is inadvertently dragged into the "jungle" of crime after a spectacularly unsuccessful boxing career. The scenes in the ring looked authentic as O'Brien hit the canvas once too often. Vincent Sherman was an efficient director who made some good films including *Mr. Skeffington* (1944) and the noir *The Damned Don't Cry* (1950). His first reaction when he read the original story on which *Backfire* was based was that it was "confused and pointless." His two writers, Ivan Goff and Ben Roberts, worked on making sense of the story, but despite their talent and eagerness, Sherman was not convinced it could be done. "When I told Warner I could not do it, he urged me to reconsider. 'I know it's not a great story, but I've got six actors sitting around and doing nothing but picking up their checks. I have to put them to work; so, do me a favor: make the picture and do the best job you can. I'll do you a favor sometime.'"[4] It was anathema to the notoriously miserly Warner to pay anyone for doing nothing. O'Brien was one of those idle actors.

The same writing duo, Goff and Roberts, surpassed themselves when they wrote the screenplay for *White Heat* (1949). Regarded as one of the finest of noirs, this marked a sensational return to Warner Bros. gangster

O'Brien (*left*) played the man on the inside in *White Heat* (1949) opposite James Cagney (*right*). It's come to be regarded as one of the finest noirs of the classic period.

films for James Cagney as the mother-fixated Cody Jarrett. Virginia Mayo played Cagney's wife with Margaret Wycherly as his mother and O'Brien as a federal agent on the inside. The action never let up in what was hailed as one of the most startling films of the year. "In the hurtling tabloid traditions of the gangster movies of the thirties," declared *Time* magazine, "but its matter-of-fact violence is a new postwar style."[5] Indeed, although the reviews were positive, the depiction of violence drew words of caution from such established commentators as Bosley Crowther, who wrote, "*White Heat* is also a cruelly vicious film and that its impact upon the emotions of the unstable or impressionable is incalculable."[6] Most of the attention was on Cagney, who was aided by a first-rate cast, especially Mayo and Wycherly. O'Brien caught the attention too; one leading critic noted, "O'Brien kicks in with a persuasive performance,"[7]

There were some great lines full of mordant wit, mostly uttered by Cody. He hears the man struggling in the trunk of the car and asks, "Getting stuffy in there?" as he chews on a chicken leg; he says, "Let me give you a little air," after which he shoots holes in the trunk. When it dawns on him that his "friend" Vic Pardo (O'Brien) is not all he seems, Cody's response was priceless delivering the immortal line "And I was going to split 50–50 with a copper!"

O'Brien was somewhat in awe of Cagney, but found him to be a generous performer. When the cameras stopped rolling, Cagney quietly took O'Brien to one side and showed him a poem he had written; "Would you mind telling me what you think of this?" he asked, adding, "Please don't tell anyone about this."[8] It had been 11 years since Cagney had appeared in a gangster role. He had been offered dozens of similar parts but had turned them all down. Cody brought him back to the genre. "I'm glad to be playing this particular hoodlum," wrote Cagney, "primarily because he's one of the most challenging and interesting characters of this sort that has ever been written in a screenplay."[9] O'Brien learned a lot from Cagney who, he said, put his heart into his work, and never played a scene the same way twice.

For some of the fight scenes, O'Brien was instructed in judo by expert John Halloran of the U.S. Marine Corps.[10] The young actor certainly went through the mill in this one and dislocated his shoulder in one fight sequence.[11] During the prison riot scene, he was "clonked on the noggin" by a guard with a billy club and lost consciousness for half a minute.[12] He later maintained that the hemorrhages in his eyes he had suffered in the war returned when he was hit on the head in such fight scenes.[13]

O'Brien had been promised equal billing with Cagney, but found that

Cagney had top billing. This made O'Brien angry, and he was hardly placated when given the excuse that the audience would be confused into thinking that this was a reissue of a Cagney enterprise with his familiar cohort Pat O'Brien.[14] Billing was always a sore point with Edmond, but he had no cause to worry because *White Heat* thrust him into the limelight, and he was now much in demand. It was even reported that his asking price had doubled.[15] Producer Richard Straus sought him for a leading role as an American colonel in postwar Germany in *Temper the Wind*, which had been a Broadway play, but the idea did not bear fruit.[16] Writer Gene Fowler hoped that O'Brien could star in his proposed life story of ex–New York Mayor Bill O'Dwyer. This was a role the other famous acting O'Brien—Pat—had long sought, but in the event the project was not brought to the screen.[17] Eddie was one of a number considered for the role which went to Gary Merrill in the Joseph Mankiewicz classic *All About Eve* (1950).[18] He was one of many actors discussed for the leading role in *Twelve O'Clock High* (1949), which eventually went to Gregory Peck.[19] Among other proposed but discarded ideas was *Metronome*, opposite the great French actress Danielle Darrieux, to be filmed in Italy.[20] O'Brien was keen to make the film, which would have seen him as an Irish tenor who coaches music students.[21] O'Brien tried to convince producer Harry Popkin to film Irving Shulman's novel *Pachuco*.[22] In 1950, there was the prospect of the lead in a film version of Jack London's life story *Sailor on Horseback*, opposite Mercedes McCambridge.[23] Five years later, the project was realized as a television play starring Lloyd Nolan as London. There was also *Flesh Peddler*, a proposed movie about unscrupulous Hollywood agents; perhaps unsurprisingly, the idea failed to receive any financial backing in Hollywood.[24] In addition, O'Brien was considered for the light-hearted *The Best Things in Life Are Free* opposite Ann Blyth, which did not materialize.[25] O'Brien often expressed a desire for a co-starring vehicle with his wife Olga which was also never realized. O'Brien was set to appear opposite Lucille Ball again in the proposed comedy *The Gentleman and the Redhead* with Ball as a New York salesgirl. The story was written by Edmond's brother Liam.[26]

The classic noir *D. O. A.* (1949) gave him one of his best remembered roles as a man who is poisoned by luminous toxin and tries desperately to discover the identity of his own murderer. Beginning with the iconic image of Frank Bigelow (O'Brien) arriving at police headquarters to report a murder (his own), the chain of events was told in flashback. The story was related in a terse, urgent manner befitting the subject. Often the scurrying figure of O'Brien appeared dwarfed by the sheer scale of the build-

8. "I want to report a murder."

A classic noir, *D.O.A.* (1949) gave O'Brien one of his greatest roles as Frank Bigelow, a man who solves his own murder. Pamela Britton played his fiancée.

ings in the urban jungle, which added to the mounting sense of doom. There was great use made of San Francisco and Los Angeles locations, such as Fisherman's Wharf and the St. Frances Hotel. The sense of fatalism was underscored by the intensely dramatic music of Dimitri Tiomkin. The script was first-class: ironic, hard-boiled and perceptive. The early scene establishing the "salesman on vacation" scenario was well-judged, although the inserted wolf-whistles as the girls walk by at the hotel seemed out of place in a classic noir and more at home in a Bob Hope movie. Nonetheless, the shafts of muted humor had their place too. The conversations on the telephone with his fiancée (Pamela Britton) showed a real understanding of human nature; "There's nothing you can do that you have to feel guilty about," she assures him. Immediately he begins to feel guilty. There was a striking scene in the Fisherman Club during which Bigelow is poisoned; the bop music group increases the feverish sense of disorientation. Oddly enough, considering their crucial appearance in this key scene, none of the personnel were credited in the movie. The quintet as featured appear to have been James Streeter on sax, Shifty Henry on bass, Al "Cake"

Wichard on drums, Ray La Rue on piano and Teddy Buckner on trumpet. Despite their prominence, the music was re-recorded later by a big band led by Maxwell Davis on saxophone.[27] Producer Leo Popkin sought advice from aficionado "Hot Licks" Howard to get just the right atmosphere in the jazz club. Howard said that among the Be-Bop enthusiasts there should be at least four males sporting beards a la "Dizzy" Gillespie and one wearing a smart beret known as a "pinch top."

The San Francisco police objected to some parts of the script, specifically the location in which Bigelow was poisoned. Therefore, the location was changed to an unnamed town.[28] All in all, it was a superb achievement by cast and crew to create a classic with the minimum of fuss in only three weeks. The United Artists publicity department enlisted the help of two retired New York homicide detectives, who toured key cities promoting the film.[29] The cast was perfect. Neville Brand made a striking debut as a psychotic heavy given some memorable lines: "I've knocked off guys I could like," he asserts. "But I don't like you, Bigelow. I've never liked that puss of yours from the minute I saw it." The excellent script was co-written by Richard Rouse and Clarence Greene, who worked together on a number of films including the tense racial drama *The Well* (1951) and the low-budget noir *Wicked Woman* (1953) which starred Rouse's wife Beverly Michaels. Director Rudolph Maté, formerly an esteemed cinematographer, had worked in Hollywood since 1919. He turned to directing in 1947 and was at the helm for *Union Station* (1950) and *When Worlds Collide* (1951) among many others. *D.O.A.* was partially inspired by the 1931 German comedy *Der Mann, der seinen Mörder Sucht* (in English, *The Man in Search of His Murderer*), directed by Robert Siodmak. That film, of which only 50 minutes survives, was co-written by a young Billy Wilder and was based on a stage play by Ernst Neubach.

Actress Beverly Garland made her debut in the film under the name of Beverly Campbell. She recalled her surprise when O'Brien personally supervised her audition and read lines with her. She reflected on working with the star and his dedication to his art:

> Edmond O'Brien was gregarious. He loved acting. It was his life. He couldn't get enough of it. He was a very intense actor and very into himself. Everything revolved around him and he came first. I wasn't intimidated by his demeanor. I adored the idea that he was so dedicated. You didn't have to waste time making idle conversation with Eddie. You could do what you were hired to do – which was to act. That's what he was doing and I thought that was great.[30]

There were not too many mishaps during filming, although in one scene O'Brien accidentally fired his revolver and the wadding from the

8. "I want to report a murder." 57

blank cartridge hit producer Popkin on the forehead. Among the cast, Luther Adler delayed rehearsals on his prestigious Broadway play *Night Tempest* in order to appear as the sinister underworld boss Majak.

D.O.A. has been analyzed time and again by cineastes who concur that it is one of the most cynical of all noirs. Many of the finest in the genre are shot through with fatalism, but surely none quite so fatalistic as a man investigating his own death. Here was an ordinary accountant from the small desert town of Modesto who just happened to notarize a certain bill of sale. The means of death—a slow-acting luminous toxin—was perhaps another unhappy by-product of the war—a conflict which opened a Pandora's Box of ills, seemingly without even leaving hope at the bottom. Again, Bigelow was not a naturally heroic figure, just an ordinary man with flaws like everyone else. This ordinariness gave him an Everyman quality, so that when he proves how remarkable he could be, by discovering his murderer in 48 hours, it added to the pathos of his life.

D.O.A. caught the attention of contemporary audiences and critics

Frank Bigelow (O'Brien) is suddenly galvanized into action when he realizes his time is short in Rudolph Maté's masterful *D.O.A.*

alike. It was different and more inventive than most other films of the era; indeed, it was ahead of its time. O'Brien was widely praised for his "real and poignant" study of Bigelow.[31] As Beverly Garland recalled, "Edmond O'Brien poured his all into this role." It was a deeply human portrait, beautifully acted. His achievement was hailed by critics as "one of the most striking portrayals in years" before the film was even released.[32] He was seen as a potential Oscar winner, but neither he nor the film were even nominated. The film has been remade several times but for many, nothing comes close to the poignancy or power of the original.

◆◆ 9 ◆◆

711 Ocean Drive

Time wounds all heels.—Mal Granger, *711 Ocean Drive* (1950)

Exposing the murky world of illegal gambling, *711 Ocean Drive* (1950) began with a bold statement claiming that all those involved in the making of the film were threatened by the organized crime syndicates in the spotlight. Lloyds of London insured the stars against kidnap.

O'Brien starred as Mal Granger, a disgruntled telephone engineer who has big ambitions. Through small-time bookmaker Chippy, he meets Vince (Barry Kelley) and is invited into the organization to use his technical knowhow to improve the flawed system of taking bets. Before long, Granger is an integral part of the set-up and pushes Vince for 20 percent of the business. After Vince is shot, Granger takes over, but the powerful eastern syndicate headed by Carl (Otto Kruger) wants to take over entirely and Granger's life becomes increasingly complicated. This was the kind of role that suited O'Brien down to the ground, and he played with ease. His natural style and mastery of dialogue made it seem that he was not acting. He was able to convey a lot of meaning with his eyes or a half smile, such as in the poolside scene while Kruger talks business and Joanne Dru sunbathes. The film sometimes employed a semi-documentary style, and ended with a chase inside Boulder Dam, which made a dramatic backdrop. The true villain of the piece, Carl, is not punished and escapes scot-free. This perhaps served the wider purpose of the film, that action is still needed to bring the evil men behind the numbers racket to book. "Maybe the picture won't change a committed gambler any more than say *The Lost Weekend* would change an alcoholic," observed O'Brien at the time of the film's release. "But it ought to make the two dollar bet guys think about what happens to their money."[1] When asked if the film was based on the career of Bugsy Siegel, O'Brien replied, "It's the story of an antisocial fellow who thinks he has climbed too high to respect human dignity and the simple rules of the game. It could be the saga of Siegel or Hitler. Only the Hitler yarn would need DeMille bathtubs to make it spectacular."[2]

The film was something of an ordeal to make because of the attention it received from the criminal underworld. "I got kicked around plenty when I was making it," recalled producer Frank Seltzer. "Every big-name hoodlum in the business tried to stop me."[3] It was reported that the Las Vegas authorities would not allow the crew to film in and around Boulder Dam for too long because of the tense situation brought on by "increasing threats of violence." In all the locations, at Doll House in Palm Springs and elsewhere, the cast and crew were assigned bodyguards by the Los Angeles Police Department, who maintained a presence until the picture was finished.[4] O'Brien was full of admiration for Seltzer: "Frank is a guy who has the guts to do what almost everyone is afraid to do—get the real dope on syndicated crime and film it," he remarked.[5] O'Brien was pleased with the film because, he said, "it seemed to be what the public enjoys, it

A telling scene at the poolside in *711 Ocean Drive* (1950), a noir about the gangsters behind betting syndicates. Left to right: Don Porter, Joanne Dru, Otto Kruger and O'Brien.

9. 711 Ocean Drive   61

did well at the box office, made a lot of money, and it was, I think, a powerful story."[6] The public did enjoy it, even if the critics were not as enamored. O'Brien was commended for his "well-rounded portrait" by *Film Bulletin,* who called the movie "an absorbing action tale that is top drawer for the fans who like their screen fare tough, tense and to the point."[7]

A special preview screening of *711 Ocean Drive* was given for Sen. Kefauver and the members of his special Senate committee at the behest of Sen. Alexander Wiley of Wisconsin.[8] Kefauver was distinctly impressed and afterwards asked Seltzer to show it to Congress. "So, I ran it in an auditorium for the Senate and the House," recounted Seltzer. "I didn't pass out review cards. But something better than that happened. A newsreel company interviewed the Congressmen afterwards and they gave me glowing endorsements." In addition, Seltzer was allowed to use all their remarks in publicity materials.[9]

To promote the opening of the film, O'Brien embarked on a brief personal appearance tour. On the opening two days, he appeared with

711 Ocean Drive (1950) delved into the murky world of the numbers racket. Left to right: Charles La Torre, O'Brien, Barry Kelley.

Louis Jordan and His Tympany Five. Others on the bill included the Fontane Sisters and Ruby Cardenas.[10] Edmond had his own specialty act worked out for such occasions: "I recited a hunk of Shakespeare," he revealed.[11] His profile was high and he was invited to be a guest of honor at the Chicago Fair of 1950 in which he greeted all those by the name of O'Brien in the first "O'Brien Day" and "Illinois Day" combined.[12]

The same team, producer Frank Seltzer and director Joseph Newman, were set to collaborate again with O'Brien on *The Kansas City Story*.[13] This was based on the true tale of a corrupt political machine run by Republican senator Tom Pendergast from the 1920s onwards in Kansas City, Missouri; the racket was finally exposed by a Catholic priest and a rabbi.[14] O'Brien was looking forward to playing the priest.[15] In a familiar pattern, it was reported that a man who Seltzer had sent to the city to do research had been "approached by several hooligans."[16] Plans for the film were well-advanced and according to Erskine Johnson there was "a whisper that President Truman's name will be woven into the script."[17] Despite the months of planning, the project was dropped.

Shortly after the premiere of *711 Ocean Drive*, O'Brien was involved in a well-documented *contretemps* with Serge Rubinstein. A former Wall Street journalist, Rubinstein made a fortune during the war but was later convicted of avoiding military service, for which he spent 18 months in a federal prison, and was forced to pay a $50,000 fine. In September 1951, when the incident with O'Brien occurred, Rubinstein was due to appear at a deportation hearing. The incident took place at the Villa Nova Café in Los Angeles, where O'Brien was discussing his radio contract with his agent. According to witnesses, Rubinstein approached their table and O'Brien objected to his "loud, abusive and vulgar language." After that, "three or four blows were exchanged with blood appearing on the face of ... O'Brien." When Rubinstein appeared to make a sudden reach for his hip pocket, O'Brien caught him in a judo hold, with Rubinstein threatening to call the police. Eventually they were separated by friends.[18] The café owner played down the incident and said that Rubinstein had only grabbed O'Brien by the lapels and that no blows had been struck.[19]

After his terrific success in the postwar years, O'Brien was offered all kinds of interesting projects, only some of which actually came to fruition. He hoped to appear in *Bernardo O'Higgins*, a proposed film about the life of the Chilean independence leader. Both Edmond and his wife were invited to go to Santiago by Gabriel Gonzalez Videla, the president of Chile, who was backing the company planning to make the film. This never materialized.[20] Edmond bought a half-interest in a comedy called

Penthouse, owned by Jane Greer, which they hoped to co-produce independently but which never saw the light of day.[21] Around the same time, O'Brien was touted to play Christian in *Cyrano de Bergerac* (1950) starring Jose Ferrer.[22] In the event, William Prince played the role.

Despite his great success in the genre, he felt he was becoming too closely associated with crime dramas. "The public seems to want that kind of picture, so I don't mind," he once observed. "But I think I could use a change of pace."[23] Hence, he switched back to romantic comedy with *The Admiral Was a Lady* (1950). The silly plot involved a girl (Wanda Hendrix) who appears to have been abandoned by her fiancé Henry, and is taken in hand by four work-shy ex-servicemen led by Jimmy Stevens (O'Brien). The joke was that they would do anything to avoid working and Pedigrew (Rudy Vallee) will force them to take jobs if they don't keep her from meeting Henry. A boisterous affair played at fever pitch for much of the time, it was all rather tiresome. O'Brien's comedic touch was often present even in his serious roles, but he seldom found a true comedy vehicle that played

Poster for *The Admiral Was a Lady* (1951), a passable comedy which gave O'Brien a welcome change of pace from too many crime dramas.

to his strengths. There were moments when it clicked, such as when he dishes out an impromptu advertising spiel for a music store over the loudspeaker from the van. Another moment was using the same device to hail the bus and stop Hendrix from getting to Walla Walla. There was the memorably painful sight of the totally out-of-shape O'Brien trying to fight a professional boxer in order to get $100. But for the most part, the humor was alternately too loud and too saccharine. Everybody seemed to be shouting too much, but if a line isn't funny when said normally, it is no funnier when delivered at the top of one's voice. Nonetheless, comedy is an entirely subjective thing and the film had decent production values and a few songs. *Variety* called it "a neatly concocted piece of fluff that will rate a lot of laughs in its general release."[24]

❖❖ 10 ❖❖

Between Midnight and Dawn

> The important difference between being a crook and being a cop on screen is that the cop must never smile or show any satisfaction when he kills somebody. The crook can. This is something you gotta remember.
> —"It's a New Experience," *The Singapore Free Press*, July 28, 1955, 17

Nineteen fifty was a great year for classic noir films, and for O'Brien in particular. His succession of outstanding roles in *White Heat, D.O.A.* and *711 Ocean Drive* established him as one of the most exciting actors of the moment. Film work, combined with the success of the *Yours Truly, Johnny Dollar* radio series, helped to bring him a substantial salary for the year estimated at around $300,000.[1] His decision to go freelance in 1949 proved to be one of the best decisions of his entire career.

After his flirtation with comedy, O'Brien was back in familiar territory in Columbia's *Between Midnight and Dawn* (1950), an underrated noir about the ordinary cops in prowl cars. The original title was *Prowl Car* and Larry Parks and Barbara Hale were slated to star.[2] Parks dropped out and was replaced by O'Brien. Hale was disappointed at the substitution and said she would "rather have someone more important career-wise" than O'Brien. Before long, Hale walked away from the project and Gale Storm was cast in her place.[3] Mark Stevens played O'Brien's partner and rival for the affections of switchboard operator Katherine (Storm). The two offered interesting contrasting character studies: "Junior" Rocky (Stevens), young and hopeful, Dan (O'Brien) bitter and weary. "Some of them rate a second chance," offers Rocky, reflecting on the people policemen have to deal with on a daily basis. "You have to look inside." Dan retorts, "I can read 'em from the outside. Wait until you've had your fill of the scum."

65

Rocky Barnes (Mark Stevens, left) and Dan Purvis (O'Brien) at home in the underrated noir *Between Midnight and Dawn* (1950), a look at the lives of the ordinary cops in prowl cars.

The film centered on police procedure, and the myriad difficulties of the job came across well. There was no more glamor in the life of a prowl car cop then there was that of a beat cop. Both were treated with equal contempt by crime big shots and even members of the public. The long hours prowling the streets at night showed the work to be trying on the nerves, consisting mostly of long periods of monotony with sudden bursts of frenzied activity. Obviously, danger was never far away. Naturally, they rely on humor as a safety valve to help them cope with the nature of their occupation.

Once again, the billing issue came to the fore; both actors insisted on top billing. In the event, Stevens was billed first although his was technically the lesser role.[4] Despite appearances, Stevens was only a year younger than O'Brien. Director Gordon Douglas had a long and sometimes interesting career beginning with comedy shorts in the 1930s. Along the way, he made the outstanding noir *Kiss Tomorrow Goodbye* (1950) and the memorable science fiction drama *Them!* (1954), and was at the helm of several of O'Brien's later films including *The Big Land* (1957).

The screenplay was written by Eugene Ling from a story by Gerald Drayson Adams and Leo Kotcher. Between them, the team had fine noir credentials. Ling was known for documentary-style yarns such as *Behind Locked Doors* (1948) and *Scandal Sheet* (1952). Oxford graduate Adams had written *Dead Reckoning* (1947) and *The Big Steal* (1949) as well as *A Girl, a Guy and a Gob* and a couple of Elvis pictures; Kotcher wrote *Party Girl* (1958). These three writers fashioned an insightful and gritty tale which occasionally employed some hardboiled humor. The device of two buddy cops in love with the same girl was hardly new but the actors suited their roles so well that it worked perfectly. Gale Storm was excellent as the girl who is wary of getting involved with cops because of her own traumatic family experience.

Filming took place in several Los Angeles locations including the vicinity of the Pacific Electric building. While shooting night scenes, Douglas was approached by two policemen in a squad car who told him that there was too much gunfire for two a.m. Once they were told about the subject of the film, they became intrigued and were keen to know if the police were being depicted accurately. The two officers ended up staying on the set for an hour or so as "technical advisors."[5] O'Brien and Stevens certainly looked convincing. Once when the two actors were wearing their police uniforms, they went for lunch at Lucey's restaurant with the assistant director. On entering, the headwaiter picked out a table for the assistant director and told the two cops to go and eat in the kitchen.[6]

There was to have been a fierce fight scene between Stevens and O'Brien, but the director and studio decided against it, chiefly because of concerns about the overseas market and particularly the British censors, who at that time took a hard line against unnecessary brutality.[7] Contemporary reviews were lackluster. However, it had an often witty and observant screenplay and was played with great judgment by a fine cast. Donald Buka was compelling as the villain of the piece. The domestic scenes were warm and believable and although the story was familiar, there were some memorable noir sequences. All in all, *Between Midnight and Dawn* remains an overlooked noir which deserves to be more widely known and appreciated.

One of the least heralded of O'Brien's films of this era was the pseudo-noir *Two of a Kind* (1951). Down-on-his-luck gambler "Lefty" Farrell (O'Brien) is asked by the enticing Brandy (Lizabeth Scott) to pose as the missing son of a rich elderly couple in order to get money from them.

O'Brien was at ease as an opportunistic gambler with a heart in *Two of a Kind* (1951), a decent crime drama with a good cast. Terry Moore is shown here behind the wheel.

Some of the posters made this one look like a true classic: the dynamic O'Brien about to kiss the sexy Scott. However, posters are often misleading and the film never quite caught fire for noir buffs. At times, the screenplay hovered indecisively between hard-boiled noir and light comedy. For instance, in an early scenes, the enigmatic Brandy asks him to lose the tip of his little finger, and he does so, by slamming the car door on it. But the scene with Terry Moore when he hides in the station wagon after inadvertently setting off the burglar alarm might have made him think he had suddenly strayed into a Deanna Durbin picture. No matter, because whatever the inconsistency of treatment, O'Brien was equal to all that was required and held it all together. When necessary, he was tough, sensitive, jaunty and quick-witted. It was a testament to his talent that he managed to make this film quietly compelling. He was aided by a good supporting cast, particularly Scott and Alexander Knox, and the curious story which made the outcome less than predictable. There was fine cinematography by Burnett Guffey, who also worked on *In a Lonely Place* (1950) and *From Here to Eternity* (1953). *Two of a Kind* was adapted from a story by James Edward Grant, who was mostly associated with westerns but who also provided the inspiration for *Johnny Eager* (1941). Director Henry Levin enjoyed a good career beginning in the 1940s. Among his highlights was an interesting biopic, *The President's Lady* (1953), and the Jules Verne adventure *Journey to the Center of the Earth* (1959). Levin was also at the helm for the film version of Liam O'Brien's *The Remarkable Mr. Pennypacker* (1959).

O'Brien enjoyed working on the film, having come in as a replacement for Rick Jason, who had hurt his back in a swimming accident.[8] Things augured well for Edmond when he reported for duty on the first day of filming at the beach in Balboa, California, when he was greeted by the sight of Lizabeth Scott and Terry Moore in their swimsuits. "Oh, boy," he declared, "I'm glad I get to do love scenes with both of you."[9] He was sought to star alongside Scott again in *The Hyde Side*, a project suggested by Hal Wallis. The story was written by Tom McGowan, a former picture editor for *Life*, and was announced for Gotham Productions, but never came to fruition.[10] O'Brien also coveted the lead role as the ruthless photographer in Nat Dillinger's story *Shakedown*, originally known under the title *The Red Carpet*. Howard Duff was cast instead.

O'Brien had several ideas of his own which he hoped to pursue including *Hester Street*, based on a magazine story by Aleen Leslie. It was the tale of an Irish immigrant who becomes foreman of a railroad gang and makes good after studying law.[11] He was always proud of his Irish roots and once attempted to persuade the State Department to finance a film to encourage American tourists to Ireland, with the help of the Eire Bureau of Tourism. His idea was to narrate a travelogue for which he would give his services free. No such film has yet come to light.[12]

◆◆ **11** ◆◆

An Easterner Goes West

> I think audiences like action pictures best. As far as I'm concerned, I just like good roles.—Helen Bower, "Star Gazing: Track Is Safer Place If You Have to Bet," *Detroit Free Press*, August 13, 1950, 26

O'Brien was identified so strongly with the noir genre that it is often forgotten that he also made several sprightly and effective westerns. His natural dynamism suited the great outdoors setting and the characters he played were not of the standard cowboy stereotype. His piquant performances made the films interesting and raised many of them above the plethora of run-of-the-mill horse operas churned out by the studios in the postwar era.

In these films, O'Brien seldom played an out-and-out cowboy; usually he was a qualified man, a mining engineer, surveyor or military officer. In fact, he was not often seen riding a horse and was one of the few western stars who spent most of his time on foot. In common with his appearances in noirs, he was usually a wronged man seeking redress in his own way.

It was O'Brien's compelling performance in *711 Ocean Drive* which directly led producer Nat Holt to cast in him in his first leading western role in *Warpath* (1951).[1] This was in essence a revenge drama set at the time of the Indian wars of the 1870s. O'Brien played a lawyer turned cavalry officer who has spent eight years trying to track down the men who killed his fiancée during a robbery. An action-packed spectacle made by Paramount, it was one of many movies that took in the events of the Little Big Horn and the famous Seventh Cavalry under Custer. It was directed with gusto by the often-underrated Byron Haskin, who enjoyed a long and varied career as a cinematographer, special effects artist and director. As a director he began with two fine noirs, *I Walk Alone* (1947) and *Too Late for Tears* (1949). He brought a suitably bold and breezy quality to such

11. An Easterner Goes West

In the early 1950s, O'Brien appeared in several westerns, mostly for producer Nat Holt and director Byron Haskin; the first was *Warpath* (1951) with (pictured) O'Brien (left), Polly Bergen and Forrest Tucker.

rousing adventures as *Treasure Island* (1950) and *His Majesty O'Keefe* (1954). He also made a number of notable entries in the science fiction genre including *The War of the Worlds* (1953) and *Robinson Crusoe on Mars* (1964). His westerns had the same spirit of adventure but with some noir undercurrents. When he was out west, he liked to have lots of trains in his pictures, but was disappointed to find when he first arrived at the Billings, Montana, location for *Warpath* that there were none available that he could use. All rolling stock was tied up due to defense service during the Korean War. Haskin borrowed two sets of wheel trucks from the Northern Pacific roundhouse and arranged for two replica period carriages to be built, so that the principals could be seen alighting from the train as originally planned. For the long shots of the train arriving, footage from one of Haskin's previous films, *The Great Missouri Raid* (1950), was used.[2] The Indians were from the Crow reservation. Other filming locations included the Yellowstone River.[3]

Warpath was beautifully shot by Ray Rennahan, and the stirring

Fawcett released a collectible comic based on *Warpath*.

music of Paul Sawtell added greatly to the atmosphere. Among the large cast there was strong support from Forrest Tucker, Dean Jagger, Harry Carey, Jr., and Wallace Ford. O'Brien's character was a driven man who displayed remarkable tenacity and also loyalty to the army. His dynamism made him suited to the role and he showed that he could carry a western.

11. An Easterner Goes West

He was tutored in gunplay by the Chickasaw Indian actor Rodd Redwing, who helped many other actors to learn.[4] It was reported at the time that O'Brien secured a comic role in *Warpath* for an old Broadway buddy, Sidney Cantro; however, Cantro does not appear in the cast list.[5] An 18-year-old local, Darlene Hogan, was given a screen test with which O'Brien helped her. She was offered a role in the film but turned it down and decided to concentrate on becoming an air hostess instead.[6] O'Brien embarked on several short personal appearance tours in such Ohio towns as Cleveland, Youngstown and Columbus to promote the movie.[7]

O'Brien's next, the black and white *The Redhead and the Cowboy* (1951), was essentially a detective story transposed to a western setting. The stars were Rhonda Fleming and Glenn Ford and the tale was set towards the end of the Civil War. Shorn of the western trappings, the movie was more akin to a noir at times, and presented an interesting three-way dynamic between the leads. O'Brien played a mysterious character who appeared friendly on the surface, but always kept his powder dry, so that it was not clear what his motives were or whose side he was on. Naturally, the same was true of Rhonda's character; she was essentially a typical noir *femme* who might or might not be *fatale*. "It's *39 Steps* on horseback," quipped O'Brien.[8] Most of the attention was on Ford and Fleming. The working title was *Beyond the Sunset*. Once, when the stars and producer Irvin Aschler were discussing a change of title, O'Brien mischievously suggested "Why don't we just change to *Beyond Glenn Ford*."[9] Despite his third billing, O'Brien, underplaying, drew much of the attention. The scenic setting and the presence of the beautiful Rhonda seemed to cry out for color, but monochrome heightened the story's noir quality. The director was Leslie Fenton, an English-born actor who took to directing in the late 1930s and was fond of western subjects. *The Redhead and the Cowboy* was his final feature. He hired two dozen Navajos for the film but was informed by their spokesman, Chief Hoskie Thorne, that they had no traditional dress; "That's only in the movies," said Thorne. Fenton had to wire the studio to send the costumes out to the location.[10]

It was O'Brien's first experience at riding a horse, which he enjoyed; according to the director, he insisted on doing all his own riding.[11] Several commentators noted his conviction and surprising ease in a western setting.[12] The film was shot at several locations in the Indian lands at Sedona, Arizona, mostly about 35 miles from Flagstaff. The locale was hit by a twister described by residents as one of the worst seen in the area for many years. A portable radio mast was brought down and a full-size prop barn ripped from its moorings, among other damage. Far worse, the brakes failed on

O'Brien (*left*) with Glenn Ford in a scene from *The Redhead and the Cowboy* (1951), a decent western set towards the end of the Civil War.

a rented truck in which all the main actors and the director were traveling. A report stated: "Only the skill of the driver who pulled his emergency brake and brought the vehicle to a halt by nosing into a hillside, saved the passengers from crashing through a safety fence and down the sheer cliff."[13]

Rhonda Fleming had cause to remember the film because of one particular incident that could have been serious:

> They wanted to get a close-up of me rearing a horse without using a stunt girl but never told me it was up a hill. So, in the scene I was riding up the hill and I reared the horse up too high and it almost fell back on top of me. By the grace of God, I was not squashed like a bug. I was knocked unconscious. How I got up and walked away and finished that film was another miracle.[14]

In those days, promoters tried to be inventive to engage interest in films. One novel idea used to promote *The Redhead and the Cowboy* was a tie-up with Copley Fabrics. This used photomontages from the film featuring the three stars which were printed directly onto a range of French crepe and satin dresses, scarves and blouses, etc. Movie theater staff were encouraged to model the clothes which were on sale in lobbies.[15]

11. An Easterner Goes West

Silver City (1951) was a splendid color western based, like many, on a *Saturday Evening Post* story and known in Great Britain under its original title *High Vermilion*. It was filmed at Bronson Canyon in Los Angeles and in Sonora, California, and had one of the highest budgets of the six Paramount westerns Byron Haskin made at that period.[16] O'Brien headed the cast as an assayer who goes on the run after being double-crossed by his partner in a robbery. This was a treat even for non-western fans with a well-judged performance from O'Brien as a quick-witted man of action. His gusto was matched by the majesty of the scenery and Ray Rennahan's superb cinematography. Rennahan had a prolific career stretching back to the early 1920s which included such highlights as *Drums Along the Mohawk* (1939) and *Duel in the Sun* (1946). His use of color was masterful. He worked on all three of the Haskin-O'Brien westerns and was responsible in large measure for their success. The rousing music of Paul Sawtell was also important. O'Brien is not generally thought of as a western actor, but his natural dynamism made him ideally suited to the genre. He preferred to do as many of his own stunts as possible but he drew the line at

O'Brien insisted on doing most of his own stunts in his westerns, and literally went through the mill in *Silver City* (1951).

some things and it was reported that stuntman Harvey Parry was the one seen leaping from the moving logging car into the river 95 feet below. Parry's only reaction afterwards was "The water's darned cold."[17] It was definitely O'Brien who was seen in the exciting climactic chase through the lumber mill and railroad yard, some of the most effective scenes in this enjoyable yarn. O'Brien had good support from a fine cast, especially Yvonne de Carlo and Edgar Buchanan. A standout was the veteran Barry Fitzgerald, who eschewed his usual charming eccentric persona to portray a shrewd villain. He was ably abetted by the black-clad Michael Moore as his henchman. The always-welcome Gladys George put in an appearance as an alert hotelier.

Unsurprisingly, there were several hazardous incidents during filming. At Tuolumne, O'Brien was injured when he fell off a floating log on the river.[18] At Sonora, he and de Carlo were having some publicity shots taken while on a logging flat car. Suddenly the train started unexpectedly

Silver City (1951) was a likable western yarn about a valuable mine. O'Brien showed to great effect as an energetic assayer who seeks to get even with a double-crossing partner. Above: O'Brien and Yvonne de Carlo.

11. An Easterner Goes West

and they had to wait for it to stop at a switch and walk five miles back to the location shooting.[19] Some considered O'Brien physically unsuited to the image of the western hero, but he received good notices generally; *Film Bulletin* declared, "[His] easygoing heroics are first-rate."[20] Director Haskin enjoyed working with him and recalled how most of the action was for real: "Eddie was pretty athletic, he did most of the stuff.... He was a gutsy guy."[21]

Arguably one of the best of his 1950s westerns was *Denver and Rio Grande* (1952), also shot in glorious color with a familiar story of rivalry between railroad companies in the early days of the trains. Sterling Hayden played the head of the rival Canon City & San Juan Railroad, a fictional representation of the real railroad known as Atchison, Topeka & Santa Fe. A good cast of stalwarts was employed including J. Carrol Naish, Dean Jagger and Lyle Bettger. The comedy was provided by the veteran comedienne Zasu Pitts, who enjoyed a near double act with Paul Fix as a far-

Lobby card advertising *Denver and Rio Grande* (1952), a colorful and entertaining western about rivalry between railroad companies. O'Brien (second from left) starred as a two-fisted ex-army captain.

from-brave train driver. Originally, Hayden had been cast as O'Brien's sidekick and Naish as the villain-of-the-piece, but, at Hayden's suggestion, they swapped roles just a week before filming began. O'Brien was perfectly keyed to the role of the two-fisted ex-army captain, dynamic and astute. Haskin kept the action flowing swiftly along and the fast-moving storyline kept pace with the trains.

Denver and Rio Grande (1952) publicity still showing (*left to right*) J. Carroll Naish, Kasey Rogers, O'Brien and Dean Jagger.

The film was shot in Colorado near the Rockies, mostly around Durango. The grandeur of the location was beautifully captured once again by the redoubtable Rennahan. The veteran cinematographer once gave his assessments of the leading actors he had known and declared that O'Brien was "excellent in virile, he-man roles, popular and cooperative."[22] In his generous way, Edmond reportedly secured a first break on the film for Mike Lewis, with whom he had previously worked on radio.[23] When it came to the dialogue in all these films, much of that was worked out by O'Brien and the director, who hammered it out between them. Haskin recalled, "Eddie O'Brien would sit me in a corner of the hotel lobby after dinner, he was good at dialogue ... and I would block out a rewrite. I'd work most of the night putting it on paper."[24] The sequence where two locomotives collided head-on was surely one of the most spectacular rail crashes ever seen on screen. Shot at Rio de la Perdita, it took five days to film and as many cameras at a cost of $165,000.[25] It would seem like sacrilege now to steam railway enthusiasts to deliberately destroy two irreplaceable nineteenth century engines. However, at that time the old rolling stock was being replaced the world over and the two that were wrecked were due to be scrapped.

There was much ballyhoo during the week-long premiere in Salt Lake City, Utah, including a Rotary Club luncheon and civic reception at which the governor and the mayor were present. Afterwards there was a parade and the stars of the film were presented on the stage of the Paramount Theater.[26] Approximately 10,000 people also attended a fete at the D & RG western railroad yards to see the narrow-gauge engine *Cinder Ella* celebrate its fiftieth anniversary.[27] All the Haskin-O'Brien films did decent business; *Denver and Rio Grande* made a respectable $1,800,000 at the box office and *Silver City* just over $1,000,000.[28]

O'Brien was considered so convincing in western roles that he was touted for more. Paramount hoped to tempt him with a long-term contract that would have seen him in parts that had been planned for Alan Ladd, who had recently departed the studio. Many of these would have been westerns, but O'Brien did not take them up on their offer.[29]

Cow Country (1953), sometimes known under the title *Lawless Territory*, was probably O'Brien's least successful western. It followed three separate storylines and contained an odd scene involving a whip. A rather dour affair, it was more akin to the predictable fare of the kind that made non-western lovers' eyes glaze over. Shot in monochrome for Allied Artists, it had none of the punch of the Haskin Technicolor efforts. It did have Barton MacLane as the bad man, but he was not given any decent material to work with. The film was made in just three weeks and showed all the signs. "You know," remarked O'Brien, "on the Allied Artists lot they don't stall. They just make a movie and get it over with, period."[30] Of *Cow Country*, a contemporary reviewer commented:

> It is mortifying to see the brilliant talent of Edmond O'Brien wasted on this piece of childish banality.... The film includes one cattle drive, eight individual shootings, and, for those who prefer them, one sumptuous slaughter of baddies in the last reel. It is suitable for hard-boiled children.[31]

O'Brien was, as usual, convincing as a would-be cattle baron and the picture was competently made with some attention paid to historical detail.

Later in the decade, O'Brien returned to the western genre with *The Big Land* (1957), based on the novel *Buffalo Grass* by prolific pulp writer Frank Gruber. Although the novel was set in Kansas, it was stated at the time that some of the filming took place in Arizona, but most of it in Sonora and Tuolumne County in California. The story explored the famil-

O'Brien (*left*) gave a fine portrayal of an ex-alcoholic architect in *The Big Land* (1957). He is seen here with Alan Ladd. The two became good friends.

iar western theme about the inability of the wounds of the Civil War to heal. It starred Alan Ladd as an army captain turned rancher who seeks to help build a new future postwar but who is forced to battle those bad men who still carry bitterness in their hearts and want to destroy everything. This interesting film gave O'Brien an excellent role as a reformed alcoholic architect. The prospect of building a new town in the wilderness spurs him on to make something of his talents while battling his own weaknesses. Once again, he was far more than the all-too-familiar western "hero" in the taciturn John Wayne mold; on the contrary, he was a man full of flaws and all the more fascinating as a result. The film might have lacked the brio of the Haskin movies but in compensation had an intriguing story superbly handled by the leads, Ladd, O'Brien and Virginia Mayo. Mayo did especially well as O'Brien's sister and love interest of Ladd. An occasionally witty script was employed, and O'Brien made the most of the ironic humor of the situation. In one scene, after days spent crossing the arid land, Ladd asks O'Brien if wants a drink of water; O'Brien retorts, "Water? What am I, a trout?" The screenplay was co-written by David Dortort and Martin Rackin. Dortort was mostly known as the writer of a run of 1960s television western series, principally *Bonanza*. Perhaps the offhand ironic wit was provided by Rackin, because a similar streak was at play in some of his other work, noticeably *Riff Raff* (1947), *Race Street* (1948) and *A Dangerous Profession* (1949). Mayo sang an odd song, "I Leaned on a Man," although actually her voice was dubbed. There was a friendly, relaxed atmosphere on the set; O'Brien delighted in telling jokes and regaling cast and crew with humorous stories. There was spontaneous applause among the crew for one of Mayo's crucial emotional scenes.[32]

Ladd had been so impressed with O'Brien's performance in *A Cry in the Night* (1956) that he signed him for the co-starring role.[33] The two became good friends and Ladd was a frequent guest at O'Brien's parties. When Ladd died in January 1964, O'Brien was asked to read the eulogy.[34]

O'Brien was considered for a number of other westerns over the years including *The Gun* for director Albert S. Rogell. Leif Erickson was named as O'Brien's replacement but the film was not made.[35] He was also in the running for *Guns of the Timberland* produced by Alan Ladd but the role was given to Noah Beery. When Howard da Silva was fired from *Slaughter Trail* for his alleged political affiliations, O'Brien was touted as a possible replacement, but in the event Brian Donlevy filled the breach.[36] O'Brien was one of the candidates for the role of reformed drunkard Dude in Howard Hawks' *Rio Bravo*, a part which went to Dean Martin instead.[37]

For O'Brien, his 1950s westerns came as a change from his noirs, although of course the best of them were essentially noir-westerns. Again, he played embittered or painfully wronged men who seek redress in their own way. In *Silver City* he was the victim of a vendetta by his ex–business partner who blackened his name and made it impossible for him to get work in the territory. In *Warpath* he was a driven man out for revenge, and in *Denver and Rio Grande* he was up against it because of a femme's belief that he murdered her brother. In *The Big Land* he had to fight not only the destructive forces in society but those in his own nature. He was equally handy with his fists whether atop a fast-moving train in the Rockies or the sidewalks of New York. The villains got their comeuppance in 1870s Durango just as they had in contemporary San Francisco. He was often the hunted victim even in the great outdoors which could afford him no escape. The sheer scale and majesty of the scenery emphasized the insignificance of human affairs. For some he looked too beefy to play the western hero convincingly. It might be churlish to point out that with all the cattle on display in film after film in this category, perhaps more real heroes of the west resembled him than the lean hombres usually cast.

Genre purists had no cause for alarm; normal service was soon resumed. O'Brien's dalliance with the west was a brief one, and although he made three more in the 1960s, the abiding image of him will forever be linked to an urban setting. Even so, his westerns are worth seeking out for showing a different side of him at a crucial time in his career and emphasizing above all that his range was never limited by genre.

❖❖ 12 ❖❖

Broadway Interlude

> I don't just want to stick to pictures. The theater is my first love and I want to come back to it.—Robert Francis, "Candid Close-Ups: Edmond O'Brien's Brooklyn Flier is Top Flight in *Winged Victory*," *The Brooklyn Daily Eagle*, December 12, 1943, 34

O'Brien maintained his love of the stage and discussed numerous projects over the years since his last New York appearance in 1940, but his marriage and Hollywood success meant that he was away from the Broadway stage for some time.

Many promising stage offers came along in the postwar years. He often wanted to appear in the plays of his brother, including *The Mazda Mines*.[1] In 1945, he was set to star in a revival of Noël Coward's *Design for Living* with husband-and-wife team Peter Lind Hayes and Mary Healy, but that did not come to fruition.[2] Three years later, O'Brien tried to organize a Shakespearean repertory company in Hollywood and had interest from his fellow players including Kent Smith.[3] O'Brien was offered the lead opposite Madeleine Carroll in *Goodbye My Fancy* by Fay Kanin, but he had a contract with Warner Brothers, who would not agree to it.[4] When he first signed with Universal in 1948, he even had a clause which allowed him seven months of the year to appear on stage.[5] He sometimes played on the "straw hat" circuit. For instance, in June 1949, he was cast in the lead role of a stage version of F. Scott Fitzgerald's novel *The Last Tycoon*. The production at the La Jolla Playhouse was based on the play by Henry Kraft, with the eventual hope of a Broadway run that did not happen.[6] In the same year, after his success in *White Heat*, he was offered the lead opposite Katharine Hepburn in a West Coast tour of *As You Like It*.[7] O'Brien was also among those considered for the role of Stanley Kowalski in Tennessee Williams' *A Streetcar Named Desire*.[8] In 1950, he was tipped to co-star with James Mason in a stage play in London but in the event, neither were able to appear.⁹

O'Brien's actual return to Broadway came about in an unexpected fashion and was as much inspired by his wife as anyone else. When they were at a Hollywood party, several of the famous guests there started entertaining and Olga was encouraged to sing; "I auditioned for this show without knowing it," she recalled. "I was not only a bit awed by it all but I was noticeably pregnant and I certainly didn't feel like doing anything when my husband urged me to sing. However, I did and I'm glad. [Alan Jay] Lerner was at the party and heard me and a short time later offered me the part [in *Paint Your Wagon*]."¹⁰ Edmond always encouraged his wife to pursue her performing ambitions: "Olga's too talented to give up her career," he said. "She's given me two wonderful babies and a happy home. I think I'd be a heel if I stood in her way."¹¹

O'Brien hoped to find work in New York at the same time as his wife was there and talked with his old friend and mentor Maurice Evans about a possible Broadway play, but that did not come to anything.¹² When Olga started to prepare for *Paint Your Wagon*, he came close to a deal with Lee Sabinson to appear in Samuel Grafton's *Out of the Sky*.¹³ It was not until the year following Olga's triumph that Edmond returned to the Great White Way. Surprisingly, the play that drew him was *I've Got Sixpence*. He was persuaded by the author, John Van Druten, with whom he had enjoyed previous success in *Leave Her to Heaven*. Van Druten thought of him for the role in his latest and called the actor to tell him about it. "But he said he was very happily settled with his wife and children and couldn't think of a thing that would take him away from California," Van Druten recalled. "However, he did consent to read the play, and the afternoon of the day he received it he called me and said that *Sixpence* was the thing that would take him back to New York."¹⁴ O'Brien again moved his family to Westchester during the play's run.¹⁵

In November 1952, the play—Van Druten's nineteenth—premiered in a tryout run at Philadelphia's Walnut Theater, where it attracted some good, if qualified, reviews. One local critic wrote, "Whatever appeal the play possesses depends largely on the actors in the virtually flawless cast."¹⁶ However, once it transferred to Broadway's Ethel Barrymore Theater in December, it was a different story. Despite a strong cast, which included Viveca Lindfors and the great Patricia Collinge, it was not generally well received. Few were attracted by religious themes, and critics found Van Druten's portrait of a marriage confusing and dissatisfying. Nor were many persuaded by O'Brien's performance and some felt he was miscast. One commented that he "substitutes shouting for passion and relies on the swear words in his text to carry meaning."[17] Brooks Atkinson considered the play too slight for its heavy themes; of O'Brien he commented, "In the part of the villain, Edmond O'Brien gave a harsh and honest performance. Although the author seems to have some hope for his character, Mr. O'Brien's forceful performance ought to dispel any easy notions."[18]

Louis Sheaffer declared Van Druten's play to be "bad, sometimes embarrassingly bad," but said the actors did their best under the circumstances; "Mr. O'Brien is persuasive as the self-centered, self-pitying writer," he wrote.[19] Another reviewer noted that O'Brien gave it a good try but said that the actors "spout soliloquies which come uncomfortably close to sophomore twaddle, adding nothing new or arresting, in this decidedly sententious drama."[20]

O'Brien was well aware of the difficulty of finding the right play, the right part and the right audience. "One look over the footlights will tell you," he observed. "Either you've picked them up and they're with you in the part, warm and alive, or you've lost them and they're inert, cold as ice. You can tell by the chill."[21] The Broadway run of *I've Got Sixpence* lasted only 23 nights, and O'Brien never returned to the New York stage. He did, however, take part with his wife in a summer theater workshop at the UCLA with *The Four-Poster*, a play about the vicissitudes in the life of a married couple over a thirty-five-year period.

13

Turning Points

> The way I figure it is that you've got to make people sit up and take notice. They'll pay a lot more attention to you if you shoot an old lady than if you coo at the ingénue.
> —"Here's One Place That Crime Pays—It's Crime Role in Films," *Democrat & Chronicle,* Rochester, New York, May 21, 1950, 3F

O'Brien did some of his best work on screen in the early 1950s, at which time he was busy in three and sometimes four media. In addition to his radio series *Yours Truly, Johnny Dollar,* he began working on television and enjoyed a range of roles on the big screen that even included a return to his beloved Shakespeare.

The Turning Point was one of several films inspired by the Kefauver Senate hearings into organized crime. Whereas others such as *Hoodlum Empire* (1952) focused more on the criminal side of things, *The Turning Point* honed in on the man running the committee and those around him. O'Brien played John Conroy, a law professor appointed to head the investigation, with Alexis Smith as his girlfriend and William Holden as a cynical reporter and lifelong friend. Based on the Horace McCoy novel *Storm in the City*, the story centered on the investigation into the business affairs of Eickelberger (Ed Begley), which reveals that crime is endemic in the city on every level. The film was beautifully acted, and although Holden had arguably the better role, O'Brien brought the well-meaning Conroy fully to life. With his "clean hands, pure heart and no political future," O'Brien made this Sir Galahad real. He was understated, and proved that he could be highly effective when he underplayed. The film was tautly directed in a semi-documentary style by the veteran William Dieterle, who had been at the helm of *The Hunchback of Notre Dame.* Although set in a fictional Midwest town, there was some fine location work around

13. Turning Points

In *The Turning Point* (1952), O'Brien plays a man on a mission who loses every illusion he ever had. William Holden (*left*) was equally fine as a cynical reporter.

downtown Los Angeles, especially the funicular railway at Angel's Flight. Dieterle is unlikely to ever become a fashionable director but he proved highly effective over his 45-year career both in Hollywood and his native Germany. Among his highlights were such varied fare as *The Story of Louis Pasteur* (1936), *The Devil and Daniel Webster* (1941) and *Portrait of Jennie* (1948).

Contemporary critics were unconvinced by *The Turning Point*. One leading reviewer dismissed it as "a wild and febrile fabrication."[1] Undoubtedly, television was now setting the pace for the big screen, to the likely detriment of the art of the cinema. Those televised hearings that viewers could watch every teatime made crime bosses look ordinary and had marked a turning point in other ways. O'Brien remarked; "The Kefauver telecasts have shattered the illusion of most Americans as far as the glamor of gangsterdom goes."[2] In a wider sense, they had arguably also contributed to the deglamorization of cinema.

Man in the Dark, originally known as *The Man Who Lived Twice*, was one of the earliest 3-D films. For all the technology, it was a familiar

The French poster for *Man in the Dark* (1953), an entertaining 3-D feature on the familiar noir theme of amnesia.

monochrome noir on the amnesia theme, but with a twist. Steve Rowley (O'Brien) has experimental brain surgery to remove his criminal tendencies. While he recovers at a sanitarium, his old gang reappears and abducts him, expecting him to lead them to a stash of stolen money. Also in pursuit of the money is a hard-nosed insurance man. At first Rowley cannot remember anything but begins to have dreams about a fairground; as his memory returns, he seems to be reverting to his former self. *Man in the*

Dark was an entertaining noir boasting many familiar faces and a sometimes witty script.

At some points, there was a straining for chances to use the new 3-D technology. One such scene was during the surgery when the frame is filled with masked doctors and scalpels lunging towards the camera, which must have seemed effective to those watching through their special glasses. The same device was used again when Ted de Corsia threatened to burn O'Brien's orbs with a cigar, and to best effect when a bird flies out of an abandoned house straight at the camera. The script also offered some appealing gallows humor. When O'Brien is wheeled into the lab, the doctor asks him how he feels about undergoing the risky surgery. "How would you like to have your lid open?" O'Brien responds. "I was born on a Monday, might as well go out on one, like the dirty laundry."

Director Lew Landers was a ubiquitous presence in Hollywood from the 1930s to the 1960s, latterly on television. He tried his hand in most genres, without great distinction in any. *Man in the Dark* was shot in only 11 days and utilized Columbia's own "depth-dimension" process which involved two cameras and no mirrors, as some 3-D processes did.[3]

The final showdown at a funfair made good use of many aspects of the terrain, particularly the rollercoaster. That was not a scene that O'Brien enjoyed filming. "I've had it," he declared. "Once was enough. They ran us 18 times just for one scene on that blankety-blank rollercoaster. I kept my nerve up but I couldn't keep my food down."[4] During a dream sequence, there was an especially surreal scene in which O'Brien is chased by cops who take potshots at him while seated in what look like rotating teacups. The sequence involved one of those annoying fat mechanical laughing figures in a glass booth, providing a suitably absurdist comment on the proceedings.

In between noirs and westerns, O'Brien appeared in a brief role as a barker on the midway at the end of the Cecil B. DeMille all-star epic *The Greatest Show on Earth* (1952). He spent a whole day working on the film but like many was unbilled.[5] A critical and commercial success, it was the top-grossing picture of the year, earning $12 million at the box office.[6]

A Double Life had a Shakespearean background, but O'Brien's only real screen foray into the works of the immortal Bard was director Joseph Mankiewicz's *Julius Caesar* (1953). Louis Calhern played the title role, with Marlon Brando as Marc Antony and James Mason as Brutus among a stellar cast. According to one story, O'Brien was so desperate for any role in the film that he approached production head of MGM Dore Schary and said he was willing to accept whatever salary was on offer so long as

For many critics, O'Brien as Casca was the surprise of Joseph L. Mankiewicz's *Julius Caesar* (1953). Those who had followed O'Brien's career closely knew of his love for the Bard since his earliest days in the theater. The film is widely regarded as one of the best-ever Hollywood adaptations of a Shakespeare play. In this shot, O'Brien is about to stab Julius Caesar (Louis Calhern).

he could appear. He was paid $10,000 for his role as Casca.[7] O'Brien was energized by the project and was gratified that Shakespeare was finally being given the full Hollywood treatment he deserved. "It's a lot of fun," he observed, "and I was curious to see what could be done with the play. It's the most exciting of Shakespeare's plays, and it's one every school kid studies.... Maybe it's a gamble, but it's a good gamble."[8]

The film was widely praised; an Australian critic wrote that it was "beautifully acted, with some scenes of extraordinary intellectual vitality.... American accents are used with remarkable aptness for some scenes and characters—notably for the ironic, irreverent Casca drawn with Yankee flourish by Edmond O'Brien."[9] *The Times* of London considered O'Brien to be "the surprise" of the film.[10] The *New Yorker* agreed, commenting on the contrast with his usual roles in crime films: "He didn't seem to be at all overwhelmed by his translation to higher things; indeed, he read lines grown gray with familiarity as though they had just occurred to him on the spot, and ... he deserves special commendation."[11] He also drew much praise from his fellow actors, including Spencer Tracy. Several observers noted that O'Brien could have done full justice to the title role given the chance.

It was an extraordinary achievement to assemble such a cast of some of the finest British and American actors around including Deborah Kerr and Greer Garson. There was some egotism on display and some tension on the set; Mason felt that too much attention was being given to Brando at his (Mason's) expense. However, the mix of actors worked well, at least on screen. Sometimes derided as the king of the mumblers, Brando sounded as clear as a bell after much tutoring from John Gielgud. Gielgud, who played Cassius, was one of the driving forces behind the project and among the first to see a rough cut of the film. He considered Calhern "dreadful" but praised O'Brien as "excellent."[12]

James Mason later reflected in his memoirs,

> I thought at the time, and, having caught it again on television, I still hold that the only impeccable performance by a member of our cast was that of Edmond O'Brien as Casca. Here was a man who had established himself as an actor of style before he appeared in his first movie. Ultimately, he assumed the tough guy so indelibly that Mank had the greatest difficulty in persuading the rest of the top brass that Eddie could play Shakespeare to the manner born.[13]

O'Brien owed his elevation to an old friend, producer John Houseman, who recalled; "For the small but crucial role of Casca, I chose Edmond O'Brien who was only cast as detectives and crooked lawyers, but who I remembered as a young Shakespearean."[14] Houseman hoped to persuade O'Brien to join him in a Broadway play he planned to do, but the actor's schedule was too full at that time.[15]

Julius Caesar stayed true to its source, which was probably its greatest strength. "I didn't cut or add anything," revealed Mankiewicz, "It's Shakespeare to the syllable."[16] The director hailed the Bard as "the genius of geniuses" and achieved what many others had hitherto failed to do in bringing his work successfully to the screen.[17] The scenes of battle were arguably the weakest areas, but such is true of many adaptations of Shakespeare's work.

O'Brien went on a road tour promoting *Julius Caesar* during which he talked about the film and gave readings from Shakespeare. Over the course of several weeks he visited colleges and universities in twenty-seven cities, expounding on the art of Shakespearean acting. He conveyed his enthusiasm to captive audiences and showed that the roles he essayed in crime films and those of the classical stage were not so far removed, "Anyone who knows Shakespeare knows that the Bard's characters can be as brutal as anything Hollywood ever turned out," he remarked, "His plays are full of murders, suicides and mayhem – and so are most of my pictures."[18]

It was a shame that O'Brien did not seek to appear in more of the playwright's works. The movie proved popular with a wide variety of people, especially college students and those studying the works. There were even special prices to attract them. A college newspaper in Sacramento commended O'Brien as the best in the strong supporting cast: "The naturalness with which he assumes Casca's character is one of the highlights of the picture," wrote a young critic.[19] The film still stands as one of the finest screen versions of any of Shakespeare's plays, and was a significant picture for O'Brien personally because it led directly to his role in Mankiewicz's next film, *The Barefoot Contessa* (1954).

Edmond still harbored stage ambitions, many of which were centered on Shakespeare. However, he was chary of Broadway; he had been acutely disappointed with the reception of *I've Got Sixpence* and put some of it down to the old animosity that existed in some circles for those who had forsaken the stage for the bright lights and big money of Tinsel Town. "You know, all you Broadway people look down on us Hollywood expatriates who've sloughed legit for movies like what we're doing is a form of whoring," he once declared.[20] He never lost his love of Shakespeare, and was involved in an ambitious film series planned with Laurence Olivier *et al.*, *The Best of the Bard*. It consisted of a series of scenes from some of Shakespeare's most famous plays.[21] One of Edmond's dreams was for seven leading actors to give their interpretation of *Hamlet*. "It would have to be a labor of love!" he said, "But what comparisons we'd get."[22] He spoke of his long-term plans for Shakespeare: "I'd like to give the toughest of all a fling—Lear," he revealed, "I could build up to it."[23]

❖❖ 14 ❖❖

Working with Ida

> I cannot tolerate fools, won't have anything to do with them. I only want to associate with brilliant people.—William Donati, *Ida Lupino: A Biography* (Lexington KY: University of Kentucky Press, 1996), 27

> You have to play the guy from the inside out, not the outside in.—Joseph Finnigan, "Free-Lancing Pays Off for Edmond O'Brien," *Schenectady Gazette,* November 19, 1964, 36.

O'Brien made memorable contributions to two extraordinary films directed by Ida Lupino. *The Hitch-Hiker* and *The Bigamist* (both 1953) were widely recognized almost immediately as being works of outstanding merit by a uniquely talented lady.

An unforgettable noir, *The Hitch-Hiker*, originally known as *The Difference*, starred O'Brien and Frank Lovejoy as friends on a fishing trip who give a lift to a man, Emmett Myers (William Talman), who turns out to be a cold-blooded killer. Myers forces them at gunpoint to drive to Mexico. The scenario was inspired by the real-life case of Billy Cook, who murdered six people in 1950 and '51 in Missouri and California. Initially, Lupino tried hard to make the film a factual reconstruction of the murders, but was told it was impossible to depict a convicted criminal. Lupino interviewed the two men who had been held at gunpoint by Cook and based the story on their testimony but, by necessity, had to stress that the film was fictionalized.[1] "The picture may have been inspired by Cook but it is not his story," she insisted. "Our story is the fight of an insane mind to drive two men insane."[2] The tale was originally written by the blacklisted author Daniel Mainwaring without a screen credit. Locations around Long Point, California, were used. The Palos Verdes peninsula and Long Point bluffs doubled for the coast of Mexico.[3]

The picture was gripping from start to finish and the tension never let up. Collins (O'Brien) was the more emotionally wrought of the two and the one less able to contain his anger and frustration with Myers. In one memorable scene, he expressed all his pent-up frustration when he appealed directly to the heavens; this was brilliantly shot by an overhead camera which panned out, showing how small and insignificant such human problems seemed in such a vast landscape. Even during the times when O'Brien was not speaking, it was clearly apparent what he was thinking as he looked for a chance to get even with his captor. Bowen (Lovejoy), the cooler of the two, kept his head most of the time. The casting was perfect. The ordinariness of the two friends underlined the arbitrary nature of the crime, and the film's opening titles that said it could happen to anyone. Lovejoy and O'Brien were both fine actors around the same age whose naturalness was completely apposite for the scenario. More glamorous

Ida Lupino's tense noir *The Hitch-Hiker* (1953) was perfectly cast with Frank Lovejoy (*left*), William Talman (*middle*, holding map and gun) and O'Brien (*right*).

star names would not have worked, and would have made the whole thing seem artificial. Lupino's attention to detail was apparent in such things as the clothes they wore: Their casual "weekend" clothes complete with jeans and baseball caps emphasized their complete unpreparedness for what occurs and reinforced the opening message. They were not two slick Joes in smart business suits with an answer for everything but two Everyman characters with wives and children and myriad worries of their own. In the noir universe, their simple act of kindness leads them into a nightmare situation from which there appears to be no escape. To Myers, their humanity is their weakness; even their friendship means they will not try to escape unless they can both get away.

Ostensibly set in the west, this was so far removed from the terrain of movie legend. For all its use of the vast landscape, the film had the claustrophobia of an urban noir. There were numerous interior shots of the car at night. The great outdoors provided no escape for the friends. Making the film was something of an ordeal for cast and crew. It was particularly difficult for cinematographer Nicholas Musuraca, whose distinctive photography was a key element of the film's success. Musuraca has been rather overshadowed by other names, but did as much as anyone to define the look of noir, his variety of tone and deep blacks being a feature of his work. Beginning as a projectionist, the Italian-born Musuraca had a full career as photographer with such outstanding credits as *Stranger on the Third Floor* (1940) and *Blood on the Moon* (1948). While working for a major studio, he was able to develop his own style in such expressionist psychological dramas as RKO's *The Seventh Victim* (1943) and *The Curse of the Cat People* (1944). The night shots in *The Hitch-Hiker* give that film its special atmosphere.

Gossip columnist Dorothy Manners intimated that there was a difference of opinion between Lupino and O'Brien concerning the portrayal of his character. It would be unsurprising if two fine actors with strong opinions did not hold differing views about such things but these matters were of little consequence.[4]

Despite the difficult conditions, O'Brien enjoyed working on the film and spoke of his "intense admiration for the Lupino name in this business."[5] Talman remarked, "She was one of the guys; in fact, our leader, who met everything with an unbeatable sense of humor. She set the pace for the 70 men who made up the troupe, and held it."[6] (It was perhaps Talman's greatest role. He was so convincing that he was once hit in the face by a man who recognized him from the film.) O'Brien neatly summarized the qualities of Ida: "She has a sense of taste, a wonderful ability to avoid cliché, to do things in a discreet, offbeat, interesting way."[7]

The background characters were well-realized, and several familiar faces popped up including Jose Torvay as the policeman. Torvay was a veteran of many Mexican films; he had even appeared in the nation's first talkie, and was memorable as one of the bandits in *The Treasure of the Sierra Madre* (1948). It was a refreshing change to see both Mexicans and the police in a positive light. For once, the Mexicans were seen as people, not caricatured as sly cutthroats, and the police were astute and efficient instead of dunderheads running around in circles like *the Keystone Cops*. The ease of American and Mexican cross-border cooperation was also heartening.

The Hitch-Hiker was widely appreciated at the time of its release. The *Film Bulletin* called it "an example of intelligent and economical filmmaking at its best."[8] It soon received classic status and has long been the subject of forensic analysis. Some have interpreted it as a social and political comment, or discussed it in terms of gender politics. Over-analysis can kill art, the best of which defies all attempts to define it. Bowen and Collins show no personal bravery, and some have even accused them of being selfish, but surely if they had been selfish they would have each tried to make a getaway at the first opportunity without considering the other. They have been viewed by various writers as representative of the comfortable, complacent postwar generation whose experience in war has made them cautious. However, although most go along with the negative view of them, Bowen and Collins surely display the finest of human instincts by offering a hitch-hiker a lift in the first place.

Lupino's economy was striking; the way she used the opening titles to tell the preliminary story and set the stage for what follows. This comprised a series of impressionistic montages which proved the power of auto-suggestion. She had great observation and skillfully used her radio sensibility in subtle ways. For instance, the dialogue was pared down to a minimum, almost in the same way such writers as Samuel Beckett worked; this gives the film a spare, taut feel and adds to the tension. It is a moot point whether the existentialism of film noir is the same or independent of the European tradition. The same undercurrents inform both.

Lupino made clever use of such things as the dead eye of Myers which appears to be watching them all night. Note also the use of the radio and the incongruity of the romantic classical music at a crucial juncture in the middle of the desert when they reach a well and Collins and Bowen are near breaking point. With its taglines such as "When did you last invite death into your car?" it was unsurprising if many were dissuaded from ever giving a lift to a stranger again. *Hobo News* thought so and campaigned unsuccessfully against the release of the film.

14. Working with Ida

The Bigamist told the story of Harry Graham, a deep-freeze salesman. His wife Eve (Joan Fontaine) is unable to have children; hence the couple try to adopt a child. The investigation into the parents' background by adoption official Mr. Jordan (Edmund Gwenn) uncovers Graham's double life with waitress Phyllis (Ida Lupino) in Los Angeles. The film handled a potentially sensationalist story with a rare emotional depth. This was notably the first movie in which Lupino directed herself. Her touch was very apparent—it was directed with skill, intelligence and sensitivity. The acting, particularly of O'Brien and Lupino, lifted this venture immeasur-

O'Brien gave a sensitive portrayal of a man torn between two women in *The Bigamist* (1953), a mature film for its time which explored a difficult subject with great understanding. Joan Fontaine (pictured) is one of his wives.

ably. Both actors had a naturalness which rendered all their scenes perfectly realized. Again, O'Brien was telling even when he wasn't speaking; one could see his mind racing at crucial points when his double life was in danger of being exposed. His sensitive portrayal of an essentially lonely man who makes a terrible mistake was arguably one his best and most dramatic roles. "Except for *Julius Caesar*, this will be his first highly dramatic role in some time," remarked Ida.[9] O'Brien, who was always fascinated by the filmmaking process, even assisted in directing her acting cenes along with her film cutter Dick Harris.

It was a difficult subject to explore in a feature film at that time, and Lupino broke new ground in her treatment. The original source of the story was *Two Loves Have I*, written by Larry Marcus and Lou Schor. Those authors were even commended by Joseph Breen and his Production Code Administration for their thoughtful handling of the subject matter.[10] There were some lighter moments, especially during the scene on the bus. "It's a very delicate kind of theme," said O'Brien, "and you have to look out for

O'Brien and Ida Lupino worked exceptionally well together on screen in *The Bigamist*. They were good friends with great mutual admiration for each other's work. Lupino later directed three episodes of O'Brien's television series *Sam Benedict* and also acted in another.

the wrong laughs. If we get a bad laugh, we're up the creek."[11] Lupino showed great observation and understanding of human nature. Such things as the clockwork toy that Eve buys for the child-to-be was poignant. Lupino always invested her characters with a life of their own, even the background personnel such as her employer at the Chinese restaurant or the landlady of her apartment house (who, incidentally was played by Joan Fontaine's mother Lillian). They are drawn with the minimum of fuss; her economy is one of the most striking things about her films.

Harry Graham does not wittingly set out to deceive both women but ironically, he becomes trapped in an impossible situation by his desire not to hurt Phyllis *or* Eve. Although he is not naturally deceptive, it is surprising how easily he adapts to the double life. In reality, the net result might have been that he would have lost both. However, a romantically ambiguous note was struck by the ending, which made the key point that bigamy is undoubtedly far more common than anyone will ever know. There was good support from the veteran twinkly-eyed character actor Edmund Gwenn, who was perhaps most famous as everybody's favorite Santa Claus in *Miracle on 34th Street* (1947). Moreover, he was an actor of vast experience and wide range who memorably essayed an assassin in Hitchcock's *Foreign Correspondent* (1940). Gwenn fitted into the fabric of the film surprisingly well. Lupino told him he could ad lib in his sequences, which delighted him. Before long, he was stealing scenes; "I'd rather have a scene stolen by Mr. Gwenn than anyone I can think of," remarked O'Brien.[12] During filming, Gwenn invited Lupino and O'Brien to stay at his house.[13]

The Bigamist was essentially a sad tale about three lonely people, and at times tapped into postwar malaise and the increasing sense of dislocation. Despite technological advances brought on by the war, there was a concomitant feeling of unease that underscores many films of that era. A major city in the United States, the most materially advanced nation in the western world at that time, offers nothing for Graham on a lonely Sunday other than a confirmation of his own feelings of isolation. "On that particular Sunday my aloneness was like a kind of pain," he explains to Jordan. Hence, Harry joins a bus tour of movie stars' houses. "I like movies," he says, "although I really don't care where Clark Gable lives. But here were people going someplace. And I went along with them." From the spur of loneliness, everything follows. It is there he meets Phyllis, who informs him that she's "just crazy about bus rides." O'Brien displayed great sensitivity and understanding as Harry Graham and showed what a subtle actor he could be.

Lupino loved working with O'Brien; she remarked,

> When Eddie or Bogie were in a picture, they ... grabbed your attention. I've never seen Eddie be bad in a picture or fair which I think is even worse. Eddie was always offbeat, different. He never came off as an actor acting.... If you saw him in a film, you'd say, "This is interesting. This is going to be colorful...." No, they're not going to say rotten things about Eddie O'Brien.[14]

After two films for Lupino, O'Brien was touted for a third, *Private Hell 36* (1954). This time Lupino was the actress and the director Don Siegel, but Steve Cochran appeared in O'Brien's place.[15]

Not all the pictures he made were classics. In the same period as the Lupino films, he also appeared in such poor fare as *Cow Country* and the trite *China Venture* (1953). This latter was an unconvincing feature about U.S. Marines whose mission is to find an important wounded Japanese general in Chinese-held territory and bring him back to safety, alive if possible. O'Brien headed the cast as the captain at loggerheads with his commander (Barry Sullivan). Jocelyn Brando was the sole woman of the party. It all felt too artificial and studio-bound. Although the actors did their best, the cheapness of the whole thing was all too apparent. O'Brien attempted to inject humor into the proceedings but the weak script gave him nothing to work with. Rather surprisingly, Fritz Lang had first been assigned as the director, at which point the film was known as *Operation 16-Z*. Lang wisely switched to *The Big Heat* instead and Don Siegel took over duties on the war film. Siegel commented, "I had a marvelous relationship with Edmond O'Brien, but I started out disastrously."[16] He invited O'Brien to a script rehearsal at his home, but he didn't show. Later Siegel realized that O'Brien was not able to read the script because of his eye problems and had to have a stand-in to read it for him. By 1954 he had already undergone two operations on his eyes and was advised by a specialist that he needed a third.[17]

Among other touted roles, Edmond almost played Sgt. Warden in *From Here to Eternity* (1953), a part which famously went to Burt Lancaster. If the other casting suggestions of Joan Crawford or Joan Fontaine in the Deborah Kerr role had been followed through, it would have been interesting to know how the famous beach scene would have turned out.[18] In May 1952, Edmond was invited to London to play the lead in *Murder in the Tate Gallery*, and intended to travel there with his wife. This minor British noir was retitled *The Fake* (1953) and the part of the American insurance agent was played by Dennis O'Keefe.[19] O'Brien was penciled in for a leading role in the Korean War drama *Battle Zone*, due to be filmed at Camp Pendleton Marine Base in California by Monogram.[20] However, his role went to John Hodiak. An interesting European venture was the chance to play the manager of boxer Primo Carnera, in the life story of "the Ambling Alp." Carnera was said to be behind the financing of the project, due to be filmed in Rome. The fascinating idea was never realized.[21]

❖❖ 15 ❖❖

O'Brien the Director

> I'd rather be regarded as a young director than a fading leading man.—Erskine Johnson, "Angel Allyson Gets Devilish Job," *The Tennessean*, Nashville, Tennessee, June 25, 1954, 26

O'Brien had long harbored an ambition to direct, ever since his earliest years in Hollywood, and his name was linked with many projects which never came to fruition. In 1954 he finally found his chance when he co-directed an intriguing noir, *Shield for Murder*.

O'Brien expressed an interest in a great many ideas over the years since he had first directed on the stage in the 1930s. In 1952, it was announced that he would direct and star in *The Murder*, from a Chester Erskine story about an engaged couple who plan to murder her parents so they will have enough money to marry.[1] There was some speculation that the plot was based on the 1947 Beulah Overell case in Newport Harbor, California. O'Brien sought Linda Christian to play the girl, having been impressed by her performance in *The Happy Time* (1952).[2] When she proved unavailable, he hoped to secure Faith Domergue for the role.[3] The project did not happen for him, because the producer who first hired him sold the script to RKO. There it was eventually handed to Otto Preminger, retitled *Angel Face* (1953), and starred Jean Simmons and Robert Mitchum. O'Brien hoped to star in and direct *A Few Flowers for Shiner*, from a story about two aviators by Richard Llewellyn, author of the classic *How Green Was My Valley*.[4] Paulette Goddard was slated to co-star and filming was due to start in Italy.[5] Arthur Godfrey was sought for the role of the other aviator.[6] However, the project was delayed because of Godfrey's commitments and finally abandoned altogether. Another idea was *The Blind Mirror*, from a story by Edmond's brother Liam; it was described as a mystery along the lines of *The Maltese Falcon*, set in Paris.[7] Working with Ida Lupino had inspired him as much as anything to try his hand at directing.

Edmond was also keen to follow the example of fellow actors John Wayne and Burt Lancaster and involve himself in the technical and production side of filmmaking. "They have gone out of their way to learn," he

The Spanish poster for *Shield for Murder* (1954), in which O'Brien (at left) starred and co-directed. It was a startling picture and a *tour de force* for O'Brien as a cop who turns spectacularly bad after 16 years' service.

noted. "So have I." Over the years he had studied the work of the great directors and watched cutters at work. He expounded on his long-term plans: "My intention, eventually, is to work myself out of acting. I want to build up a solid future with equity in pictures, not just work for a salary the rest of my life. Taxes get most of my income anyhow." With his brother, he formed another company, Story Tellers Present, and had several other properties he hoped to explore including *The Money Man* and *The Orloff Whip*. Out of four potential projects he intended to direct three and act in only one.[8] Nothing came of all this. "Maybe I'll try directing yet," he said. "When I get a script that means something."[9] The chance came far sooner than he imagined with *Shield for Murder*, of which he was both co-director (with Howard W. Koch) and star.

Shield for Murder was adapted from a novel of the same name by William P. McGivern, whose work provided the basis of *The Big Heat* (1953), *Hell on Frisco Bay* (1955) and *Odds Against Tomorrow* (1958). *Shield for Murder* was an unrelenting story of a thoroughly corrupt cop. Whereas the cop in *Between Midnight and Dawn* grumbled about his lot but eventually came good, Barney Nolan (O'Brien) is determined to do something about his predicament—and does so, spectacularly. There are definite parallels with *The Prowler* (1951), in which Van Heflin played a disgruntled cop who sees a chance of escaping his humdrum existence to the kind of life he always dreamed of. Nolan goes further and takes far more drastic action. There was a startling scene in a restaurant where, watched by astonished diners, he begins beating two private detectives viciously. The plates of spaghetti, the horror of the patrons and background jazz music added to the power of the scene. Just before this segment, he was chatting up Carolyn Jones and then spoke to his fiancée on the phone. There is the sense that something is about to happen but it is still surprising when it does. "Call the police!" yells the mortified restaurateur. "You've *had* the police," O'Brien says on the way out.

There was great support from John Agar as Nolan's partner and best friend. At this stage of his career, Agar had become a doyen of B-movies, but always enjoyed making them. He described Shield for Murder as "lots of fun" and said O'Brien was "a lovely, nice man." Emile Meyer was excellent as the harassed police captain. Marla English did well in the difficult role as the girlfriend. In one scene, O'Brien was required to hit her but found it hard to make it look convincing. "Look," she exclaimed, "this is my first chance in my two years in Hollywood. If getting my face slapped, my eye blackened or my nose bent out of shape is going to help me look like an actress, let's get on with it."[10] She was still only 19 and, although this was her first credited screen appearance, she had actually made five previous films, all uncredited. Her last had been a bit as a girl at the songwriter's party in Hitchcock's *Rear Window* (1954). A six-time winner of beauty contests from San Diego, English showed promise but retired from the screen after *Voodoo Woman* (1957) in order to get married.[11]

Shield for Murder is the kind of film which is perhaps more appreciated now than at the time. The lack of pay and demoralizing nature of police work is a recurrent theme on screen. In many a noir, the poor remuneration of all ranks of police is used as a constant reason for those who go off the rails. In *The Big Combo* (1955), for example, smug crime boss Richard Conte taunts Cornel Wilde about the difference in their salaries. Despite everything, *Shield for Murder* was not particularly well-received on its release. One forthright critic observed that O'Brien "deserves better material than the stereotyped thuggery" of the film.[12] Some commentators pointed to the discrepancies in the storyline, and many felt that a cop with 16 years' experience would not have overlooked vital clues. However, such things seemed entirely likely because by that stage, Nolan was not thinking logically at all; his eyes were on the prize and he was not able to see anything else in his quest for the money that seemed to be the answer to all his prayers. O'Brien's achievement as director was commended in some quarters; for instance, the highly popular British magazine *Picture Show* declared that the film was well-directed and expressed great anticipation of all his future efforts behind the camera.

Nolan was by far O'Brien's most disturbed and disturbing character, but he was such a skillful actor that he was able to show how things might have been otherwise. In one scene, he is suddenly appalled by his own actions but unable to stop himself. The dehumanizing aspect of police work is seen as a contributing factor to his downfall, but the main cause is the destructive nature of his inherent greed. Perhaps the wider ills of the capitalist system, or at any rate, consumerism, were also under attack. Nolan was not the first or last policeman to be tempted in order to get the things he wanted and reach the life he thought he deserved, but cops are only human despite having to appear that they are somehow more.

The film is shot through with a startling cynicism about the postwar world. For instance, the new house represents everything to which many young married couples aspired. However, the show house full of all the latest gadgets becomes, as one critic noted, "a symbol of decaying middle-class values."[13] The house feels like a façade hiding the misdeeds of a corrupt cop. From a director's perspective, there were several memorable scenes, chiefly that in the restaurant as previously mentioned, but also when the wounded detective chases Nolan around the swimming pool as bathers try and flee the bullets. The sequence when Nolan tries to make his escape wearing his old uniform across the dark streets was also well handled, and the final scene of all was eminently fitting for all that has gone before. Much of the story took place at night, and the whole film felt like a nightmare ride through one man's subconscious, exploring all the malignant desires that are suppressed in the daytime by the thinnest of veneers.

O'Brien has been dubbed the Prince of Noir but if he had been able to follow through on all the films that were proposed but never made and the roles he missed out on, he might have been the undisputed King of Noir. For the same indie company as *Shield for Murder*, he was to have starred in *Big House, U.S.A.* (1954) in a role which went to Broderick Crawford. The intended television series of the same name was never made.[14] While in New York, O'Brien was offered the leading role in *The Killer Wore a Badge* for director Rudolph Maté.[15] O'Brien, Maté and Philip Waxman set up an independent company to produce the film, partially based on a *Saturday Evening Post* story by Thomas Walsh. O'Brien was to play the villain with Jack Palance as the hero.[16] However, the plans did not bear fruit at that time and the movie was not made until two years later, with entirely different personnel. It was eventually released as *Pushover* (1954) starring Fred MacMurray.[17] Edmond was announced to play opposite Gloria Grahame in a crime story called *Cry Copper* for Universal-International. The film was later retitled *Naked Alibi* (1954) and his part went to Sterling Hayden.[18] O'Brien expressed a desire to play the FBI boss J. Edgar Hoover in a biopic of his life. He even took a trip to Washington to meet Hoover to discuss the project.[19] The minutes of the meeting were never released but the answer was firmly in the negative. It was not until several years after Hoover's death that he was portrayed on screen (coincidentally, by Crawford).[20] Edmond and his brother Liam considered using the Gordons' novel *The Big Frame* as the basis of a movie, but that too failed to happen.[21]

Some of the movies that did come to pass were a mixed bag. For instance, *The Shanghai Story* (1954) was a period curio about a group of American expats in China after the Korean War, held captive in a Shanghai hotel. O'Brien starred as an embittered doctor doing humanitarian work, unwittingly caught up in events. The powers that be, in the shape of Colonel Zorak (Marvin Miller), believe that one of the Americans is a spy, and begin interrogating them. All the guests are suspicious of the alluring Rita King (Ruth Roman), who is allowed to come and go as she pleases. In time, the truth becomes apparent and O'Brien faces great danger.

15. O'Brien the Director

The Shanghai Story (1954) was a typical Cold War thriller in which Red China was the enemy. A curiously appealing and atmospheric yarn, it was enlivened by good performances from O'Brien as an embittered doctor, Ruth Roman as a mysterious femme and a cast of familiar faces.

A rather obscure movie, *The Shanghai Story* had all the hallmarks of the low-budget Republic Studios. It contained some noirish moments but was essentially an old-fashioned espionage adventure given a topical twist in which Red China is the bogeyman. The enemy is so heartless they shoot dogs and Nationalists with the same casual abandon. O'Brien had the leading role and played well opposite Roman, showing that he could easily assume the mantle of dashing romantic hero. Many familiar faces popped up in support, including Richard Jaeckel as his main ally, Barry Kelley as a pompous arms dealer, and Frank Ferguson as a heroic Norwegian. The career of Scottish-born director Frank Lloyd stretched back to Hollywood's early days. He was Oscar-nominated five times and won for his version of Noël Coward's *Cavalcade* (1933) but surprisingly not for *Mutiny on the Bounty* (1935), which was perhaps his most widely remembered film. After the death of his wife, he retired from filmmaking in 1945. Following a nine-year hiatus, he returned with *The Shanghai Story*, his penultimate picture. The film contained some atmospheric cinematography by Jack Marta which added to the noir ambience.

The movie was not generally well-liked; a contemporary London critic considered it "a violent film ... uncompromising ... unimportant in itself, yet symptomatic of the times."[22] Many felt that O'Brien acquitted himself well; *Variety* noted that he was "lusty and vigorous in his role of a hard-hitting doctor."[23] Once again he played a cynical and disillusioned figure with a jaundiced view of the world. His doctor was a long way from the prevailing screen image of the reassuring medical man. O'Brien made far more of the uneven script than seemed to be there. "The things I was going to do as a doctor," he says to Roman in an early scene in the hotel lobby. "Come to China and cure the ills of mankind. But you get ground down; the apathy, the greed, the rake-off, the double-cross." He made it sound as though the medical profession was run by gangsters. *The Shanghai Story* remains a curiously enjoyable and intriguing artifact, with a fine portrait of distilled disillusionment by O'Brien. The picture is something of a guilty pleasure; it would give students of mid–twentieth century history food for thought for its political and sociological insight into its era and the minds of those who dreamt it up.

❖❖ 16 ❖❖

An Oscar for Oscar

> If it hadn't been for Humphrey Bogart, God rest his soul, I might not have had an Oscar today.—James Bacon, "Ed O'Brien Shrugs Off Star Billing," *Press and Sun- Bulletin*, Binghampton, New York, March 2, 1963, 9

> You could fill a big, thick book with what I haven't been able to figure since I was 12 years old.—Oscar Muldoon in *The Barefoot Contessa*

Joseph Mankiewicz's brilliant fable *The Barefoot Contessa* (1954) was a searing indictment of Hollywood and the international set. O'Brien won an Oscar for his performance as the harassed press agent Oscar Muldoon.

It almost never happened. When O'Brien flew to Rome, he discovered that he would have to take lower billing. Humphrey Bogart's contract demanded that only he and Ava Gardner were billed above the title. "Bogie and I were the best of friends," recalled O'Brien, "but billing among actors is something that excludes friendship. He wouldn't budge and neither would I. My first Irish impulse was to go home."[1] However, after a few drinks with Bogie, he agreed to take lower billing.

Beginning with the funeral of famed actress Maria Vargas (Gardner), the film related her story in flashback from the perspectives of three people who knew her: Harry Dawes (Bogart) who discovered her and directed all her pictures; Muldoon (O'Brien), press agent of millionaire Kirk Edwards; and Count Vincenzo (Rossano Brazzi) who married her. *The Barefoot Contessa* was the first film Mankiewicz wrote, directed and produced. It was entirely his vision; "I am essentially a writer who directs," he once asserted.[2] He assembled a great cast and some of the best behind-the-scenes workers in the business, including the veteran Jack Cardiff who contributed some sublime cinematography. It was the height of the era of glamor and the sumptuous gowns by Fontana of Rome were ideal for the fairy tale nature of the story. The lush score of the prolific Italian composer Mario Nascimbene was perfectly suited to the occasion, being at once romantic and deeply melancholic. His expert use of lush orchestrations, gypsy violins, Spanish guitars and the flute for the haunting "Maria's Theme" gave the film a sense of place and time, but was, paradoxically, timeless. The main theme was later given lyrics and recorded by Anne Shelton as "The Song of the Barefoot Contessa" and was also known under the title "My Gypsy Heart" which was released on the HMV label. The Italian singer Katyna Ranieri also recorded the song along with another based on the film on her 1955 LP *Girl on the Spanish Steps.*

The way the story was told, Mankiewicz employed a great deal of narration, which worked particularly well in the hands of Bogart and O'Brien, past masters in the art. They could suggest so much with their dry delivery of the astute script. Brazzi's faltering English was a problem for the final narration, and indeed, the last portion of the film is arguably

Oscar Muldoon (O'Brien) with Maria Vargas (Ava Gardner) in a key scene from *The Barefoot Contessa* (1954), a bitter Cinderella fable. O'Brien won the Academy Award as Best Supporting Actor for his performance.

16. An Oscar for Oscar

the weakest. The director's first choice for the role of the count was James Mason, who would have been ideal, but MGM executive Nicholas Schenk wouldn't release him. Schenk and Mankiewicz had rowed in public at the opening of *Julius Caesar,* and Schenk had never forgiven him for it. "And I ended up with Rossano Brazzi," recalled Mankiewicz, "who cannot act, cannot be sensual ... can hardly speak English, for God's sake, so we had to hire someone to teach him his lines phonetically."[3]

Although the director considered others for the role of Harry Dawes, he always wanted O'Brien as Muldoon. It was a happy symbiosis of actor and role, and O'Brien intuitively understood the character. He recognized that the long telephone scene could do a lot for his Oscar chances. Mankiewicz stressed the importance of him being word perfect in the scene and urged him to learn by heart all ten pages of dialogue. True to form, O'Brien tried to do just that, to the extent that he became somewhat obsessed by it.

> I went over the lines every spare minute I had," he admitted. "When we came back from location, I'd read the part before we went downstairs and had some drinks with Bogart. Even when I was in the shower, Ollie [Olga] would feed me the lines. When I went out on location every morning, I'd go over the scene in the car, rather than the lines I was supposed to do that day.[4]

When it came to the actual filming of the scene, his memory failed him completely. After one whole frustrating day spent on it, he was in despair that he would never be able to do it. That night he repaired to the bar of the Excelsior with Bogart and David Hanna, a publicist working on the picture. O'Brien, nursing his drink, was feeling extremely low that he was not able to remember the lines. However, Bogart jolted him to life: "Don't be a chump," he exclaimed. "To hell with the lines. Stop worrying about them. That's not what the director wants. He wants that fat, pudgy face of yours; the sweat, the excitement a good actor like you knows how to generate. The woods are full of actors who can memorize a long speech. But can they play it?"[5] It was exactly what O'Brien needed. The next day he was able to do the scene in one take.[6] Despite his preoccupation with the telephone scene, O'Brien's understanding of the character showed in more subtle ways—for instance, in the scene after the trial at which Maria testifies. Everyone files out and he stands still as the crowds pass him by. "Imagine you're me," he muses, "and what the public wants and thinks is your business. You're standing in the middle of them and you ask yourself, where did you lose these people?" It was a perfect moment of self-realization; the point at which Muldoon becomes a more interesting and distinctly human character.

One of the most memorable aspects of the character was his constant perspiration. "The sweating was my own piece of business," he recalled. "Then we began to enlarge upon it. But it's cold in January, February and March in Rome. To keep up the illusion, we used glycerin and water, and the makeup guy kept hitting me with it."[7] The use of overlapping flashbacks gave the film a distinct texture. In a similar way to *The Killers*, this built up a many-sided perspective of the subject and her story.

Oscar Muldoon was said to have been inspired by Johnny Meyer, the right-hand man of Howard Hughes. Indeed, Kirk Edwards was modeled on Hughes; as such, he was one of the least successful characters on show because Hughes was a complex personality and Edwards came across as a mere cypher. Conversely, Muldoon existed as a personality in his own right, brought vividly to life by O'Brien. He made the potentially dislikable press agent into a thoroughly human and believable character. He not only won the Academy Award as Best Supporting Actor, but was a runner-up in the New York Critic's Circle and winner of the Golden Globe for Best Single Actor.

The distinguished Spanish film critic Angel Fernandez-Santos writing in *El Pais* wrote perhaps the most perceptive obituary of O'Brien, in which he talked of his great ability to convey ambiguity. Writing about his appearance as Muldoon, Fernandez-Santos wrote: "The single qualities of the New York actor were condensed in this interpretation, and especially the proverbial intensity of his gestures, which made him an unmistakable, peculiar and resounding actor, with a quality of ambiguity."[8]

The making of the film was not one of star Ava Gardner's favorite experiences. The tension on set and the lack of empathy between her and Bogart has been well-documented. The good-natured O'Brien wanted everyone to get along; he was friends with both and never ceased to be. He and Ava even tried to learn Italian together between scenes. Ava was grateful for his presence. She recalled,

> The only good thing on that picture was Eddie O'Brien. He deserved his Oscar. I first met him on *The Killers*. He was a wonderful actor, and he knew I was struggling. He would say little things like "Don't be in a hurry to say that line. Wait a beat. It's a good line, it's important." Eddie knew more about Maria Vargas than Mankiewicz did—and Mankiewicz created her.[9]

The film was shot in several locations in Rome, San Remo, Tivoli and Portofino, with interior shots at the Cinecitta lot outside the capitol. While in Rome, Edmond and Olga enjoyed spending their days sightseeing. One evening they went to see Vittorio Gassman in *Hamlet* and the two actors met afterwards and talked of their mutual admiration for the Bard.[10]

16. An Oscar for Oscar

As soon as filming finished, Mankiewicz, Bogart and O'Brien all expressed an interest in working together again on *The Life of Nick the Greek,* by Hank Greenspun. The career of professional Las Vegas gambler Nick Dandalos would have been an intriguing project for them but this never came to pass.[11]

The Barefoot Contessa's world premiere in September 1954 at the Capitol in New York was the first theatrical event sponsored by CARE, the European relief charity, and some of the proceeds went towards food and clothing textile packages to those areas most in need.[12] *The Barefoot Contessa* has often been more widely appreciated by a European audience. Few American critics at the time knew what to make of it, except that they didn't like it. Especially liverish, Bosley Crowther called it "a caustic and cynical report on the glittering and graceless behavior of the Hollywood-International set." That was his most positive remark.[13] Even so, audiences were intrigued and the cast alone was enough to generate excitement; the premiere went into a seventh week and continued its run into November.[14] François Truffaut wrote the most percipient analysis of the work; he called it "a subtle and intelligent film, beautifully directed and acted.... What is beyond doubt is its total sincerity, novelty, daring and fascination. I myself value it for its freshness, intelligence and beauty."[15]

In the wake of his performance in *The Barefoot Contessa,* O'Brien was offered several other projects in Europe. He was sought by Carlo Ponti and Dino de Laurentiis for a role in *Always Tomorrow,* based on the life of the great Italian actress Eleonora Duse. Deborah Kerr was approached for the lead; however, the idea came to naught.[16] Director Hugo Fregonese wanted O'Brien to star in *The Black Sword* opposite Mrs. Fregonese, Faith Domergue. Although filming was due to take place in Spain, this was also abandoned.[17] Earlier, Roberto Rossellini had intended to film a version of Eugene O'Neill's *Anna Christie* with Ingrid Bergman as the star and O'Brien as Mat Burke. O'Brien agreed but the film was never made.[18] With his brother Liam, Edmond planned to bring the stage play *Portrait in Black* to the big screen. This murder-mystery was set in England and the intention was to shoot it in Italy, but it did not transpire at that time.[19] The film was made six years later and starred Anthony Quinn. Edmond also planned to branch out into comedy with his brother and sought to make *The Phoniest Game on Broadway,* but that was also dropped.[20]

His name was often to the fore when big-budget productions were being cast. For instance, he was on the shortlist for the role of Baka in *The Ten Commandments* (1955) and would have been signed had Vincent Price not been available. O'Brien was wanted by British producer Alexander

Salkind for the role of Guido Orlando, unscrupulous agent to the stars, in an intended adaptation of his self-inflating memoir *Confessions of a Scoundrel*. The film was to have been shot in England but the rights were passed to another producer and eventually shelved.

Being an inveterate worrier, O'Brien's nomination for the Academy Award was both a blessing and a curse. In the time between his nomination and Oscar night, he received numerous communiqués regarding the award. He admitted to fretting about it incessantly. By the time the big day came, he had tortured himself about it to the extent that he was convinced *On the Waterfront* would sweep the board and that he had no chance. It was the proudest night of his life to be awarded the accolade from his peers. His daughter Bridget, then almost six years old, remembered the night vividly, primarily because she wet the bed in her excitement. She could hear the happy throng in the house and then the sure tread of Daddy getting closer. He entered her room full of exuberance, clutching the gold statuette. "Bridge, look what Daddy got," he said, beaming. "Your ol' man did it."[21]

17

Family Man

> I guess my essential hobby is my family.—"*The Long, Hot Summer* to Emphasize Single Episode," *Sunday Times-Union*, Albany, New York, August 22, 1965, H-3

Off-screen, O'Brien was a devoted family man who enjoyed a long and happy second marriage. He loved his home and enjoyed giving parties, but also found ways to relax such as fishing and photography.

He liked to go fishing in the Pacific: "I keep a tiny beach apartment right on the ocean at Malibu," he once revealed. "I go out there a lot on Sundays during the winter when the crowds aren't there."[1] At times, he went fishing with friends and co-workers. For instance, he and Elisha Cook, Jr., once went up to the High Sierras on a fishing trip. While there, they met up with John Wayne and Laraine Day who happened to be shooting *Tycoon* (1947) in a nearby location. O'Brien and Cook, two of Hollywood's hardest-working actors, even managed to get involved in the film and, dressed as Indians, spent a day working on the picture.[2] Edmond fulfilled one of his lifelong dreams when he bought a small boat which he christened the *San Juan* in honor of Olga. Twelve feet long, it was suitable for short trips.[3]

A self-described "camera nut," Edmond loved taking pictures and brought his camera everywhere. His favorite subject was Olga. His house was full of photography equipment and he had his own darkroom where he developed everything. Even this linked back to his working life and he felt it was helpful for him with his background as a stage actor: "I believe that by taking photos, still as well as movie, an actor can improve his film technique," he observed. "He'll learn more about what the cameraman and director are striving for."[4] As with all things, he was quite enthusiastic about it. "I can't think of a more satisfying hobby than the particular one

I'm addicted to—that of home movies," he said, "It keeps me out in the open when I'm shooting movies of my wife, Olga and the little O'Briens.... Of course, they're able to sleep during the evening. I'm up half the night in my den cutting together all that's come back from the lab."[5]

He put a lot of time and effort into supervising the design and building of his ranch-style home in Brentwood. It had ten rooms, five of which were bathrooms. The living room, built like a miniature stage, had a concealed movie screen with theatrical lighting which used dimmer switches. He later built a guest house in the grounds.[6] He was justly proud of the work he had put into designing the house. "Olga and I took a year to get this thing on paper," he once revealed. "We planned every detail."[7] He bought $150 worth of books on the subject and watched numerous DIY shows on television. At one point he even hoped to interest a television crew in filming the builder's progress.[8] "I got books on blueprints and lighting and plumbing and heating installation," he said. "Who needs an architect? I laid out the whole thing myself." He didn't actually do the building work; that was entrusted to Ed Sebastian.[9]

Edmond loved his house, which was built on a hill overlooking the Pacific. It was described as contemporary with a Provincial feel; there were lots of sloping beams and plenty of cupboards—around 100 in total. Although he maintained that it was a joint effort with Olga, she admitted that the only thing she got her way on was using fieldstone for the fireplaces rather than brick as Eddie wanted. It cost around $50,000 to construct, a substantial amount at the time. "We had to wait a few years to add the pool and the other buildings," he said. "What with taxes and all, there wasn't enough to complete it all."[10] In time, the family also employed servants.

When he and Olga married, Edmond still liked "the nightclubs and the gay evenings."[11] In those days, they did the rounds of the Hollywood night spots and were often sighted dancing at Ciro's. He once told a reporter, "I'm the noisy and loud one here. Olga's very placid and quiet."[12] Olga often preferred nights in. If he couldn't go to where the party was, he would bring the party to him. "We do quite a bit of entertaining," he related, "especially in the summer, when we can use the large terrace off the swimming pool. It easily accommodates 30 or 40 guests."[13] Among the guests were Alan Ladd, Burt Lancaster, William Holden, Hoagy Carmichael and Vic Damone. "Eddie was an inveterate party-giver," wrote Mel Tormé. "Those were Eddie's two-fisted drinking days. Late in the party, Eddie, in his cups, would get up and deliver Shakespeare brilliantly. He was already having trouble with his eyes, and one could sense the problem worsening with time."[14]

Edmond relished the comforts of home and sometimes enjoyed cooking. Olga described him as a messy cook and said his specialty was stews. His favorite lunch at one time was a large bowl of fruit compote and a minute steak.[15] He enjoyed shopping for food and clothes, and was a quick shopper, never stopping to look at the price tags. He said he had about 30 suits but only wore a couple of them.[16] He loved to play records and had all the latest hi-fi equipment. The family also enjoyed having sing-songs around the piano and Eddie would record their warblings on his tape-recorder. He was an avid reader and by all accounts had one of the largest private libraries in Hollywood. He also liked to show movies, although, conversely, hated seeing himself on screen and did all he could to avoid it.[17] He had a 16mm projector and used to rent films so he could study the work of some of the best directors such as John Ford and William Wyler. He enjoyed playing practical jokes on Olga, such as the time he ran a Bela Lugosi horror film for her and some friends. Just at the scariest moment when two policemen lifted a coffin lid, a ghastly green face like a Chinese mask lit by a flashlight appeared at the French windows. It was one of Eddie's friends, Mary Hatcher, made up.[18] Olga appreciated his offbeat humor and he in turn enjoyed making her laugh. "She's a great giggler," he said. "I get up in the morning and play different characters for her. She never knows who she's waking up with."[19] She used to help him with his work, and even admitted that when they got married, she spent several hours on the first day of their honeymoon in their flower-bedecked suite in Bel Air going over his lines with him for the film scene he was next due to play.[20]

He was perhaps typically Irish—and a typical actor—in that he was superstitious. For instance, he wore a sapphire ring that he believed warded off evil. The friend who gave it to him had traveled in India and gotten it from a Hindu priest. Edmond was convinced that it had brought him nothing but good luck.[21] In September 1955, he was a willing participant in an astrological TV show, *Thank Your Lucky Stars*. In "Mysteries of the Zodiac," he was profiled and his star chart analyzed by astrologer Alan Wilder.[22] Eddie displayed many of the widely acknowledged traits of the Virgo, being hard-working, down-to-earth with a deep sense of humanity, a perfectionist in his work with attention to detail, but defensive and rather private for all his sociability.

In his younger days, O'Brien used to play sports; he always preferred team games such as football and softball to individual sports like golf. He enjoyed the friendly rivalry and banter between teams.[23] In his early Hollywood days, he regularly went ice skating with Nancy Kelly, Cesar Romero and Ann Sheridan at the outdoor Tropical Gardens Ice Rink in the Westwood Hills.[24] He seldom played sports in later years, although he did sometimes play tennis with his brother Liam, who, he said, usually won. Eddie was a big fan of baseball and a lifelong supporter of the New York Giants.[25] He was a man of great enthusiasms and a hearty supporter at prizefights and ball games.[26] He had a yen for sports paintings and collected baseball pictures. When he was filming in Hawaii, he bought one by the artist Edmond Kohn. He had several of Kohn's vivid and atmospheric pictures including "The Late Throw" and "Batter Up"; this latter was once hailed as "the baseball painting of the century."[27] At the same time, he bought some native paintings as a present for Olga.

Edmond was generous, romantic and impulsive, often buying presents for loved ones.[28] He bought Olga a new Cadillac for their eighth wedding anniversary after he happened to spot it in a showroom window as he was passing.[29] One time at breakfast, he presented her with a big box which contained a marabou coat in what she described as an "ugly violet-red." He looked so happy, she hadn't the heart to tell him she didn't like it. He said he wanted to surprise her with something that she would never have bought for herself. "You certainly did!" she replied. After a few days he came to realize it was not what she wanted and exchanged it for a white one.[30] She was always tactful and understood him totally. When he used to get angry, she would just laugh at him or call him king and he didn't stay mad for long. "He loves affection," she once observed. "He'd give you the world if you were affectionate with him."[31]

Edmond was plagued by tax problems over the years. As early as 1943, the Internal Revenue Service filed an $18,295 tax lien against him.[32] A further incentive to work in Europe in the mid–1950s had been the tax breaks involved. "Uncle Sam's income tax has kept me busted," he once declared.[33] He hoped that his endeavors in the production side of filmmaking would eventually prove financially rewarding. He did several newspaper advertisements for such products as Pepsi Cola (with Lucille Ball), Rheingold Beer and Van Heusen shirts.[34] He also advertised Gruen watches on television in the early days of the medium.[35] In common with several in the film colony, he sometimes acquired unusual business interests; for instance, he once owned a half-interest in a mice circus that was popular at carnivals and fairs.[36]

Like many couples, the O'Briens argued but their marriage seemed far stronger than most in Hollywood. Unlike some acting couples, their shared professional life was a strength for them rather than a hindrance. Edmond explained, "When I asked Olga to be my wife and she accepted,

I didn't expect her to drop her personal individuality and just become Mrs. O'Brien.... Olga is as interested in her career as I am in mine."[37] They boosted each other, and Olga said that she felt far more confident because of him. She said, "Some of our happiest moments are spent talking about our work."[38] They shared duties in the home and rearing the children. Olga returned to her career at intervals; in the early 1950s, she had much success in the musical *Paint Your Wagon*. She even had a small role in *The Barefoot Contessa*. She once discussed the possibility of her own television show, *Fiesta*, based on a radio series of that name in which she previously appeared.[39] "Try and sublimate the creative force in either party in the marriage deal and you're buying a ticket for Reno," commented Edmond.[40]

Their first daughter Bridget Eileen was born two months prematurely in April 1949.[41] Maria Mercedes was born in August 1950. The family was complete with the birth of Brendan James in May 1962. Edmond doted on his children but, according to Olga, worried incessantly if he was doing the right thing. For all his outward appearance as a happy-go-lucky Irishman, O'Brien was a big worrier. Olga related, "Eddie is a highly nervous person and is given to worrying a lot. He worries tons and tons. He carries his problems around on his shoulders as though they were slabs of granite. If he isn't worrying about the house, he fusses about the dogs. If it's not the dogs, it's the garden. If he has nothing to worry about, he finds something."[42]

Edmond had recurrent problems with his weight that, to an extent, hampered his career and potentially imperiled his health. As a leading Hollywood actor, his appearance was often remarked upon and from the 1940s onwards he tried many times to diet but he found it tough, because he loved his food. "I had to talk sternly to myself," he remarked during one diet regime. "I knew I could no longer consume six rolls at dinner, endless glasses of milk, mounds of French fried potatoes and piles of butter—much less the midnight snacks, usually double portions of bacon and eggs." He also gave up drinking and at one stage lost 20 pounds in six weeks.[43] He began to exercise and eat healthily. He started getting up at six and running the four-mile course at the circuit of the UCLA athletics track.[44] When in New York, he took to jogging around the reservoir in Central Park. He initiated his new regime by reducing his intake of toast for breakfast from ten slices to two. In a relatively short time, he reduced from 220 pounds: "Now a proud 168, I can assure you I never felt happier or healthier in my life," he declared. "Slimming down has done almost as much for my ego as it has for my tailor's finances," he joked.[45]

The whole family was fond of their huge German Shepherd and the feeling was mutual. One time when Edmond was hospitalized for several days for a minor operation, the dog pined away and refused to eat until his master returned. Eddie hoped they would be able to train him and teach him lots of tricks.

Edmond's problems with his sight became increasingly noticeable as the 1950s progressed. By the middle of that decade he had had four operations with more to follow in the 1960s. At one time he underwent treatment by William Sheppard who had himself gone blind at the age of eight but regained his sight twenty years later with cornea implants.

Edmond often attended premieres and special dinners. In April 1956, he and Olga were guests at a special Testimonial Tribute dinner given by the Masquers Club for Ida Lupino. During the sentimental evening, Lupino reminisced about her long show business career and her friends and colleagues paid heartfelt tribute to her. Olga sang a song dedicated to her, and Edmond recited a *Hamlet* soliloquy which was warmly received.[46]

The previous year, he received a special award for his humanitarian work by the Al Jolson branch of the B'nai B'rith organization. The citation read in part, "To Edmond O'Brien for his commitment to interfaith tolerance and understanding by aiding numerous worldwide causes, irrespective of race or creed."[47] Keen to help youngsters, he also sponsored leadership seminars for high school students.

On one occasion, Edmond was driving along the highway in Palm Springs when the car in front of him blew a tire, overturned and caught fire. He managed to break the rear window with rocks and dragged the unconscious driver to safety just before the gas tank exploded. The rescued man, a hosiery salesman named McVeigh, recovered in a local hospital.[48]

O'Brien was perhaps a paradox. He disliked talking about himself in interviews and over the years there were relatively few articles written about him. When he did give interviews, he was expansive but wary; understandably so. Like most actors, he gave little away about himself. He loved to give parties but expressed a hatred of crowds. He was essentially a private person who cultivated close friendships and was known among them for his great generosity. Director Martin Rackin called him a "generous soft touch." Lawyer Jake Erhlich, who got to know him well during the making of the TV series *Sam Benedict,* spoke of him warmly: "This man is just great. He is a cultured, educated man, a Shakespeare student.... He is a well-read, well-informed gentleman, but he will talk about baseball too and take a drink with you. He is not the easiest man in the world to know. Most men worth knowing aren't."[49]

Edmond remained close to his siblings, especially Liam, who admired

Edmond's tremendous drive and enthusiasm. Liam maintained that Eddie didn't like talking about himself, or promoting himself, but that he was a happy and fulfilled individual.[50]

Edmond's faith was something that meant a great deal to him, and he held to the belief that there was more to life than only what was tangible. He once said, "I don't know what keeps other people going, but for me, the so-called joy of living isn't enough. What keeps me going is faith in an afterlife. Maybe other people are comfortable with morphine and booze, but faith is what I have chosen."[51]

He loved his work, but he often said that he wanted to work to live, not live to work. As he reached his forties, he sought to slow down and make only one or two pictures a year, travel more and perhaps return to the stage occasionally. His long-term ambition was to achieve a work-life balance and give himself time and space to accomplish the other things he always hoped to do. "There are many parts of the world I want to see, lots of books I want to read," he once said. "I want to write a little, maybe someday I'll write a play for myself and mount it on Broadway. I think I can do it but if I'm working all the time, I'll never know just what I'm capable of doing."[52]

❖❖ 18 ❖❖

Television:
The Early Days

> TV means for me a variety of parts you can't find anywhere else.—Steven H. Scheuer, "TV Keynotes: O'Brien Plays Pole Refugee," *The Times*, Munster, Indiana, May 3, 1956, 6

In 1950, O'Brien began a television career that lasted 24 years. He undoubtedly made an impact in the medium because by the end of his first decade in 1960, he had already earned a star on the Hollywood Walk of Fame for his contribution to television.

Unlike some of his contemporaries, O'Brien did not have disdain for the small screen. On the contrary, although he always preferred cinema, he was practical and recognized that change was inevitable in any business.

In 1950, he discussed the possibility of transferring his successful radio series *Yours Truly, Johnny Dollar* to the small screen. However, he was busy with his film and radio commitments at that time and the show never made the transition to television. It was reported that he turned down the offer of $2000 a week to make the series.[1] One of his chief concerns about appearing too often on television was the fear that audiences would stop going to see his movies. Nonetheless, he was on the lookout for a good series and many ideas came along, including using him as the host-narrator of an anthology series, *The Law Strikes Back*. A pilot episode was made but never broadcast.[2] He was announced as the principal actor in a planned series of 13 episodes of scenes from Shakespeare's plays, but the idea seems to have been dropped.[3] He also discussed with CBS the possibility of a role as a professor of drama set in a small-town college.[4] Around the same time, Ray Williford proposed a fantasy series about a heavenly visitor who straightens out various people's problems on Earth. He wanted O'Brien to play the guardian angel, but nothing came of this

18. Television: The Early Days

or the other idea.[5] Later in the decade, there was even the offer of a regular series in Europe, but that too did not come about.[6] O'Brien was eager to play the prison psychiatrist in comedy-drama *My Six Convicts,* a planned series based on the book by Donald Powell Wilson, which had already provided the basis of the film of that name. However, despite the obvious potential, the television idea did not bear fruit.

He mostly made one-off TV appearances, including several for *Lux Video Theater.* In 1951 he appeared in the psychological drama "Hit and Run" as a conscience-stricken driver. In November of that year, he made an impression as the widowed father of a teenage girl addicted to drugs in "A Matter of Life." It was the early days for such potentially controversial subject matter: CBS reportedly received an "unprecedented" response to the broadcast, with 20,000 calls asking for it to be repeated. O'Brien thus became the first film star to appear in a repeated television show.[7]

An early venture was a travelogue show made by the Filmakers, and featuring narration from Ida Lupino, Joan Fontaine and O'Brien. Initially entitled *Ports of Call,* it consisted of 39 half-hour episodes which showed such far-flung locales as Tibet, Algeria, China, Italy, Australia and Guatemala. The footage was shot by some of the leading cameramen of the time including Karl Robinson and Clifford Kamen. Co-developed by Lupino and Collier Young, it was a secret project for about a year and was distributed by Comet television and shown on several Midwest channels in 1954 under the title *Holiday.*[8]

In the early 1950s, television was only in its infancy; screens were relatively small and expensive, and the picture was not always of the best quality. Sets could also be unreliable and reception variable. Nonetheless, it was not long before the new medium found its feet and began eating into the radio audience share. By the middle of the decade, the radio audience collapsed and by 1960 that medium was almost moribund. Similarly, the movie audience drifted to television. Movie-going declined but, tellingly, movies still held sway in the public imagination. For example, a televised showing of *D.O.A.* in February 1954 attracted 24 percent of the viewing public; its nearest rival was *The Ed Sullivan Show* with 18 percent.[9] This was significant because broadcasters realized there was a big market for films, especially reruns of old films. Whatever the apparent drawbacks of television, it gave people access to countless films they may not otherwise have seen and unwittingly built up a large base of fans of old movies. Many of O'Brien's early efforts were shown even though some of them he hoped had been forgotten.

He regularly appeared in teleplays which were well-received and were aired again many times after he won the Academy Award. In "The Long Shot," perhaps the earliest version of the "time bomb on a plane" scenario, O'Brien essayed the role of the captain. A TV critic noted that his acting made the episode "tense and believable."[10] He starred in adaptations of familiar films including *Five Star Final, A Bell for Adano* and *To Have and Have Not* to great acclaim. Stage plays were popular and he appeared in "Icebound" by Owen Davis. In the oft-repeated "Charlie C. Company," he gave a thoughtful performance as the disillusioned chaplain of a dwindling band of Korean War soldiers who begins to question his faith.

He was featured in a memorable episode of the popular series *Climax*, "An Error in Chemistry," based on a William Faulkner short story. The prize-winning tale was written in 1940 and first published six years later in *Ellery Queen's Mystery Magazine*. O'Brien excelled as carnival barker and illusionist (and con man) Joel Flint, who arrives in a sleepy Southern town and quickly courts, then marries the credulous daughter of a landowner, with devastating consequences all around. Lon Chaney, Jr., appeared as the ill-tempered father-in-law with Douglas Kennedy and Tommy Ivo as the lawyer and his nephew, who play detective in the case. The adaptation stayed fairly true to Faulkner's curious allegory although the telescoping of events to fit the 45-minute running time was a distinct disadvantage. O'Brien drew praise; *Time* noted that he "played the role with a fine malevolence."[11] Tommy Ivo recalled:

> Edmond was not at the top of his game when I worked with him and he was a little aloof it seemed, because I had a fairly good part with him in the show and he never could remember my name when he wanted my attention. He was really challenged with the way *live* TV broadcasting was done. For one big thing, he had a tough time seeing and the way you had to work in live TV was like doing a play. Once you did it, out it went with any mistakes that were made and all. *I hated live TV!* There was a lump in my throat when I'd hear the on-stage speakers billow out, "Live from Hollywood"!
>
> I think he also might think the character he was playing wouldn't work well if he used glasses, which is only my assessment. Because why not just use them? Unless it was a matter of vanity. But it really got exciting, when they were running him around back stage from one scene to another and holding onto him like a seeing eye dog. On our dress rehearsal, I heard a big crash from behind the set when he tripped over something and down he went. Good grief, I was waiting on stage and he didn't show up for a good period of time. On another rehearsal, they knocked over a huge stand with a very big klieg light on it, which bouncing across the scene it came.
>
> *But*, and here comes that *but* again: All's well that ends well. When the show actually went out on air, it ran like clockwork....[12]

O'Brien seldom appeared on the popular celebrity panel game shows of the era, but he was seen on *I've Got a Secret*, in which he sought to fool the guests by donning several disguises, including as a truculent traffic warden.

In January 1955, he appeared in the first episode of the anthology series *The Star and the Story*. In "The Dark Stranger," he played a writer who thinks he sees the girl in his book and runs after her. He becomes convinced she is in danger of her life for real because of him. He was understated as the writer and Joanne Woodward was effective as the girl in a story which almost came off but not quite. It was reminiscent of the noir *Portrait of Jennie* (1948), but the 25-minute running time was not enough to satisfactorily develop the theme. O'Brien was quietly convincing as the owner of a roadside diner who takes on a dishwasher (Skip Homeier) despite his criminal past in "The Net Draws Tight" for the *Spotlight Theater*. He made an impression as a cynical house detective in *Tower Room 14-A*, based on a story by Raymond Chandler.

He made several entries in the groundbreaking *Playhouse 90* series. This showcased young directors and assembled fine casts in contemporary works. "The Comedian" starred Mickey Rooney as a demanding comic despised by all those working for him, including his younger brother (Mel Torme) who he continually runs down in his act. O'Brien played a gag writer who has run out of ideas and stoops to using a dead man's work and passing it off as his own. Director John Frankenheimer often filled the screen with people and used extreme close-ups which increased the dramatic intensity. It was the antithesis of the glamorous cinematic approach and made everyone look unattractive. Rooney tended to overplay with the result that at times the other actors tried to match him. O'Brien expertly conveyed his character's air of desperation and the pain his actions cause him. There was good support from Kim Stanley and Constance Ford. Torme did surprisingly well in the difficult role of the put-upon brother; he had been prompted to return to acting by O'Brien. The Rooney character was so obnoxious, it sometimes stretched belief that anyone would stay with him. O'Brien later played the leading role in director Frankenheimer's "The Blue Men," the tense tale of an honest cop of 18 years' service (O'Brien) whose career and personal integrity are put on the line because of political expediency and a vengeful public. It was uniformly well-acted by a cast which included Jack Warden and Eileen Eckhart. "The play is probably the first drama on television that really examines the character of a group of typical cops and the problems they run into," O'Brien commented in an interview.[13] A critic wrote; "O'Brien mixed underplaying with zealous reactions for his gripping portrayal."[14]

He found those television plays hard work. "One *Playhouse 90* is tougher than anything on Broadway," he once contended.[15] Apart from the problems caused by his poor eyesight, O'Brien once fell asleep during a scene on live television.[16] Nevertheless, he felt that the experience of working in the medium was closest to that of the theater. He once observed, "Even without an audience, a live show presents the same challenges as a stage play. You get the one chance and you have to make it good."[17]

In one of his most notable dramas from this era, "The Heart Is a Forgotten Hotel," he played a Florida hotelier with no sense of responsibility. His 14-year-old son is left to deal with the practicalities of life while he spends money he doesn't have on cars, expensive suits and chasing girls. It was described as "a striking, memorable piece ... a simple, taut story of a perpetual adolescent, well played by Edmond O'Brien."[18] The episode later inspired the film *A Hole in the Head* (1959) with Frank Sinatra and Edward G. Robinson.

In 1958, O'Brien turned again to directing with *Schlitz Playhouse*'s "The Town That Slept with the Lights On." He played a New York reporter who helps to discover the truth about a small-town murder. It was a well-acted and atmospheric drama with a fine central performance by O'Brien, whose narration set the tone admirably. There was good support from Emile Meyer as a local agitator and Robert Middleton as a level-headed sheriff. The story was written by Eddie's brother Liam and based on two real-life cases. Edmond emphasized his approach: "I'm not a private eye and I don't solve the murders. TV is full of private eyes. Even the heroes of westerns are really private eyes on horseback. I'm a reporter, I don't solve murders."[19]

O'Brien played a bigamist for the second time in *Lux Playhouse*'s "Coney Island Winter," set in the off-season at the famous amusement pier. He played the co-proprietor of a bar and grill who finds his past catching up with him when his business partner discovers his secret and tries to blackmail him, and his second wife resolves to take drastic action. O'Brien felt that the episode had the potential to make the transfer to the Broadway stage, but nothing came of his suggestions.[20] He was forceful as a brutal renegade army officer in *Laramie*'s "The Iron Captain" and as a restless U.S. marshal in *Zane Grey Theater*'s "Lonesome Road." In the latter, he was directed for the first time (a decade before *The Wild Bunch*) by Sam Peckinpah, who also wrote the episode. O'Brien played a marshal who has become inured to killing, and is practically destroyed psychologically and morally by his job.[21] He continually underlined his range and was just as effective in *Screen Directors Playhouse*'s "A Ticket for Thaddeus" as a frightened Polish refugee, complete with walrus moustache, who tries to make a new life in America but whose traumatic wartime experiences make him fearful of everyone he encounters in uniform.

O'Brien achieved a great measure of success in the medium of television, enhancing his wider reputation. What he wanted more than anything was a good series. He found *three* in the following decade, and all the while continued his film career with equal vigor.

❖❖ 19 ❖❖

After Oscar

> The older I get, the less I like acting that looks like acting. After 25 years, you gain a certain facility, but that's a blessing and a danger. That's the curse of an actor. You get loose. Me, I have to work hard. It's a business like anything else.
> —Cindy Adams, *Sunday Herald,* March 12, 1961, 26

The mid–1950s was an exciting time for O'Brien after receiving the Oscar which led to many offers of work and he was more able to pick and choose his cinema roles. *Pete Kelly's Blues* (1955) was a great showcase for several popular musicians of the day, particularly two of the greatest jazz singers of all time, Ella Fitzgerald and Peggy Lee. Set in the Prohibition Era, this told the story of bandleader Kelly (Jack Webb), who is told by a gangster (O'Brien) that he wants to be a music agent and will get 25 percent of the band's takings. This slippery slope leads to violence. The critics did not know what to make of it. "A rather odd and slightly ludicrous affair," concluded one reviewer.[1] Its strength lay in the music, not in Webb's somber direction and humorless performance. Initially, it looked as though it was going to be played for laughs but it soon became apparent that was not the case. O'Brien's character was a one-note heavy with no real room for maneuver. He was domineering with a violent streak. Lee Marvin stood out among the unusual supporting cast, which also included Andy Devine giving perhaps his most serious performance. The music and cinematography were the film's finest assets. Cinematographer Harold Rosson's long career began in 1915. Best remembered for *The Wizard of Oz* (1939), he was once married to Jean Harlow.

The Oscar certainly had a big impact on O'Brien's later career. "I've never had such a selection of—really choice—roles," he observed, "[Before] I'd sometimes get six or eight offers in a row until I found one I figured was right for me. Now I get only two or three or maybe four at a time. But the big difference is they're all great. I really enjoyed working in *Pete Kelly's Blues*."[2]

19. After Oscar

One of the most interesting offers that came along was the role of Winston Smith in *1984* (1956). George Orwell's *Nineteen Eighty-Four*, published in 1949, was one the most depressing dystopian views of the future ever, but was also a trenchant satire full of cynical humor. An unsettling but strangely piquant fable, it retains its relevance in a world in which Big Brother really does appear to be watching everything and the thought police don't need to wear uniforms. Filmed in England, director Michael Anderson's *1984* was originally set to have an all–British cast, but then the makers decided to appeal to the North American markets by handing the lead roles to O'Brien and Jan Sterling. Despite objections in some quarters, it was somehow fitting that two film noir regulars should be cast in one of the blackest noir fables of all time. O'Brien commented at the time, "In my films I have shot hundreds of people, been a cop who has chased crooks and a crook who has been chased by the police. But this is the first time I've been pursued by Thought Police. New experience."[3]

Winston Smith is a worker in the records department in Oceania,

Winston Smith (O'Brien, left) is tormented by O'Connor (Michael Redgrave) in the English-made *1984* (1956). O'Brien proved effective in the role.

whose job entails the rewriting of history to tell the "truth" as laid down by the ruling party. All life is regulated and the party dictates everything; everywhere there are cameras which watch everyone's movements. Any suspicious behavior is reported to the Thought Police. Smith smuggles a diary into his house in which he writes "Down with Big Brother," a treasonable offense. All interaction between the sexes is discouraged, but Smith arranges a clandestine meeting with Julia (Jan Sterling). He befriends an antique dealer and moves into the apartment above his shop. Believing Inner Party man O'Connor (Michael Redgrave) to be a secret member of the underground movement, Smith and Julia meet him and admit their love for each other and that they would betray their country if they were asked. Smith realizes too late that O'Connor is loyal to the party, and is tortured to submit to the logic of the party that two and two might not always equal four, if the party should so decree.

The screenplay strayed from Orwell's original, but the finished film was on the whole successful in getting across much of the atmosphere and intent of the novel. Few, if any, works of literature have ever been realized perfectly on screen to everyone's satisfaction, but this version of the book does compare favorably to earlier and later attempts. Much of the author's ironic humor was missing, but then the same was true of the other films. O'Brien added to his laurels with his portrayal of Smith, admirably capturing the desperation and bemusement of a human soul trapped in a nightmare world where every thought is potentially lethal.

Some commentators considered O'Brien far too dynamic for the role of Smith, and found it difficult to imagine that he had not rebelled earlier. However, it is O'Brien's dynamism that adds to the power of his eventual defeat. He transitions from belligerence to confused acceptance after being "cleansed" in an entirely believable fashion. Two alternative endings were made. One wrapped with Smith thoroughly defeated and shouting "Long live Big Brother!" (as in the novel). The other ending—running contrary to everything Orwell intended—finished with Smith shouting "Down with Big Brother!" The former ending was made for the release in Britain, and the latter ending was intended for the American and overseas markets. But according to the director, "it was the middlemen and retailers who chose [to release them] the other way round."[4] The version that is loyal to the book is the only one that makes sense and it was a pointless exercise to change it.

Of the other players, Michael Redgrave made the greatest impact as O'Brien's chief tormentor. Donald Pleasence played Smith's friend and neighbor who is denounced by his own daughter, and David Kossoff was a seemingly benign antiques dealer. Some of the filming took place on the streets of London, but too often a crowd would gather and there were sometimes so many interruptions that it became impossible to continue. When O'Brien was involved on one particular scene, a bystander constantly interjected, shouting, "Attaboy, Eddie, you tell 'em!"[5]

The career of director Anderson encompassed an early attempt at social drama [*Waterfront* (1950)], an excellently judged war movie [*The Dam Busters* (1955)], the all-star hit *Around the World in Eighty Days* (1956), the spy drama *The Quiller Memorandum* (1966). *1984* benefited greatly from the music of the prolific British composer Sir Malcolm Arnold, which was dramatically intense and spoke to and for the human spirit at the core of the story.

After *1984*, O'Brien hoped to stay on in Britain to work on *The Remarkable Mr. Pennypacker* with his brother Liam.[6] The play had been a minor success on Broadway and when it transferred to the New London Theatre, it became "the solid hit of the summer."[7] However, the film project was abandoned because Edmond could not get an extension for his work permit to stay in England after August 1955.[8] He considered going into partnership with *1984* producer Peter Rathvon on another project. Edmond bought an option on the story *It Happened Yesterday* by Allen Mintor, with the intention of making a film of it on his return to Hollywood, but nothing came of the idea.[9]

Michael Redgrave spoke of his plan to make a five-hour full-length version of *Hamlet*, and he hoped to persuade O'Brien to appear as Claudius, but that didn't happen.[10] In 1958, Redgrave played the role in Glen Byam Shaw's production at Stratford and received rave reviews.[11] While in Britain, O'Brien went to see several West End shows in which some of his friends were appearing, and also Rosemary Clooney at the London Palladium.[12] He also took some time off to visit Ireland, where he made a pilgrimage to the family seat and had lots of fun with his movie camera to show to his mother on his return.[13] Edmond and Olga later hired a car and toured France and Spain for a month or so. By the time they returned to the States, he had amassed many reels of home movies.[14]

During his time in Europe, the opportunity arose for him to fulfill a longstanding ambition to act in a Greek drama. He was invited to appear with Katina Paxinou and her husband Alexis Minotis in an English verse production of Sophocles' tragedy *Oedipus Rex*. The play was to be staged in Athens as part of an International Music and Drama Festival, sponsored by the Greek government. When Minotis starred in the production, O'Brien was not part of the cast.[15]

Several years later, when Edmond and his brother Liam were scouting possible locations in London for their television series *Johnny Midnight*, they went to the Old Vic in hopes of seeing Laurence Olivier. Unfortunately, they were no tickets available for the show, so Eddie sent a message to Olivier backstage: "From the world's worst Mercutio." Eddie was going to sign it but his brother said there was no need, because Olivier would know who it is. "I've never forgiven him," said Eddie "because I didn't sign the note and [Olivier] *did* know who was out front. He came rushing out of the theater door looking around the lobby and saying 'Eddie, my boy, where are you?'"[16]

D–Day, the Sixth of June (1956) was a weak movie which used the momentous events of June 1944 as mere background for a soap opera–style love story in which two men, one British (Richard Todd), the other American (Robert Taylor), fall for the same girl (Dana Wynter). O'Brien was fourth-billed as an unorthodox lieutenant who tries to steal a march on a rival officer by leading an advance battalion of Canadians to Dieppe prior to D–Day without any authorization. For that and breaching security, he is not allowed to take part in the eventual attack. The war action was confined to the last ten minutes but seemed rather contrived to accommodate all the strands of the plot. There was a good attempt to recreate a European setting, although the film was actually shot mostly in Malibu and the Long Beach Naval Shipyard. Taylor and Wynter made a handsome couple and the appealing color made up for many deficiencies in the screenplay. Taylor said he was first attracted to the project because it reminded him of his 1940 film *Waterloo Bridge*, but expressed disappointment with the finished product. The film itself was poorly received, and O'Brien was singled out for most of the praise: "The only performance that makes any sense at all is that of Edmond O'Brien as a loud-mouthed, aggressive Milwaukee automobile salesman bucking for a colonelcy," wrote Harold V. Cohen. "He puts a sort of nameless drive into an otherwise leaden drama."[17] The international critics concurred; "It is a pity he falls victim to security before D–Day," lamented a London reviewer, "for Mr. O'Brien's is the only part to throw light on the qualities that win battles though not wars."[18] Doctor's daughter Wynter was concerned about O'Brien's eye trouble during filming and particularly his hypersensitivity to light. She prescribed him some eye drops to help alleviate the problem.[19]

Returning to Hollywood, O'Brien was back in familiar crime territory in *A Cry in the Night* (1956), in which he played a police captain whose daughter (Natalie Wood) is abducted by a psychotic mother's boy in the familiar shape of Raymond Burr. The cast also included Irene Hervey as O'Brien's wife and Brian Donlevy as a fellow officer assigned to the case. O'Brien was suitably distressed as the father, constantly on the edge of exploding, who eventually realizes that his over-protective nature is a contributing cause of the situation.

A number of the actors were on diets during production; O'Brien, Donlevy and Burr all had to watch their waistlines. Burr and O'Brien even held an impromptu contest to see who could lose the most weight; O'Brien lost 25 pounds while Burr lost 38.[20] It was reported that Natalie Wood was the only one who tucked into huge breakfasts while the others waited around suffering at the thought of bacon and eggs, toast, jam and *café au lait*, etc. Around mid-afternoon she stopped for a cream-and-cake break and developed a yen for ice cream sundaes while cast and crew waited patiently for her return. On the last day there was relief all around when there were refreshments served for everyone.[21]

Producer Alan Ladd was so impressed with Edmond's *Cry in the Night* performance that he cast him in the western *The Big Land* (see Chapter 5). Ladd admired O'Brien's versatility and was surprised by his performance as a Polish refugee cabinet-maker in the television drama "A Ticket for Thaddeus." Ladd announced two new projects set in Greece with O'Brien in mind. The first was *Uprising*, based on a novel by Alexandros Tantagos, for which Ladd hoped to acquire the rights.[22] That fell through, but then Ladd intended to produce *Day of Triumph*, from a novelette by Francois Georges. The story concerned an American artist who is rehabilitated when he finds romance with a singer. O'Brien was to have starred, with Abbe Lane as the singer. It was never made.[23]

The Rack was a competent legal drama about an army captain (Paul Newman) who returns from three years in a Korean POW camp to face charges of collaboration with the enemy. Newman's defense attorney (O'Brien) puts forward a good case but is ultimately defeated by his own client's testimony. The ending left matter hanging; for some reason, a verdict was passed but no sentence given. This made the film feel unfinished. O'Brien was assured in his role, expansive when necessary and eloquent in his summation. The lead role had been intended for Glenn Ford, who turned it down. Walter Pidgeon did well as Newman's confused father, and Anne Francis was effective as the widowed sister-in-law. An occasionally thought-provoking drama, it was based on a teleplay by Rod Serling and betrayed its television roots, lacking any cinematic feel whatsoever.

In one of the great rock'n'roll films of all time, *The Girl Can't Help*

It, O'Brien had one of his most appealing roles. Ostensibly a comedy vehicle for Jayne Mansfield, it was effectively overtaken by the music. The "plot," such as it was, concerned a drink-addicted agent (Tom Ewell) who is forced by gangster "Fats" Murdock (O'Brien) to make his girl Jordan (Mansfield) into a singing star, against her wishes. Ewell (of course) falls in love with her. The film was based on a Garson Kanin story. Broderick Crawford was first assigned the gangster role. After he fell ill and dropped out, Dick Powell was ordered by his studio to replace him; Powell refused. Luckily, O'Brien was available and said yes.[24] He enjoyed himself immensely as the cigar-chomping boss with a penchant for outlandish clothes, such as bright red smoking jacket, cummerbund and tartan cap. It was interesting to compare this film to the previous music-inspired films in which O'Brien had played a gangster. But where he had been coldhearted and unpredictable in *Pete Kelly's Blues,* in *The Girl Can't Help It* he was a cuddly comedy baddie. He had a lot of fun with his lines, such

The Girl Can't Help It (1956) captured some of the early greats in their prime for all time. Left to right: Jayne Mansfield, O'Brien, Tom Ewell.

as when he watches old newsreels of himself in his heyday as a big shot and laments, "I used to be 'Slim' Murdock in those days." But the story was mere window dressing for the music, which was the *raison d'etre* of the whole thing. From the first bars of Little Richard belting out the title song, the music was everything. Presented in CinemaScope and shot in beautiful De Luxe color, this was a great document of its era, and the sight of Gene Vincent, Eddie Cochran, Fats Domino *et al.* in their prime was captured for all time. Only Elvis was missing. O'Brien really entered into the spirit of it and he even got to "sing" a song, "Rock Around the Rockpile," and jive to it as only he could, accompanied by the Ray Anthony Orchestra in a rousing finale which was later released on the soundtrack LP. "I never had more fun making a picture," recalled O'Brien, who especially enjoyed his dance routine which he choreographed himself. "I worked out the dance at home with my wife ... as advisor and critic. When I first showed it to [director] Frank Tashlin ... he flipped." There was the possibility of starring again with Jayne Mansfield in *The Wayward Bus*, loosely based on the John Steinbeck novel, but O'Brien's role went to Dan Dailey instead.[25] Sammy Lewis, the entertainment director at the New Frontier Hotel in Las Vegas, was so impressed with O'Brien and Mansfield together that he tried hard to convince them to do a nightclub double act at the hotel in April 1957, but that did not happen.[26]

In the spring of 1956, Allied Artists announced an ambitious multi-million-dollar investment in a run of seven films to be made in four months.[27] Among the titles was *Poppaea,* in CinemaScope, starring Jeanne Crain as the notorious Roman empress and O'Brien as Nero.[28] It was unfortunate that such an outlandish venture never made it to the big screen. A remake of the boxing drama *Golden Boy* was considered by Columbia Pictures, starring Eddie's old friend Mario Lanza. O'Brien was lined up to play his manager, but the project did not get past the planning stage.[29] Lanza wanted O'Brien to play his sidekick in *Seven Hills of Rome* (1957), but that didn't happen.[30]

He was due to start with Alan Ladd in *The Deep Six* (1958), but O'Brien injured himself while doing household chores and suffered a slipped disc. He was laid up for several weeks and William Bendix was assigned his role instead.[31] O'Brien next flew to Japan to make *Stopover Tokyo* (1957) for 20th Century–Fox. This beautifully shot espionage thriller made use of many famous Japanese locations but it was ultimately let down by a rather ordinary story. Robert Wagner starred as Mark Fannon, an American special agent decoyed from his scheduled destination in Korea and diverted by persons unknown to Tokyo. He meets two fellow agents, but one of them, Naboki, is killed and Fannon sets out to find his murderer. His investigation leads him to the Pacific Coal and Iron Company which appears to be planning a high-level political assassination. He suspects there is a link to mysterious American George Underwood (O'Brien), a Communist who often turns up at regular intervals. Along the way, Fannon befriends Naboki's young daughter Koko (Reiko Oyama) and an airport receptionist, Tina (Joan Collins), with whom he falls in love.

Collins recalled her immense surprise that the actors were greeted on their arrival at Tokyo airport by thousands of screaming fans.[32] O'Brien enjoyed his time in the country. He remarked that Japanese women "[have] an aura of mystery that American women in general do not. This is especially so when they wear their traditional kimono." He was also struck by the children; "Japanese kids are simply mad about baseball," he observed. "[Y]ou find them everywhere—and apparently they learn baseball practically as soon as they're able to walk."[33]

There were two incidents involving firearms during the making of the picture. In one, a stray shot smashed a pane of glass which showered several technicians, but no one was hurt.[34] The second incident involved O'Brien: He was caught off-balance and his gun fired too soon, and the other actor in the scene, Ken Scott, was hit in the right side of his face. He was not badly hurt but doctors spent two hours removing cartridge powder grains.[35]

All the actors did well, but the languid screenplay, based on John P. Marquand's *Saturday Evening Post* story "Rendezvous in Japan" was a letdown. Marquand had been asked to write a Mr. Moto adventure, 15 years after his last. He rose to the challenge and the story was later released as a novel, variously titled *Right You Are, Mr. Moto* and *The Last Case of Mr. Moto*. When it came to making a film version, the decision was made early on to drop the Moto character and cast a big star in the main role. William Holden was considered; the role went to Wagner after Robert Stack refused to fly to Japan.

O'Brien's role was limited and rather underwritten, but the actor did his best as an unctuous villain and made an impact in all his scenes. The movie began promisingly but, as one critic observed, "never begins to get underneath the skin of [Japan]."[36] Its slow pace and familiar storyline tended to mean that interest soon waned. The great compensation of the film was its sumptuous color and the spectacular cinematography of Charles G. Clarke which made this one worth seeing. O'Brien expressed a desire to return to Japan with his wife and family for a holiday. He became a devotee of steam baths and one day spent three hours relaxing in one. He found that the next day he had to film a scene in a steam bath and spent a further eight hours there.[37]

The World Was His Jury (1958) was a rather ordinary little courtroom drama concerned with the trial of an inexperienced captain held responsible for the deaths of 162 people on board a luxury liner through criminal negligence (a fire broke out in the hold). O'Brien played an ambitious lawyer who forsakes his usual clients—gangsters and grafters—to defend the captain. In the process, he hopes to win back his lady love, Mona Freeman. It contained some neat plot twists but O'Brien was not stretched. One commentator noted that it proved the adage "A good lawyer is better than a clear conscience."[38]

Sing Boy Sing (1958) was yet another example of television and rock'n'roll setting the agenda for cinema. This began life as the *Kraft Television Theater* episode "The Singing Idol," which was inspired by the story of Colonel Parker's shepherding of the career of Elvis Presley. For *Sing Boy Sing*, Presley was sought for the role as the Southern boy who shoots to stardom, but Parker turned down the offer and suggested singer Tommy Sands instead. Parker even paid Sands' airfare to go to the audition show.[39] Several songs were added to the film and one of them, "Teenage Crush," sold a million copies and reached #2 on the *Billboard* chart. As a boy, Virgil Walker (Sands) starts singing at the tent revival meetings of his preacher grandfather (John McIntire). Virgil remains close to his grandfather but his manager Sharkey (O'Brien) continually tries to sever the link between them. O'Brien was effective as the ruthless and seemingly callous manager, who has his own reasons for acting the way he does. Nick Adams did well as the ultimate freeloader along for the ride. A soundtrack album was released the same year.

In the fall of 1958, O'Brien was invited by a Franco-Australian team to make a film, *L'Amitieuse,* in Tahiti. (The producers had been impressed by his work in *The Girl Can't Help It.*) O'Brien accepted because he liked the role, which he called "a rare combination of Wallace Beery and Humphrey Bogart." He was initially looking forward to traveling to such an exotic locale. However, he soon discovered that the islands were not the paradise he envisioned. The location shoot took three months in Tahiti and Tuamotu Island. "There were no studios," he explained, "so we had to shoot our interiors where we could. One place had a tin roof, and you can imagine how that was, combined with our lights from the color camera." He described the weather as murder. "Hot? That doesn't begin to describe it. I sweated right through a mattress every night," he remarked.[40]

Ambitious Dominique (Andrea Parisy) persuades her reserved husband George (Richard Basehart), scion of a wealthy mining family, to move from Paris to Tahiti. Here she becomes the secretary of American adventurer Buchanan (O'Brien), owner of a profitable phosphate mine, and soon concocts a scheme to discover a fortune. The screenplay was based on the novel *Manganese* by Francois Ponthier.[41] The renowned French director Yves Allegret began his career with comedies such as *Tobias Is an Angel* (1940) and made his reputation with atmospheric noirs including *Une Si Jolie Petite Plage* (1949) and *Les Miracles N'ont Lieu qu'une Fois* (1951). Prior to *L'Amitieuse,* Allegret had attempted to work with O'Brien in an adaptation of Molière's *Tartuffe,* to be filmed in Paris, with O'Brien augmenting a cast of well-known French actors including Fernandel and Martine Carol, but that project was ultimately discarded.[42]

L'Amitieuse was variously known in English as *The Ambitious One, The Restless and the Damned, The Climbers* and *The Dispossessed.* Partially financed by Australian actor Chips Rafferty, it was shot in Eastmancolor which showed the locale to great effect. The picture also benefited from the plaintive score by Henri Crolla. There were some noir elements to the story but Allegret didn't have the magic touch this time. Two versions were released, one in English and the other in French, both directed by Allegret. The movie was not given a theatrical release in the United States, Great Britain or Australia, and only a limited showing in three Paris cinemas in October 1959. Unsurprisingly, it was a box office loser. An edited version was occasionally shown on U.S. television. Difficult to find, it remains one of O'Brien's most obscure titles.

O'Brien was forthright in his views of Tahiti, commenting that the island attracted "the worst that western civilization could have brought in." He decried the lack of white beaches and the lagoons where the coral was so sharp it could cut a swimmer to ribbons. He observed, "[T]he natives hate the French who ... have treated them with little regard, [and] everyone hates the Chinese who control the island's economy."[43] He admired some of the outlying islands, particularly Moorea and Bora Bora, and found some of the girls as beautiful as their reputation. He brought back some valuable native paintings as a gift for his wife.[44] One of Tahiti's most famous residents was painter Paul Gauguin, and O'Brien met one of his sons. Edmond found time to relax during his stay and even started writing a stage play, *The Tropics.*[45]

O'Brien was tempted to return to Broadway in a production of Shaw's *Caesar and Cleopatra* with Eartha Kitt, but the tantalizing idea ran aground.[46] He was sought by Harry Horner for the lead in *Ottawa After*

Dark, a proposed thriller about narcotics smuggling from a script by DeWitt Bodeen, but that did not come about.[47]

The standard wartime adventure *Up Periscope* (1959) starred James Garner as a Navy frogman assigned a covert mission: photograph a code book at a radio station on a Japanese-held island. He gets there on a submarine skippered by O'Brien, who is disliked by his crew because of something that happened as a result of his insistence on going by the book. Although Garner was pleased to be making a picture with O'Brien, he was dismissive of the film.[48] *Up Periscope* is much better than he thought; the photography by Carl Guthrie was impressive and there were moments of genuine tension. Retired Naval officer, Vice Admiral Charles A. Lockwood, acted as chief advisor. However, the running time of 112 minutes was trying for those not enamored of the submarine genre. O'Brien's intense yet understated portrayal of the captain was its greatest asset.

◆◆ 20 ◆◆

Johnny and Sam

> I have mixed feelings about the series. You certainly reach a large audience in America every week, but you run the danger of losing whatever world audience you have gained through movies.
> —Vernon Scott, "*Sam Benedict* Series Keeps Edmond O'Brien Busy," *Tonawanda News*, May 3, 1963, 11

In the early 1960s he appeared in two TV series, *Johnny Midnight* and *Sam Benedict*. He put a lot into both ventures, but neither proved to be a hit. He later had a prominent role in the Southern saga *The Long, Hot Summer*, but found it unrewarding and left partway through the run.

Johnny Midnight was based on a novel premise by Edmond's brother Liam. Set in New York, it starred O'Brien as an actor-turned detective who owned his own theater. The Broadway background gave scope for some unusual theater-based stories and even presented opportunities for him to don disguises. Initially, the intention was to have the show set in foggy London, but it was decided that Broadway was more suitable. The character was initially described as "slim," and the program's producer Jack Chertok asked O'Brien to lose weight before the series began filming. He had already reduced in the previous two years. However, in three months he lost the required weight by following a special protein diet combined with regular exercise. According to O'Brien, "There were times during the period of reducing when I was certain I would turn into a protein myself, so much of that commodity did I consume."[1]

An appealing but largely overlooked syndicated series, *Johnny Midnight* ran between January and September 1960. Each episode began with the strains of "Lullaby of Broadway" and a shot of wet, dark streets, from which the familiar figure of O'Brien emerges. "Broadway, the world of make-believe," intones O'Brien. "But I found that the curtain never comes down on the real street of dreams. That's why I gave up acting to become a private investigator." His laconic voiceover enhanced the noir ambience of the series. Some episodes followed the conventional route, but the more interesting ones were those which delved into the actor's psyche or explored the particular and sometimes bizarre world of those who pretend for a living. For instance, "Voice of the Dummy," an atmospheric tale concerned with the disappearance of a ventriloquist; "He was a shabby little man with a big heartbreak. Back from the nowhere of his lost past and waiting to salvage whatever was left of his future." The curiously insular and inverted world of the stage and show business in general was sometimes captured. Some of the characters were semi-regulars, such as Midnight's Japanese houseboy (Yuki Shimoda) who provided comic relief, and a Puerto Rican police sergeant (Arthur Batanides). There were guest appearances by some familiar names such as Adam West, who was soon to find fame as Batman, and Alan Reed, the voice of Fred Flintstone. In some episodes, O'Brien was able to demonstrate his ability with Shakespeare and knack of mimicry.

O'Brien had been looking for the ideal vehicle, and believed *Johnny Midnight* was it. He had many previous offers of TV series: "I've turned down about twenty of them," he revealed. "Eight of which have been on the air."[2] He explained what attracted him about the show: "It had a concept and setting totally different from anything in the mystery-adventure field. It was a story about the real drama of life as contrasted with Broadway play life. I made the deal quick, knowing that this series would give me a wide range of performance as an actor."[3] The format was suitable for a family audience.

Midnight did not usually carry a gun. "We are shunning the violence thing," he explained. "I saw some figures not too long ago that the normal schoolchild is exposed to something like 472 homicides in a year of average television viewing. We like to think of our show as entertainment. We don't pretend that it's true."[4] Promisingly, the pilot episode "Double of Nothing" was to have been shown in May 1959 on *Stripe Playhouse*, but was snapped up by the sponsors before it was even seen by the public, such was the pull of the O'Brien name.[5] He made the most of the dry humor of some of the lines; such as when he visits an arty joint frequented by beatniks: "It was one of those jazz and black coffee dives, where a man could feel conspicuous without a beard and sneakers. I went in anyway." Despite his high hopes for the series, the reception was lukewarm at best and hostile at worst. A storyline involving an embittered gossip columnist hardly helped the cause. When viewed now, it is difficult to see why the show was not a hit. It was the longest-running video series he made and he was ideal in the role, relaxed and understated. All 39 episodes are available on DVD.

In O'Brien's next big series *Sam Benedict,* he played a flamboyant San Francisco attorney who takes on seemingly impossible cases—and often wins. The character was based on trial lawyer Jake Ehrlich, who worked as advisor on the series. O'Brien was impressed with Ehrlich and the feeling was mutual, "He gets right at the meat of the thing," Ehrlich observed. "He portrays a good, solid trial man in that every time he moves, it means something."[6] Benedict had two regular supporting characters, young lawyer Hank Tabor (Richard Rust) and secretary Joan Tompkins (Trudy Wagner). The show attracted some fine actors during its run including Claude Rains, Vera Miles and Gloria Grahame. Ida Lupino directed three episodes, "Everybody's Playing Polo," "Sugar and Spice and Everything…" and "Hear the Mellow Wedding Bells." She also acted in a fourth, "Not Even the Gulls Should Weep" along with her husband Howard Duff. Paul Henreid directed one episode, "Run Softly, Oh Softly," and Richard Donner also directed several. O'Brien got to play two parts in "Seventeen Gypsies and a Sinner Named Charlie," in which he enjoyed himself as a confidence trickster and was tipped for an Emmy award. His 12-year-old daughter Maria made her television debut in the same episode. Producer E. Jack Neuman had been so impressed with a poolside theatrical show that the children had given when he visited the O'Brien house one Sunday that he suggested Maria could appear.[7]

As always, O'Brien put a lot into the role. "Since we started last June, I've had four full days off," he remarked. "We've done a lot of localities in San Francisco, where we work a six-day week." He was required to learn 80 pages of script a week; he studied at night and over the weekends. Olga and the girls often fed him lines. "I work all day on the set, go home, have a shower, eat dinner in bed and study the next day's lines," he said. "My kids are beginning to call me 'uncle.'"[8]

The show tried to be different from other, similar programs such as the perennially popular *Perry Mason,* and did not follow causes in the manner of *The Defenders.* Instead, *Sam Benedict* went for the human-interest angle. The flamboyant Benedict was renowned for his fancy waistcoats and mastery of the courtroom. O'Brien attacked the role with a will, but seemed to some too forceful. He thrived on what one critic termed his "sheer nervous drive."[9] Nevertheless, he impressed many of his fellow actors with such things as his delivery of a speech from Shakespeare in one of his final summations to a jury. Audience feedback after the first few episodes indicated that there were too many plotlines which made the story difficult to follow. This was addressed midway through the season. Although the show was in direct competition with Jackie Gleason, the numbers for *Sam Benedict* were good. But it was not long before the plug was pulled. This rankled O'Brien, who remarked a couple of years later, "They turned us off just as we were really gaining audiences. To prove it—MGM's number one seller in the rerun market is *Sam*."[10] Contemporary reviews indicated that audiences warmed to the series as it went on, and a small but loyal following was built up. Since then, it has seldom been discussed and would appear to be largely unremembered. There was no DVD release until 2016, when Warner Bros. issued the complete series. Tellingly, it was in the Manufactured on Demand format, available only through their online store or via Amazon; but at least it was rescued from complete oblivion.

O'Brien compared the two media: "When you work in television, its demands are so great and the need for speed so important that I stay at a high pitch all day. In films, the pace is so much slower that I found that for days together I'd coast along. After all, if we do ... 32 TV shows in one year, that is the equivalent of 20 full-length motion pictures."[11] He was reluctant to commit to a long series, and never enjoyed playing the same part too often. "I don't mind it once in a while," he explained, "but I'm afraid of becoming a hack ... grinding them out every week.... [T]he danger for an actor is falling into his own clichés. If something works well one time, there is a tendency to do it again and again."[12]

O'Brien appeared in one of the earliest television movies, *The Hanged Man* (1964). Set in New Orleans, it was based on the Dorothy B. Hughes novel *Ride the Pink Horse* that had previously been filmed under that title. The director was Don Siegel and the taciturn star was Robert Culp. O'Brien appeared as a corrupt union boss, with Vera Miles as his wife. He made a naturally convincing heavy, his bullying swagger especially evident in a short scene when he holds court for the press. The scenes during the climax at the carnival were well realized. However, the film as a whole was forgettable, and compared unfavorably to *Ride a Pink Horse* (1947) which had starred Robert Montgomery and Thomas Gomez. Several of Hughes' works provided the basis for memorable noirs (notably 1950's *In a Lonely Place*). Color and the televisual approach added nothing but detracted. One of the few bright spots was the music of Astrud Gilberto and a fine performance of the famous song "The Girl from Ipanema." In the same year, O'Brien did sterling work in an episode of the hospital-set drama series *Breaking Point* which dealt with psychological crises. In "Tide of Darkness," he played a widower whose 14-year-old daughter goes into shock after being attacked.

Television gave him scope for a wider variety of roles. He was featured in several episodes of the popular children's series *The Wonderful World of Disney*; he enjoyed hamming it up as an old-time newspaper editor in "The Further Adventures of Gallagher." He drew praise for his powerhouse portrayal of larger-than-life political lobbyist Ollie Crown in "The Invisible Government," an episode of *Target: The Corruptors*. His scenes with fellow noir veteran Stephen McNally showed both actors to good advantage. For all his bombast, Crown was shown to be curiously naïve for the political game he was playing.

O'Brien appeared as an escaped convict who terrorizes his brother's family in "Killer in the House" for *The Dick Powell Theater*. He garnered fulsome praise for his appearance in the television movie *Flesh and Blood* alongside E.G. Marshall and Kim Stanley, directed by Arthur Penn. He played an aging construction worker uncertain of himself at great heights and continually tortured by his inability to save a young worker who fell many years before. A reviewer wrote, "[T]he high point was Edmond O'Brien's poetic recollection of a daredevil contest he engaged in with the young iron worker on high before the boy plunged to his death."[13] Written by William Hanley, it was originally intended for Broadway. However, it was decided that it would be premiered on television first.[14] It was one of O'Brien's outstanding later roles.

His best television film by far was Rod Serling's *The Doomsday Flight* (1966), in which he starred as an embittered engineer who phones an airline to say there is a bomb on board a flight from Los Angeles to New York. The security men dealing with the case (Jack Lord and Ed Asner) have to take him seriously, and even agree to give him the $100,000 he demands to tell them where it is hidden. The bomb is set to explode when the plane drops below a certain altitude. Meanwhile, the crew tries desperately to find the bomb, without success. When the van delivering the money to the man is destroyed in a freak accident, he gets drunk and starts to relish his newfound power over people's lives, saying that he might not tell where the bomb is hidden. This was a tense and generally engrossing drama, although the scenes on board the plane held far less interest than the ones on the ground involving O'Brien and his telephone conversations with an airport security agent. The characters on the flight were too clichéd; the real drama was with O'Brien, wearing his thick-lensed glasses, talking on the phone. His distinctive voice conveyed all his conflicting emotions; at first, he is precise and decisive, giving instructions, then wheedling and mocking, finally triumphant. Here was a man who was tired of "being nothing, wanting everything." The scene in the bar was a *tour de force*; he is drunk and incoherent, seemingly ill, but curiously lucid at the same time. He bemoans his constant lack of success: "I've never had an eight-course meal" he laments, and has just "ten bucks in the bank." Suddenly he becomes belligerent: "I want my change," he demands. If anything, the actual ending was an exercise in bathos. The movie was considerably enhanced by the music of Lalo Schifrin. "I loved that script," recalled Ed Asner, "and I thought Edmond O'Brien gave lessons on acting with [his performance]."

Teleplay writer Serling had based the *Doomsday Flight* idea on an actual case when a plane had to make a forced descent into Denver because of altitude. There were worries that the film might give people ideas, and before it was broadcast the Airline Pilots Association wrote to Serling asking that it be withdrawn. He responded by saying that it was out of his hands and was a matter for the network. However, he later said he wished he had never written it, as there were three cases where someone had tried and succeeded in extorting money from airlines by placing hoax calls. There were two incidents in the United States, one involving National Airlines and the other with Western Airlines; the money was paid in both cases and only in one instance was the money ever recovered. Shortly after the film was shown in Melbourne, Australia, another hoaxer demanded and got away with $520,000 from Qantas Airways. Serling commented, "I have done a vast disservice to the airlines."[15] Incidentally, O'Brien was among those considered for the role of the bomber D.O. Guerrero in the later theatrical film *Airport*.[16]

O'Brien popped up in other made-for-television movies including a better-than-average western, *The Intruders*, made in 1967 and first broadcast in 1970. This starred Don Murray as a marshal who loses the confidence of the townspeople when they are threatened by outlaws. O'Brien was full of authority as a colonel and saloon owner among a good cast who were given a decent storyline. Some of these "movies," such as *The Outsider* starring Darren McGavin, were actually pilots for series.

O'Brien was an excellent choice as the narrator of an interesting documentary series, *Men in Crisis* (1964–65). Each of the 32 half-hour episodes analyzed historic events through the personalities of the men involved. Titles included "Hitler vs Chamberlain" and "Castro vs Batista." Produced by the prolific David L. Wolper, the series was often repeated. One critic wrote of the episode "Grant vs Lee," "[T]he reality of the past and of the present are coalesced into a profoundly moving documentary narrated by Edmond O'Brien."[17]

O'Brien was excited by several television projects and by the mid–1960s was regularly seen on the small screen. He was not keen on doing a long TV series though, and turned down five offers before 20th Century–Fox Television enticed him with a film and television package including the offer of a central role in *The Long, Hot Summer*. The screenplay was based on three works by William Faulkner: the novella *Spotted Horses*, the short story "Barn Burning" and the novel *The Hamlet*. These had previously inspired the theatrical film *The Long, Hot Summer* (1958) with Orson Welles as Will Varner, the bombastic patriarch of a small Mississippi town. Faulkner had been inspired by the works of Tennessee Williams. O'Brien played Varner in the TV version. While in Rome making *The Barefoot Contessa*, O'Brien had been introduced to Faulkner by Humphrey Bogart in Harry's Bar, just around the corner from the Excelsior Hotel. "Faulkner was a very quiet man," said O'Brien. "He was a watcher and an observer. You got the feeling that he was observing everyone in order to put them in a scene. He felt comfortable only with small groups of people."[18] Edmond had already appeared in a previous adaptation of the author's story "An Error in Chemistry," and was familiar with his world. "I had read a good deal of Faulkner's work," he said, "and I knew that the tough, ruthless Will Varner was a very playable part."[19]

He was full of praise for the show's young star, Roy Thinnes: "He impresses me a great deal professionally and personally," said O'Brien.[20] He was happy to be working once more with Ruth Roman, although she was given little to do in the show. Thinnes was equally impressed with them both: "When Miss Roman plays a scene with Edmond O'Brien—two people of equal skills and inner strength—something magnificent happens. It's electrifying," he remarked.[21] It was rather hectic for the 50-year-old O'Brien, who had already had one heart attack. He was required on set for hours each day and the intensity of the work coupled with his increasingly obvious problems with his sight took their toll. After a dozen or so episodes in December 1965, he called it a day, and his part was taken over by Dan O'Herlihy.

Various reasons were given for O'Brien's abrupt departure: artistic differences over the nature of the character of Varner were cited, and his continually worsening eyesight.[22] According to cast member Jason Wingreen, the show was plagued with problems throughout its run and O'Brien left because he was unhappy with the way he was being treated; "They made me a lot of promises," O'Brien confided to him one day. "I was going to be very big on the series. They made me a lot of promises, and it's not working out. They're giving all the stuff to the kids. The kids are getting all the episodes." Wingreen said Edmond attended rehearsals one afternoon, mumbled his lines, then got up halfway through and went to his trailer. When the scene was ready to shoot, director Marc Daniels asked the second assistant to summon O'Brien. As he did so, the trailer door opened and O'Brien emerged wearing his overcoat. He turned to the left and walked off the set. With that, he quit the show. The producers tried to phone O'Brien that night but he was in no mood to talk to anyone.[23]

A fair audience had been built up and many viewers wrote in asking where he had gone. The series continued but the loss of O'Brien was a major blow. This, coupled with the lack of development of the characters, resulted in the show fizzling out by the following spring. Although O'Brien's TV career lasted several more years, he was never again tempted to work on a series, as a regular.

In the remainder of the decade, O'Brien popped up in guest roles in episodes of many of the hits of the day. In the circus drama *The Greatest Show on Earth*, he essayed the possessive head of a family act. He played an alcoholic ex-lawyer who has lost belief in his own ability and is reluctantly persuaded to return to the courtroom to represent a Chinese cook facing racism in an episode of *The Virginian*. He was featured in *Mission: Impossible* as a manufacturer of fake drugs who ends up receiving his own medicine. He played a boozy ex-safecracker in the Robert Wagner series *To Catch a Thief*. In the early 1970s O'Brien mostly made television movies but also appeared in guest spots in several fondly-remembered shows including *The High Chaparral* and *Macmillan & Wife*. He was especially touching in an episode of *The Streets of San Francisco* as a thirty-year cop who is shot during a robbery. Although his appearance had changed markedly, he showed to effect in his few brief scenes, particularly those in the hospital with Karl Malden, who he had known since the days they worked together on the stage show of *Winged Victory*. O'Brien invested his character with humanity and made a poignant and vulnerable figure at the twilight of his career.

❖❖ 21 ❖❖

New Directions

> I want to be a picture maker. That's where the real fun is in this town. Sure, acting's okay. But the guys who really create are the ones who make the pictures.
> —Interview with Bob Thomas, *The Milwaukee Sentinel,* "Director O'Brien Enlivens Films," March 29, 1961, 10

O'Brien began the decade brightly when he was awarded two stars on the Hollywood Walk of Fame for his work in film and television. The attention did not go to his head. Once when he visited Universal Studios in the early 1960s to settle some television projects, he found there was a new doorman who didn't recognize him and asked his name. "O'Brien," he replied. "Hugh?" asked the doorman. "No." "George?" "No!" "Pat?" "No!" he said, becoming increasingly frustrated. "Then which O'Brien are you?" "Margaret!" he said, and drove on.[1]

The Last Voyage (1960) was a well-acted film set on a sinking ocean liner, with good special effects and a semi-documentary feel. O'Brien played an embittered second engineer who lost his father on the *Titanic.* The main conflict was between him and the over-cautious captain (George Sanders), who is determined not to lose the ship. The star was Robert Stack whose wife (Dorothy Malone) is trapped in one of the cabins and it is a race against time to free her before the ship sinks. Woody Strode provided sterling support as a selfless crew member. O'Brien was reduced to barking orders at his men for much of the time as the engine room is flooded and he tries desperately to avert disaster. However, his character has a definite zeal and the actor's familiar intensity surfaces when he has an explosive run-in with his captain and tells him in no uncertain terms what he feels. Although he is reduced in rank for insubordination, his words hit home and the captain is rather dazed thereafter. Later films have followed a similar template, but O'Brien and Sanders provided living portraits of two men who cope with disaster from entirely different perspectives.

O'Brien and the cast and crew spent three and a half months working on location and the film was one of the most arduous that he ever made. Andrew and Virginia Stone had been searching for a ship they could sink for five years. Eventually they set their sights on the famed liner the *Île de France*. Built at Saint-Nazaire in the 1920s during the heyday of the great passenger liners, the glorious ship ended its days in the Sea of Japan, just off Osaka.[2] The Stones were allowed to use the liner for the film, even to the extent of setting fire to some of the upper decks and laying explosives in the interior, with the proviso that they did not sink it. However, they did sink the ship partially; it began to list, and one section flooded. It was frightening for Stack, Malone, Strode and O'Brien, who were in the climactic scenes. It was especially dangerous for O'Brien, whose sight was weak. Stack recounted in his memoir, "Eddie O'Brien, according to scripted instructions, fought his way through the waves and stumbled over the sandbags to the main dining room. He had to battle his way through thousands of gallons of water and arc lights spitting sparks like Dr. Frankenstein's infernal machine." Incensed, O'Brien walked off the set. "It is understandable that he found the experience unusually terrifying," observed Stack. "So much water had come into the superstructure that the ship began to list. Eddie couldn't see that well, and the ship really appeared to be going down."[3]

There was the prospect of O'Brien working again with Andrew Stone on the proposed thriller *Dark of the Sun*. Set in San Francisco's Chinatown this would have starred O'Brien as a reporter, but after his experience on *The Last Voyage* he did not feel inclined, and besides, the project never got off the ground.[4]

By far his most intriguing film of the decade, *The Third Voice* was a nifty, neatly plotted noir with an unusual slant and a compelling central performance by O'Brien. Embittered secretary Marian (Laraine Day) concocts an elaborate plan to murder millionaire businessman Harris Chapman and steal his money. She was his mistress and helped him develop his business, but he has left her for a younger model. Marian enlists a man (O'Brien) to impersonate him during a trip to Mexico. The movie was well played by the interesting cast with the sultry-voiced Julie London especially effective in support. Edmond's wife Olga made a brief appearance as a blonde prostitute. The atmosphere of suspense and mystery was enhanced by the music of Johnny Mandel. Writer-director-producer Hubert Cornfield made only a few feature films including the unsung noirs

German poster for *The Third Voice* (1960), one of O'Brien's most intriguing later films with a definite noir feel, written and directed by the underrated Hubert Cornfield. With Julie London.

Sudden Danger (1955) and *Plunder Road* (1957). He was born in Turkey and lived for a while in Paris, where he became friendly with the New Wave directors François Truffaut and Jean-Luc Godard. Cornfield is seldom spoken of by cineastes, perhaps because he made so few films, or because critics don't know what to make of them, but they all displayed an intelligent and inventive talent at work. *The Third Voice* was decidedly original and he employed some interesting touches, such as the raven which appears twice on the windowsill; ravens have always been portents of doom and forewarned many a Roman emperor that the end was nigh.

In the central role, O'Brien was a standout, reflecting in an internal dialogue at crucial moments and with great humor when the situation called for it. He thoroughly enjoyed the larger-than-life role of impersonating the aggressive businessman Chapman, but was equally effective in the quiet moments. In one sequence, he is in the hotel lobby when Chapman's friends, a judge and his wife, stand behind him. All the time he is praying that the girl at the desk will not call his name out and that he will not be recognized.

The film's peculiar appeal was not lost on contemporary critics, many of whom commented on the unusual approach and lauded a new talent in its young director. One reviewer wrote, "A great deal of credit must also go to Edmond O'Brien who is on screen for practically the entire eighty minutes or so of the picture's duration. He manages to hold attention throughout, which is quite a tribute to his performance."[5] *Motion Picture Daily* wrote that it was "a career piece for Edmond O'Brien who delivers a fascinating performance."[6] Veteran critic Harold V. Cohen called O'Brien's portrayal "perfect."[7] Edmond was fired with enthusiasm for *The Third Voice*, and reportedly turned down two projects in order to do it. One was no loss, the weak comedy *Wake Me When It's Over*; but the other was the lead in *Elmer Gantry* (1960), for which Burt Lancaster won an Oscar as Best Actor.[8] On balance, *The Third Voice* was a more intriguing and suitable vehicle for O'Brien.

O'Brien had long harbored the ambition of a return to directing since his first attempt with *Shield for Murder* in 1954. Some seven years passed before he found another chance with *Deadlock*, which was retitled *Man-Trap* (1961) on its release. Originally, the star was announced as Tony Curtis, but he dropped out.[9] O'Brien wanted to call the film *Hell Is for Heroes*, but Steve McQueen claimed that title.[10] The eventual cast consisted of Jeffrey Hunter, David Janssen and Stella Stevens. The plot centered on Matt (Hunter), who saves the life of his friend Vince Biskay (Janssen) during the Korean War; Biskay vows to repay him. Some years later, Matt is unhappily married to dipsomaniac Nina (Stevens), while having an affair with his secretary Ruth. Matt is employed as a builder by his wife's domineering father, but longs to strike out on his own. Biskay suddenly returns from the past with a plan to steal millions of dollars from the diplomatic envoy of a South American dictator. The skeptical Matt agrees to take part, but the heist goes horribly wrong and everything starts to unravel.

O'Brien's finished film was strong in parts but weak in others. The best sequences were those when the two were planning their heist, and the repeated dummy runs driving on the newly constructed freeway, to the accompaniment of Leith Stevens' dynamic music. These scenes were full of tension and promised much, displaying good use of the San Francisco locations. The scene when the diplomat arrived at the airport was also well-observed, as the screams of excitement from the crowd of teenagers greeting their pop idol become screams of panic once the shooting starts. This was enhanced by O'Brien asking the girls to each try to snatch an item of the idol's clothing. "If you girls can do it, there's five bucks extra in it for you," he said. He was willing to do anything to help the cause; "I'll use any method, Stanislavsky or Shakespeare, to get what I want," he said.[11]

The annoying party guests were well-drawn; with their belligerent bonhomie and unfunny humor, they enter Matt's house seemingly at will. When they creep en masse into his living room through the patio doors at night as he sits in the dark having been beaten up by the dictator's thugs, it was like a surreal vision of a suburban nightmare. Where the screenplay fell down was on the characters and their motivations. Matt seemed to prevaricate too much; his constant uncertainty made the scenario appear muddled and rather far-fetched. There were numerous inconsistencies and too much was glossed over. For instance, when Biskay is shot he tells Matt to go for a doctor in a rich neighborhood, and to pay with some of

David Janssen (*left*) and Jeffrey Hunter in a tense scene from *Man-Trap* (1961). O'Brien's second film as director, it received a muted response, but it's a good effort which deserves reappraisal.

the money they have stolen. But the next scene moved on several weeks to show Biskay recovering in bed, with no explanation of what happened when they went to the doctor and paid him to treat Biskay's gaping gunshot wounds with unused $100 bills. Perhaps the fault was with the original 1958 novel, *Soft Touch* by John D. MacDonald. The author had his greatest success with *The Executioners* which was filmed twice successfully as *Cape Fear*. As it was, rather too much happened in *Man-Trap* to make it believable, and the use of the device of amnesia to block out Matt's memory of where he buried his wife was rather too convenient. Matt's ever-loving secretary Ruth emerged as a non-character. But overall, the film stands up today; the cinematography of Loyal Griggs was another notable aspect.

Star Hunter was initially full of praise: "Eddie is great," he said. "It's wonderful to have a director who really understands the actor's problems. He takes time with everyone. The result is we'll break our necks for him."[12] O'Brien's directing style was just as wholehearted as his acting. "It's Radio City Music Hall and 3000 people are looking at you up there on the screen," he enthused to Stella Stevens for her big scene. "Give it the full schmear!"[13] O'Brien said of Stevens, "She's a director's dream, she's a completely instinctual actress, and has that wonderful gift of letting the audience in on the mind and heart of the character she plays."[14] When asked what she thought of her director, Stevens remarked, "It's not work, it's a ball, and he gets results."[15] O'Brien's enthusiasm was decidedly infectious but sometimes, according to Hunter, he was over-enthusiastic. In an article, Hunter commented,

> Eddie, being a very strong performer, interprets each character himself; and at times this can be very very helpful, and at other times it can be terribly frustrating, only because the actor likes to feel that he is an individual and not a parrot. It was an early stumbling block, because Eddie would act it all out, play the play, play the individual scenes, and play the characters. At times it's great fun to watch but then it does become a little troubling in terms of your own stream of consciousness, or your self-conscious reaction.... Eddie is extremely resourceful; he's a good sport, he accepts suggestions, and I think he has all the makings of being a very fine director.[16]

O'Brien said that he did not care to direct himself in a film, calling it "the one-armed paper-hanger's approach."[17] He could not contain his natural exuberance and thoroughly enjoyed his six months working on the project; "Even if I bomb, I've had a great time of it," he said.[18] It was an excellent effort by O'Brien, who was lined up as director-producer for two more films by Paramount to be released under his own Tiger Productions banner. Neither of these was made.[19]

O'Brien was content to accept cameos in a range of star vehicles. *The*

Great Imposter (1961) utilized a script by his brother Liam, based on the allegedly true tale of a man who assumed multiple identities. Tony Curtis played Fred, the title role, and although O'Brien was billed second, he did not appear until two-thirds of the way into the film as a ship captain who needs his tooth extracted by Curtis, and is rendered almost comatose with Novocain. Fred's exploits seemed far-fetched at times, particularly when he performed surgery on 19 Koreans on board ship during a storm, having had no previous medical training. About the same time, Edmond was due to return to Broadway to play the father in Liam's *The Male Principle*, the saga of an Irish immigrant family. However, that did not come about.[20]

O'Brien was still receiving interesting film offers, including an invite to Paris from Louis Malle to appear in *Zazie dans le Metro* (1960), but in the event Phillipe Noiret played that role.[21] Among other proposed projects was *The Hope Diamond Jinx*, a portmanteau film about the bad luck that befell the various owners of the famous diamond. The other mooted stars were Rita Hayworth, Dana Wynter and David Niven, but the film was never made.[22] O'Brien was slated to co-star with Bobby Darin in director John Cassavetes' *Too Late Blues* (1961), the story of a dedicated jazz musician.[23] He was not able to appear in the film because of other commitments.

Gene Kelly and Kirk Douglas had been considered for the pivotal role of the American newspaperman Jackson Bentley in David Lean's epic *Lawrence of Arabia*, but O'Brien was eventually handed the part. Bentley was loosely based on Lowell Thomas, whose influential book on Lawrence first brought him to wide public attention, especially in America. Suffering from flu at the beginning of 1962 when filming was due to begin, O'Brien was called by producer Sam Spiegel to make his way to Spain, traveling via London where he had wardrobe fittings. He filmed several scenes including those set in Jerusalem and the political discussion with Ali (Omar Sharif). O'Brien enjoyed his time filming at the sixteenth century Casa de Pilatos in Seville, which doubled for locations in the Middle East. "We had to be so careful not to damage anything," he recalled. "So it was startling to watch the young heirs to the place throwing darts at the Goyas which hang on the walls."[24] He returned home at the end of February 1962, and was due to begin the next seven weeks of filming in London and Spain in the spring. However, he began to feel unwell and suffered his first heart attack. He was admitted to Cedars of Lebanon hospital where the doctor ordered him to undertake no more work until June of that year.[25] Arthur Kennedy was called in as his replacement on the film.[26]

Walt Disney's *Moon Pilot* (1962) was a so-so family comedy about a project to send a man into space to orbit the moon. Volunteer astronaut Tom Tryon was aided by a benevolent French-accented alien female (Dany Saval) who comes from some unpronounceable planet. O'Brien appeared as an exasperated security agent who has to guard Tryon and make sure he doesn't get away, which of course he does, several times. There were some funny moments along the way such as when O'Brien is unable to avert his eyes from a gangster film on television no matter what is going on around him, and especially a scene when several young beatnik girls are rounded up for an identity parade and cause minor havoc at police headquarters. But for the most part it was all too frenetic, and there was too much shouting, as though it was presumed that the youngsters watching the film might fall asleep otherwise. One Nebraska exhibitor commented, "Many youngsters came but they did not enjoy it too much."[27] The movie drew criticism from the FBI which petitioned Walt Disney, protesting that guarding an astronaut was not a bureau jurisdiction. The character became instead a Federal Security Officer, but the difference was lost on most people. The FBI was not placated and further objected to the "most slapstick and uncomplimentary manner" in which the role was presented.[28]

John Ford's *The Man Who Shot Liberty Valance* (1962) was a sometimes labored treatise on the nature of legends and the passing of the Old West. It did not see the great director at his best, but it certainly had its moments. Aging Senator Ransom Stoddard (James Stewart) returns to the town of Shinbone for the funeral of his old friend Tom Doniphon (John Wayne). Stoddard recounts his story to the local pressmen, which is seen in flashback, of how the town was rid of the violent Liberty Valance (Lee Marvin) and his gang.

A slow-moving tale for the most part, the film lacked some spark of magic. It received a divided reception on its release. Some interpreted it as a satire of westerns; one critic remarked upon its effect on a typical audience; "An adult audience in a packed public theater ... laughed, groaned and commented so audibly and derivatively that a well-disposed reviewer could only be embarrassed for its makers."[29] The limited budget was apparent and rather too much of the 123-minute running time was spent in the kitchens. Stewart seemed uncomfortable and too old for the part, and a good many of the supporting stars hammed it up a little too much. O'Brien was guilty of that, but endearingly so. *The Times* of London remarked in his obituary that he "overacted delightfully, not least in the scene where, much the worse for alcohol, he recites the St. Crispin Day speech from *Henry V.*"[30] He was so engaging as Dutton Peabody, guardian

One of O'Brien's finest characterizations was as Dutton Peabody, editor of *The Shinbone Star* and staunch upholder of the freedom of the press in John Ford's *The Man Who Shot Liberty Valance* (1962). O'Brien addresses the townspeople at the statehood meeting, with Robert F. Simon (*center right*), Sam Harris (*in top hat*) and uncredited townsmen.

of the freedom of the press that when the expected attack by Valance and his cronies happened, there was a collective sigh of relief when he was seen up and about again afterwards. He delivered his final speech beautifully when nominating Ransom Stoddard to the Senate in the rowdy hall. O'Brien caught the mood just right with his grandiloquent manner and shabby-genteel appearance; "Go west, young man," he announces to Stoddard, paraphrasing Horace Greeley, "and grow young with the country!" This scene was worthy of the master director and involved that other great Ford regular John Carradine, also at his flowery best. O'Brien was made up to look much older, with whiskers and heavy bags under the eyes. When he was first made up for the part, Ford took one look at him and joked, "Now, Eddie, if you'll just go up to make up and see if they can cover up some of those ravages of the night before, we'll start the test."[31] O'Brien enjoyed working with Ford, who, according to one witness, "called his fellow Irishman Eamon and allowed as much time as [he] needed to amplify his baroque performance."[32] O'Brien declared afterwards that Ford was "eight directors in one," and observed, "He doesn't act out a role, but touches your imagination. With one gesture, he gives you the essence. For 15 years I've been meeting Ford and he's been saying we should work

O'Brien (*left*) with James Stewart in *The Man Who Shot Liberty Valance* (1962).

together. Everybody told me he was the toughest director in town. He is, but what a sense of security knowing you're in the hands of a master."[33] He later wrote in a letter to Ford, "In all the years I never enjoyed an acting experience as much."[34]

Despite the film's lackluster reception, many critics warmed to O'Brien's contribution. One commented that despite the presence of two of the biggest stars of the time, Wayne and Stewart, "both, surprisingly, are eclipsed by the memorably good performance of Mr. Edmond O'Brien."[35] *Boxoffice* declared that he "pulls the picture out from under his co-stars with a performance of Shakespearean magnitude."³⁶ Dutton Peabody was a great Fordian creation, an expansive, warm-hearted, drink-addled dreamer with a way with words, and O'Brien invested the character with his own humanity.

Packed with star names, *The Longest Day* (1962) was arguably one of the best war films of all time and a decent account of the Normandy landings. O'Brien made few really good war movies, and this was probably the best, but he seemed to get lost in the crowd. He played a Navy commander and shared a few good scenes with Henry Fonda, who played President Franklin D. Roosevelt's son Teddy. The film cost $10,000,000 and was a massive box office hit, earning $50,000,000.

John Frankenheimer's *Birdman of Alcatraz* (1962) was a powerful drama based on the life of Robert Stroud, whose death sentence for double murder was commuted to life imprisonment in solitary confinement. Famously he became an expert on birds and their diseases after keeping them in his Leavenworth cell. Burt Lancaster was excellent in the title role, winning a BAFTA for his portrayal, with fine support from a great cast of veterans, especially Thelma Ritter, Karl Malden and Neville Brand. The highly fictionalized account was taken from the book of the same name by Thomas E. Gaddis, played in the film by O'Brien. Initially, Gaddis was going to play himself but, ironically, after a test it was decided that he was just not the type. However, he was retained as a technical advisor. It had taken Gaddis some time to find a publisher willing to publish his controversial book about a federal prisoner and even longer to convince a film studio to tackle it. Gaddis' wife Martha sometimes visited him on the set and observed the actors at work: "It was interesting to watch O'Brien study Tom's mannerisms and then assume them," she wrote. "He even expressed hope that the filming of his scenes wouldn't take too long so that he could stop smoking the little cigarillos that Tom always smokes."³⁷ O'Brien provided the expert narration for the story and linked each segment of the narrative through the two-and-a-half-hour running time. Thus, he was an integral part of the film, his familiar gruff tones providing an air of jaded realism.

O'Brien's second cinematic appearance for Frankenheimer was in the taut political thriller *Seven Days in May* (1964), based on a same-name bestseller from a couple of years earlier. President Kennedy was keen for a screen version to be made, and had been distinctly impressed by Frankenheimer's *The Manchurian Candidate* (1962). The president even vacated the White House for a week to allow the scenes of demonstrations to be filmed outside the executive mansion.³⁸ The plot concerned a five-

21. New Directions

O'Brien won a Golden Globe and was also Oscar-nominated for his portrayal of a Southern Senator who is put in harm's way in John Frankenheimer's intelligent political thriller *Seven Days in May* (1964). This lobby card shows O'Brien (*left*) and Fredric March.

star general (Burt Lancaster) who plans with the other Chiefs of Staff to stage a military coup and bring down the president. Intelligent and engrossing, the film has an admirable screenplay by Rod Serling. The urgent music of Jerry Goldsmith caught the mood perfectly and there was impressive cinematography by Ellsworth Fredericks. A fine cast was assembled with Kirk Douglas as the whistleblower and Fredric March as the president. O'Brien enjoyed a good role as an outspoken Southern Senator with a fondness for the bottle, sent to find out more about a secret military base in the Arizona desert. Douglas was the film's producer and immediately thought of O'Brien for the role, describing him as one of his favorite actors. O'Brien's performance earned him a Golden Globe as Best Supporting Actor; he was Oscar-nominated in the same category but lost out to Peter Ustinov for *Topkapi* (1964).

Frankenheimer had spent a year preparing the film and O'Brien was in his element in the company.[39] But at first, he had problems adjusting to the slower tempo in comparison to the high pitch of his television show *Sam Benedict*. He said there were between 40 and 60 setups a day on the TV series, but on *Seven Days in May* they did six or seven. On the series, they did 11 to 16 pages of script a day; "Here if we do two or three pages it's a big day." In total, the film took 11 or 12 twelve weeks. He loved working with the cast. "It's so beautiful to watch Freddy [March]," he observed. He also acknowledged which medium he preferred: "[Frankenheimer] is staging this marvelously, playing scenes all the way through. It's the difference between playing a concert in Carnegie Hall and beating a drum in some bar."[40]

22

A Last Hurrah

> I make movies for lots of reasons. Money, love and more money.—Cindy Adams, *Sunday Herald,* March 12, 1961, 26

> There are vogues in acting like anything else. But though styles in acting may change, the truth does not.—"O'Brien Starring in Faulkner Epic," *The Post-Standard,* Syracuse, New York, September 29, 1965.

From the mid–1960s onwards, O'Brien's film career consisted mostly of cameo roles. He was featured in a diverse group of movies reflecting the changing times, from science fiction to drug addiction. After falling into obscurity, he returned to wider prominence at the close of the decade for a last hurrah in a seminal western by Sam Peckinpah.

Edmond was well aware of the changes wrought in cinema since the heyday of the studios: "Hollywood has to face the truth," he asserted, "The habit of movie-going has been broken."[1] He further observed,

> Theater used to be the selective medium and movies for the masses. A few big studios owned the top stars and made material for them. Those pictures were designed to sell like clothes brushes and they sold. But the world changed and the way of making pictures changed. The onslaught of TV was responsible. It's now the mass medium and pictures the selective medium.[2]

He always preferred the big screen but was content to appear only occasionally in those roles that caught his fancy such as the maverick general in *Rio Conchos* (1964). This was a good color western full of tension and action in equal measure. Stuart Whitman starred as a cavalry captain sent after a shipment of stolen army rifles, with Jim Brown as his sergeant. The goal was to find renegade Southern General Perdo (O'Brien), who plans to sell the guns to the Apaches in return for gold. Leading Whitman and Brown through the rough country was an ex–Confederate Army

Major (Richard Boone), fired by hatred of the Apaches, and a Mexican ne'er-do-well (Anthony Franciosa). O'Brien did not appear until two-thirds of the way into the film, introduced on the veranda of a curious half-built Southern-style residence, looking for all the world like the last remnant of the set of *Gone with the Wind*. He made the most of his scenes and makes the character somehow real. Perdo is clearly overtaken by dreams of glory but despite his apparent imbalance he is nonetheless shrewd. He seems blithely unaware of the chaos he is causing, which is brought home in the closing shot as he re-enters the "mansion" while it burns and the camera pans out to the silhouette of the timber frame house and the disappearing figure framed within. During shooting, O'Brien was troubled with what was described as an eye infection while on location in Moab, Utah, and was forced to withdraw from the film. He was treated on the set by a specialist who flew in a special drug to help alleviate the marked swelling around his eye, which reduced sooner than expected. After consultations with the doctors, he was allowed to complete his scenes involving 250 extras.[3] After filming, he underwent another eye operation at Cedars of Lebanon in Los Angeles.[4]

Sylvia (1965) spent most of its 115 minutes trying to piece together the dodgy past of a millionaire's prospective bride. Is she what she seems to be? Who exactly is Sylvia? By the end of this wearisome venture, the answer might well be "Who cares?" Still, it provided several old stagers with a chance to shine, especially the eye-catching Ann Sothern as the girl's dipsomaniac roommate. O'Brien had a cameo as a harassed married man in the throes of a mid-life crisis who becomes obsessed with Sylvia (Carroll Baker). He drives her from Mexico to New York, but his love goes unrequited, no matter how much he pleads for just "one little kiss." There was little in the role to latch onto but he made it live, and his simmering anger with his lot was palpable in a scene in his back garden on a suburban Sunday, practicing his putting and cursing his obnoxious son. There was the prospect of the role as an agent in the biopic *Harlow* (1965), for the same producer and director with the same star, Carroll Baker. However, O'Brien had too much other work and could not fit it in; the part went to Red Buttons instead.[5]

O'Brien seriously considered a number of theatrical projects in the 1960s. He bought the rights to Paul Scheier's adaptation of John Hershey's science fiction novel *The Child Buyer*, intending to play the title role. The idea was for a 20-week nationwide tour followed by a Broadway run, but the idea was never taken up.[6] After producer Stuart Ostow saw O'Brien in the guise of an old man in an episode of *Sam Benedict*, he wanted him

22. A Last Hurrah 163

for the role of Santa Claus in Meredith Willson's *Here's Love,* a musical version of the classic *Miracle on 34th Street.* In the event, the role was played successfully by British character actor Laurence Naismith, giving the veteran a new lease on life.[7] In the 1965 theatrical season, O'Brien planned to make a return to Broadway and to Shakespeare in *Coriolanus* starring Richard Burton.[8] He later withdrew because of film and TV commitments and in any event Burton abandoned the project.[9]

Towards the end of 1963, O'Brien attended a Sunday brunch at the home of director Richard Quine. There he met Chuck Dederich, the founder of Synanon, an addiction treatment project based in Santa Monica, California. During conversations, the subject of a film about the pioneering work of the center came up, and Dederich said of O'Brien, "There is the man who should play me."[10] O'Brien was equally impressed with Dederich, who he said had "the most total personality I've ever met."[11] Dederich was an ex-alcoholic who had started the center from his flat with a $33 unemployment check in 1958. His approach was to tackle the root cause of addiction and cure what he called the "addiction to stupidity."[12] His methods were controversial and sometimes violent; in later years, Synanon degenerated into a criminal religious cult with Dederich as its virtual dictator. But at the time the film was made, his work was viewed with open minds and generally felt to be positive. He was even drafted in as technical advisor on the film.[13] On the plus side, several addicts had actually been "cured" during their time there, albeit temporarily, including jazz greats Art Pepper and Joe Pass. Pass even recorded a memorable album, *Sounds of Synanon.* O'Brien had tried to help the drug-addict son of a director, encouraging him to enter the center, but the son became involved in more crime after leaving prison and died young. O'Brien devoted half his salary for the film to the organization.[14]

Viewed now, *Synanon* appears incredibly modish and of its time. From the opening shots of two addicts arriving at the center after crossing what looks like a desert while the lower-case titles come up and the jazzy Neal Hefti score plays, the feeling is that this must be the 1960s in full swing. Eartha Kitt and Chuck Connors stood out in what were unexpected roles for them. There was no plot as such; the screenplay was focused mostly on the addicts and their ferocious self-examination. There was much intensity on show but some of the scenes were overlong and did not hold the attention. At times, the director achieved a semi-documentary feel. The subject may have worked better as a documentary. Former child actor Quine turned to directing in the late 1940s. He first heard about Synanon when he heard on the radio a recording of drug addicts speaking, and soon he was fired up with enthusiasm for the project. "I'm making the film because I have to," he declared. "The story of Synanon seems so vital, so important, that it has to be told."[15]

The critics were divided, but many welcomed the frank discussion of hitherto taboo subjects. Whatever else it did, Synanon kick-started many self-help groups. O'Brien gave a strong performance that epitomized the "tough love" approach of the project's founder. One commentator remarked that O'Brien and Richard Conte were "reliable as the senior citizens of the establishment."[16] *Variety* wrote, "O'Brien's performance is smooth and convincing and lends strength to the character he portrays."[17] Some felt the treatment glamorized the lifestyle: "The real drug addicts who appear in the background are plumpish, greyish and utterly ordinary," noted one critic, "but the fictional ones are glamorously handsome, and lead lives which are full of throbbing emotion and upset."[18] O'Brien had earlier narrated a half-hour TV documentary about the center, *To Slay a White Horse*.[19]

O'Brien was sought to play an American army sergeant who murders a British officer in 1964's *The Winston Affair*, also known as *Man in the Middle*, filmed in England and India. Robert Mitchum was cast as the lawyer who defends him. Mitchum appeared in the film but Keenan Wynn played the sergeant.[20] With his brother Liam, Edmond again hoped to make a number of independent features, which he planned to act in and direct, including *The Right of Way* by Malcolm Brandt, but that did not transpire.[21] The brothers were excited when they secured the film rights to Luigi Pirandello's classic stage play *Six Characters in Search of an Author*. However, although a film version was made in Australia that year, neither Edmond or Liam were involved in it.[22] Dino De Laurentiis offered O'Brien the role of Pontius Pilate in his epic *The Bible* (1966). The original intention was for the whole book, Old and New Testaments, to be committed to celluloid in a series of films. However, such a mammoth undertaking faced many problems and delays. Only the first 22 books of the Old Testament made it into the film, which was directed by John Huston and subtitled *The Beginning*.[23] O'Brien's raised profile after his Oscar nomination meant that he was in the running for interesting roles. One such was *The Diamond Orchid*, based on a Broadway play inspired by the story of Juan and Evita Peron. The film, not made, would have seen him as Juan with Sophia Loren as Evita.[24]

O'Brien next popped up in the engaging science fiction fantasy *Fantastic Voyage* (1966). He played a general in charge of a top-secret military base that has the secret of miniaturization. The novel premise was that enemy agents have tried to assassinate a scientist who knows vital things about the miniaturization process and that the only way to save his life is to miniaturize a special team of experts in a submarine and send them into his bloodstream. It was good fun, but many critics were less than enthusiastic. "The process shots are so clumsily matted," wrote Pauline Kael, "that the actors look as if a child has cut them out with blunt scissors."[25] Seen now, the effects might seem risible, but the concept was inventive, and the minimalist score by Leonard Roseman added greatly to the effect. It was a change of pace for O'Brien, although he was in the control room most of the time and had little to do except scowl and pour endless cups of coffee. Science fiction was not his natural métier but he was, as always, convincing, despite admitting, "I didn't know what half of the things I said meant."[26] A good cast was assembled, with '60s icon Raquel Welch the most prominent presence. Despite outward appearances, Welch admitted to feeling unsure of herself at that time among the company. She recalled of the shooting, "[E]very day for five months I'd sit in the commissary at lunch time with Stephen Boyd and Edmond O'Brien and Donald Pleasence and I'd hardly know what they were talking about. It wasn't only things about acting, but words I didn't know and restaurants and foods I'd never heard of. And I'd try to act sophisticated and knowing, but I wasn't."[27]

After one excursion into science fiction, O'Brien very nearly appeared in another cult classic of the era, as Dr. Zaius in *Planet of the Apes* (1968). However, the role went to his old friend and mentor from Shakespearean Broadway days, Maurice Evans.[28] O'Brien was due to begin work on the Doris Day comedy *The Glass Bottom Boat* (1966) when he had his second heart attack. He was also up for a role in the Alistair MacLean adventure *Ice Station Zebra* (1968) but was later replaced by Ernest Borgnine.[29]

He played a publisher in the European-made espionage yarn *To Commit a Murder* (1967), which starred Louis Jourdan. In this French-Italian-German co-production, Red China was the enemy. It made use of attractive locales in Paris and Heidelberg, but wasted a good cast; O'Brien was not in it much. A distinctly average feature, it was undistinguishable from all the other Cold War thrillers of the kind and did not go into general release in the U.S. until 1970. A contemporary critic remarked that it was shot in "washy color ... dreadfully dubbed into English."[30] Also lensed in Europe, *The Viscount* (1967) was a modish, repetitive thriller also typical of its period starring Kerwin Mathews as a sub–James Bond type playboy adventurer. Bosley Crowther accurately summed it up: "It's full of fist fights, karate battles, automobile chases and machine-gun duels, and is totally devoid of intelligence, humor or class."[31] O'Brien reputedly appeared in this film, but in one version he was not listed in the credits and his character was played by another actor.

As Edmond's career wound down, his daughter Bridget was beginning to show promise when she won the Bank of America Award for Acting for her performance in a school play, *Annie Get Your Gun*. She secured a place at the Syracuse University Drama School, where she began in September 1967.[32] His other daughter Maria had also embarked on an acting career.

In October 1968, O'Brien traveled to Brazil with his wife to work on the Universal television movie *River of Diamonds*, later renamed *River of Mystery*.[33] In this action-adventure, filmed in several locations including the capitol Brasilia and Rio de Janeiro, Vic Morrow and Claude Akins played down-on-their-luck oil drillers contracted by an old acquaintance (Niall MacGinnis) to use their knowledge of explosives to extract diamonds for a wealthy fugitive American (O'Brien). The scenic locations, especially at the famous Ipanema beach and above the Christ the Redeemer statue, made the film worthwhile. For the most part, the breathtaking scenery overwhelmed the formulaic story. O'Brien tended to overplay but he was nonetheless endearing. The movie was not shown on television until October 1971.

After several forgettable films, O'Brien returned to general public attention in Sam Peckinpah's seminal western *The Wild Bunch* (1969). In a good cast headed by Robert Ryan and William Holden, O'Brien gave a boisterous performance as Freddie Sykes, a grizzled old-timer. Looking decidedly older, it was hard to believe it was the same man who only a few years before had been playing leading roles. A surprising range of other actors were considered for the role including Walter Brennan, Lee J. Cobb and even the veteran comic Andy Clyde. The diversity of such players spoke well for the talents embodied by O'Brien. Nonetheless he had a number of problems on set, as Ernest Borgnine recalled: "[He] was half-blind at the time he made the film. He really had to work hard to hit his marks, but the old pro did it."[34] Working on the picture was not a pleasurable experience for any of the actors. The chief location shooting took place at the remote town of Parras, described variously as a hellhole, and Torreon. Holden's biographer recounted:

Peckinpah seemed intent on converting the actors into his own variety of wild bunch. He exhibited a unique talent for roiling the atmosphere and infuriating the cast and crew without losing their respect for him as a filmmaker. He drove everyone hard, especially himself, ordered take

O'Brien (*right*) was almost unrecognizable as grizzled oldtimer Freddie Sykes in Sam Peckinpah's seminal western *The Wild Bunch* (1969). Left to right: William Holden, Ben Johnson, Warren Oates and O'Brien.

after take of seemingly unnecessary scenes, spent long hours striving for visual effects, stormed and ranted hourly.[35]

The finished film had some scenes removed but was still over two and a half hours long. Critics were divided, but most realized its significance. One called it "a bloody lament made with a terrible beauty." The same critic defined the new world that the film seemed to inhabit: "It is a world of moral confusion, wherein revolutionary battle is in the wrong hands, every man contains a streak of violence ready to break out, and any noble action only destroys its maker."[36]

The movie enjoys a solid reputation among fans of cinema, not just western fans. It has been hugely influential for generations of filmmakers, especially Quentin Tarantino. But the constant use of excessive violence seems to some the anathema of entertainment, and its long-term effects appear corrosive. "We watch endless violence," wrote one critic, "to assure us that violence is not good."[37]

The action took place in Mexico in 1913, right at the end of the "classic western" era, and there was a palpable sense of men outliving their time. All the protagonists looked their age, which suited the theme of the movie. Peckinpah chose his actors carefully, and held out for older actors when it was suggested to him that younger men would be better. Even among the strong cast and in a far less prominent role, O'Brien still managed to be noticed. According to *Film Bulletin*, "As a broken-down old gunslinger, Edmond O'Brien is superb, although almost unrecognizable; a sort of degenerate Gabby Hayes."[38]

The fine score by Jerry Fielding made good use of the old Mexican lament "La Golondrinha" aka "The Swallow," a song about the impossibility of returning to the homeland. The sentimental song seemed curiously incongruous among all the mayhem and yet entirely apt, underscoring the general feeling of the whole thing as a tribute to the disappearing west.

O'Brien's last released film of the 1960s was the tiresome Don Knotts comedy *The Love God?* (1969). Knotts, editor of a bird-watchers' magazine, joins up with Tremaine (O'Brien), the publisher of a girlie magazine, in order to stay afloat. It was written by Nat Hiken, whose most memorable creation was the immortal Sergeant Bilko played by Phil Silvers. Hiken offered the part of Tremaine to Silvers, who gave a qualified yes but then changed his mind. The apparent sticking point was that he wanted equal billing with Knotts, which the producers would not countenance.[39] O'Brien was given the role against the wishes of Hiken, who died suddenly of a heart attack shortly after filming had finished. O'Brien was ill-suited to this kind of knockabout comedy and was wasted in the part. It was a poor end to an interesting decade.

In November 1969, O'Brien was due to make his long-awaited return to Broadway to star in *The Munday Scheme* by the acclaimed Irish playwright Brian Friel. The actor was forced to withdraw because of what was described as a "vascular condition in one leg."[40] The play opened in December with another actor in his role, but it lasted only a couple of nights.

❖❖ 23 ❖❖

The 1970s

> Once an actor, almost always an actor. The drive can't be turned on and off like a well-oiled light switch.—Walt Hackett, "Hackett in Hollywood: *King Solomon's Mines* One of Best for Year," *Lansing State Journal*, December 3, 1950, 42

For O'Brien, the decade of the 1970s started promisingly with ideas for his own productions and a key part in Orson Welles' long-awaited return to filmmaking. In partnership with his brother Liam, Edmond had set up a production company, Emerald Productions, and one of their projects was a version of the Bret Harte short story "How Santa Claus Came to Simpson's Bar."[1] That never came to pass. Once again, O'Brien almost returned to the stage when he was offered the leading role of a Supreme Court Justice in Jay Broad's *The Balding Affair*. Fellow veteran Gary Merrill was lined up to play the American president. The play was to have toured, starting in Washington and ending on Broadway, but O'Brien's health precluded his participation.[2] His increasing health problems persuaded him to accept voice-over work for television commercials. This was lucrative and earned him around $75,000 per advert.

Potentially, O'Brien's most significant film of the decade was *The Other Side of the Wind,* directed by Orson Welles, which began filming in 1970 and "finished" in 1976. This turned out to be the last movie the great director ever made, although it was never officially completed and technically it has been in post-production ever since.

The cast was headed by John Huston as a veteran director returning from Europe after years of exile to work on a new film. Most of the action took place at a party. It was full of familiar faces from the glory years of Hollywood, including Mercedes McCambridge, Paul Stewart and Lilli Palmer. O'Brien played Pat, a character described as a "red-faced, whiskey-swilling former actor who openly harbors fascist political leanings." The role was intended for the veteran actor Pat O'Brien, who turned it down with alacrity.³ Filming took place in the ironically named Carefree, Arizona. There have been conflicting accounts of the production, but all agree that Edmond was not well and appeared disorientated. His eccentricities of behavior were often remarked upon. Some cast and crew members presumed he had a drinking problem but in reality, although only in his mid-fifties, he was already suffering from Alzheimer's disease. According to several witnesses, he was in a daze and did not appear to know where he was much of the time. Some said that Welles was considerate of him but others maintained that he often berated O'Brien, who was also suffering from emphysema and deafness in addition to his other health problems. According to one who was there; "Orson would whip him and yell at him and O'Brien just took it and did his job."⁴ O'Brien could be heard muttering incoherently on set and appeared to be unaware of his surroundings. However, observers declared that once the cameras started rolling, he came to life. Said one witness, "[H]e would transform before the camera and suddenly be 100 percent there, never missing a beat and giving a spot-on performance without complaint."⁵ When his part in the filming finished, O'Brien announced, "Orson, it's been a pleasure working with you on this movie. Any time you ever need me again, you can always call my agent—care of Peking, China!"⁶ In 2015, a group of interested parties got together to try to finish it, having raised enough funds for the purpose. They hope that the film will finally be released in the not too distant future, with a projected date of 2018.

Starting around 1970, the quality of the roles O'Brien was offered began to decline. He appeared in several low-budget made-for-television movies including *Dream No Evil* (1970). This oddball horror was written and directed by John Hayes, whose debut short film *The Kiss* (1958) was nominated for an Oscar. His oeuvre contained such teasing titles as *The Farmer's Other Daughter* (1965) and *Jailbait Babysitter* (1977). *Dream No Evil* told, in a roundabout way, the tale of a troubled girl with a father fixation. She takes up with a faith healer and lives in a caravan, all the time trying to find her lost father, who turns out to be O'Brien. A low-key and rather disjointed affair, it also featured Marc Lawrence as a seedy undertaker. O'Brien looked distinctly heavier and seemed unsurprisingly lost but showed he had lost none of his ability to convey feelings in several short scenes (for instance, when he glared at the preacher while playing the concertina as his daughter danced an Irish jig). During filming in high altitudes at a desert location near Wrightwood, California, O'Brien complained of breathlessness and pains in his chest. He was taken to a San

Bernardino hospital where he was treated for a cardiac condition, the seriousness of which was downplayed in the press. He stayed there for several days and appeared to make a recovery.[7]

His next appearance was in the ABC-TV movie *What's a Nice Girl Like You...?* (1971). The film starred Brenda Vaccaro as a poor girl from the Bronx who becomes involved in an elaborate scheme to extort $500,000 from a financier (O'Brien) by posing as his long-lost daughter. The cast included a number of Golden Age stars including Vincent Price and Roddy McDowall. O'Brien's aged appearance drew much comment. He had suffered heart problems only two months before shooting started and was only able to spend one day working on the film, which left him exhausted.[8]

The rest of the films of the decade were unremarkable. He turned up as a detective in the missing persons drama *Jigsaw* (1972), a formulaic made-for-TV movie. One of his last screen appearances was as a liquor store proprietor in the murder mystery *They Only Kill Their Masters* (1972). This sluggish tale felt more like a television movie, a feeling enhanced by the presence of small-screen favorite James Garner in the starring role. Other familiar faces included June Allyson and Ann Rutherford. This was the last film made using the old Metro lot.[9] O'Brien had only one scene, looking much older and weightier, but the voice was still recognizably his. The film bore more than a passing resemblance to his next picture, the made-for-TV feature *Isn't It Shocking?* In Angel Mount, a small town somewhere near Vermont, the local police captain (Alan Alda) is puzzled by the apparently natural deaths of people in their sixties. There was really no mystery because it was revealed at the beginning who the killer was. Indeed, the opening scene was the best of the film, in which O'Brien murders an elderly-looking lady in her sleep to the strains of the plaintive, bittersweet melody "You Forgot to Remember," and then eats a chocolate bar. The resolution was disappointing and there was no real definition of his true motivation because the backstory was not sufficiently developed. The ending left a feeling of dissatisfaction and the good cast, including Lloyd Nolan and Ruth Gordon, was largely wasted. Although the case was sufficiently offbeat, the screenplay needed far more than it was given. However, when O'Brien broke down at the end, it was hard not to be moved by his plight.

Lucky Luciano (1973), an Italian-American co-production directed by Francesco Rosi, took in the years 1946 to 1962 and used flashbacks to tell the story of one of *the* most notorious twentieth century gangsters. The use of out-of-sequence flashbacks created a disjointed feel, a feeling emphasized by the dubbing of some sequences into English while retaining some in Italian. Award-winning actor Gian Maria Volonte, "the Italian Laurence Olivier," played Luciano and Rod Steiger appeared in a smaller role. O'Brien played the commissioner of an enquiry into Mafia activity in the 1950s. He was noticeably older and appeared jaded; he also sounded hoarse at times. The film was rather grim but detailed about the murky political involvement of the United States in the rise and consolidation of Mafia power. It premiered in Italy in 1973 but was not shown in America until the following year.

O'Brien played the Greek philosopher Socrates in 1974's *El Juicio de Socrates* (*The Trial of Socrates*), filmed in Athens by young Mexican director Raul Araiza. This was one of a series of five hour-long historical films, *Noticias de la Historia*, made for Mexican TV and financed by the U.S. The series featuring famous Hollywood and European actors and was shot in international locations. Other subjects included Nefertiti, Galileo and Hernan Cortes.[10] In the same year, the television anthology pilot *Rex Harrison's Stories of Love* featured three tales by famous authors. One of the tales, "Epicac," was adapted by Edmond's brother Liam from the Kurt Vonnegut short story. This starred Bill Bixby as a computer programmer who uses poems fed to a computer to woo a fellow technician, with the result that the computer falls in love with him. The poems used in the film, which one reviewer described as "very beautiful," had been composed by Edmond, revealing a hitherto unknown talent for verse.[11]

O'Brien's final significant contribution to broadcasting came in the educational documentary film *A Storm of Strangers*, which took him back full circle to his own roots. Each episode of this award-winning independent film series dealt with the social history of various ethnic immigrant groups in America, including the Italians (directed by Martin Scorsese) and the Chinese. In *The Irish*, O'Brien movingly spoke the words of Dennis Mulligan, a partly fictionalized account of one family's flight from the devastating Irish famine in the 1840s to a new life in the U.S.[12] The narrative starkly delineated the many struggles Irish immigrants faced, encompassing social, political problems and prejudice. Using contemporary photographs, drawings and some moving images, the insightful 27-minute film told the tale well with expert narration by O'Brien, which brought the whole thing vividly to life. It is available to view courtesy of the Internet Archive.[13]

Edmond was next invited to play the role of the detective in the Canadian slasher film *Black Christmas* (1974). On receiving the script, he said he was delighted at the prospect. However, when he arrived at Toronto

Airport, he had no idea where he was. It soon became apparent that he was not in a fit state to do the film. At this stage, he was frequently disorientated and it sometimes took him 40 minutes to fasten his shirt. Despite everything, director Bob Clark observed, "I would have taken a chance. I said to my co-producer, 'I think we might risk this.' It's strange, because, [like many] people with that stage of Alzheimer's, he could be coherent, he'd learned some of the script. He would go blank at times. That's all right, I can cover that. He's still Edmond O'Brien, he's still got that personality."[14] His scenes called for three nights of filming in temperatures of -5° C. It was too strenuous a task, and Edmond had to leave the project. "I had some very short and very tough words to say to his agent," commented co-producer Gerry Arbeid, "who should *never* have sent him out in such a condition. He must have known."[15] At short notice, O'Brien was replaced by John Saxon. (Bette Davis was also penciled in for a role but withdrew.) The film is regarded as a cult horror classic.[16]

O'Brien's health was now a cause for serious concern. However, he was able to complete one more big-screen assignment, *99 and 44/100% Dead* (1974), directed by John Frankenheimer. This starred Richard Harris as a hitman hired by old-time gangster Uncle Frank (O'Brien) to protect his interests against his arch rival Big Eddie (Bradford Dillman). The Roy Lichtenstein–influenced pop art opening titles and the jaunty Henry Mancini score promised a good-natured parody of 1940s gangster films. Indeed, the beginning in which a dead man with his feet in a block of cement is dumped in the sea was the prelude to the best sequence in the film. As the man sinks to the bottom, he joins all the other losers among the rusting slot machines and roulette wheels; "The East Side's got the great old bunch" intones Harris as the camera pans along a group of skeletons wearing Coolidge boaters. Unfortunately, after a car chase to the strains of a trad-jazz tune, the film settled down to a turgid crime drama which never moved out of first gear. There was a lack of coherent intent; it was not funny enough to be a comedy and nor was it dramatically convincing. The scenes were far too long and made the 98-minute running time seem like twice the amount. Harris gave a one-note performance and conveyed the impression of being completely uninterested. O'Brien was good as always, and had lost some weight; he was far more recognizably himself than he had been in *The Wild Bunch* five years earlier. He looked tired but delivered his lines well; if anything, he was more subdued than usual. Overall, an empty feeling pervaded. Frankenheimer himself was not impressed with the script to begin with; "The first time I read it, I didn't want to do it at all," he admitted.[17] His first instinct was right. *Variety* summed it up best: "Aesthetically, commercially and morally, a quintessential fiasco."[18]

In April 1978, O'Brien made his final public appearance at the 50th Academy Awards ceremony, when he joined many other past Oscar winners on stage at the beginning of the evening. Looking relaxed, O'Brien stood next to Ruth Gordon, with whom he spoke briefly. He was guided from the stage by a lady in white.

The years after his forced retirement from acting were the most difficult of Edmond's life. His eyesight had been deteriorating for many years and it was a testament to his fortitude that he had been able to continue his career for so long with such an acute problem. His friend and colleague from Mercury Theater days, Everett Sloane, was diagnosed with glaucoma, a condition which can lead to blindness. However, it can be treated with eye drops taken for life or, in extreme cases, surgery. Sloane could not bear to live with the threat of losing his sight and took his own life at the age of 55. Edmond had the added and far worse problem of memory loss, and his personality altered. For some years, his altered behavior had been noticed by those closest to him. His daughter Bridget recollected that it was in the late 1960s when the changes became marked: "At the time," she wrote, "we all had no idea why he was changing so drastically. Why lines could no longer be recalled and why names of beloved crew members were evading him. And above all why he seemed angry at everything."[19] The diagnosis of Alzheimer's disease was not made until many years later.

In 1971, the year of his heart problems, Olga suffered a stroke. With her own health in a precarious state, it became too much for her to contend with and they separated in March 1975. In December of that year, she filed for a legal separation from her husband in the Superior Court in Los Angeles.[20] After that, she went to live with her sister. Although she could no longer stay with Edmond, they remained on friendly terms for the remainder of his life. For some time, he stayed on in his beloved Brentwood home, with his children and the family helping as much as they could. His condition steadily worsened and he was forced to sell the house. By the early 1980s, he was living in a Santa Monica sanitarium.[21] He was not allowed to stay at the Motion Picture Home because they did not take anyone suffering from what was, technically-speaking, a mental disease. According to his daughter Maria, her father was suffering from a "loss of memory and sense of orientation and brain power." She also commented, "I think my father still knows us."[22]

Edmond was eventually diagnosed with Alzheimer's and in March 1983 was admitted to the Veteran's Hospital in Los Angeles. Alzheimer's is the most common kind of dementia and attacks those centers of the brain dealing with memory, thought and language; all the things an actor needs most. It is a disease which often strikes actors, writers and politicians, although normally at a later age. Rita Hayworth also suffered from it when she was in her fifties, but, as her daughter revealed, she was misdiagnosed.[23] It is a disease that is as little understood now as it was then. Despite advances in medical science and increased knowledge, it is still not known what causes it or why some are more susceptible than others. Raised awareness through a number of high-profile cases has led to greater funding to investigate the disease and perhaps one day find a cure.

Maria spoke of her father's "tremendous spirits" and commented at the time of the diagnosis, "He is battling very hard to cope with the situation."[24] With little if any sight, he had become by all accounts "combative and confused," and at one time was put in a straitjacket.[25] By then, he "had lost virtually all mental and neurological functions," said Maria. She later spoke about his time in the hospital; "He was screaming. He was violent. I remember noticing how thin he'd gotten. We didn't know because for years he'd been sleeping with all his clothes on. We saw him a little later and he was walking around like all the other lost souls there."[26] She added, "Ironically, a man who could once hold an audience in the palm of his hand towards the end had difficulty expressing even his most basic feelings of affection, recognition and love."[27]

Maria testified about the devastating effects of the disease on the victim and those nearest to him, before a Senate select committee on Aging in Washington. A medical journal reported her testimony and that of others on the lack of support for families trying to cope with a sick relative in the advanced stages of the disease,

> The burden of around-the-clock care and supervision rests squarely on the family, she said. Families suffer in silence, receiving little help. The prognosis is often poverty. Medicare does not cover the cost of caring for the Alzheimer's patient, either at home or in a nursing home. There is no insurance, no tax break, and no affordable in-home or day care program capable of caring for Alzheimer's patients, added other witnesses testifying at the hearing.[28]

Maria spoke movingly about her experience: "I cannot begin to tell you the impact Alzheimer's disease has on an otherwise healthy, vibrant person. Nor can I explain the sorrow and feelings of helplessness one experiences at seeing a loved one suffering through the prolonged stages of this disease."[29] Edmond died at the St. Erne Sanitarium, Inglewood, on May 8, 1985, at the age of 69. "In a very real sense," said Maria, "death was the only hope of release for my father."[30]

Epilogue

> I'd like to be able to say something important ... to say something to people about their relationship with each other. If it touches just one guy, helps illustrate some points of view about living, then you've accomplished something.
>
> —Bob Baker, "Versatile Character Actor Edmond O'Brien, 69, Dies," *The Los Angeles Times,* May 10, 1985, 214

There is an abiding affection for Edmond O'Brien among fans of classic films. His performances in noir films alone ensured him a kind of immortality. Sadly, his health problems brought a premature halt to his career when he was only in his fifties. He could have gone on acting for a long time if things had been otherwise; there is no age limit for character actors. He had a lot to contend with health-wise (failing eyesight and heart problems) even before the onset of Alzheimer's—surely the cruelest kind of illness for anyone, especially so for an actor of such intelligence and vitality. In the days following his death, O'Brien was given many warm tributes from friends and colleagues in the acting profession. "[He] was a fine actor who contributed greatly to every picture in which he appeared," said James Stewart, reflecting the feelings of his peers. "He will be sorely missed."[1]

Edmond himself was ambivalent about his own achievements. Among all the arts, he described acting as the least satisfying, and called it "a highly transient art form." He further reflected, "I should have liked to create lastingly. I don't think that acting really achieves that."[2] He also felt that his versatility prevented him from becoming a personality actor, and therefore a star, and when looking back on his career he admitted, "I don't think I've been that successful."[3] Nevertheless, his versatility was his strength. His daughter Bridget once asked him if he minded being a supporting star or if he would not rather be a leading man. "No, Bridget," he answered. "'Cause it's me who gets the chance to do the interesting, the different, the funny. It's from me the audience expects the unusual. I like it that way."[4] Audiences were always rewarded and never went away disappointed. Few other actors articulated the confusion of the ordinary Joe in postwar western society so profoundly as he did. A dynamic, emotional actor, he could literally play Everyman. From lovesick Navy lieutenants in light musical comedies, to desperate men in noirs, he was totally convincing. He seldom played outright heroic or noble characters, but they were all the more real and believable for that. He left a gallery of indelible screen portraits: Frank Bigelow, Mal Granger, Harry Graham, Casca, Oscar Muldoon, Dutton Peabody, to name just a few. The sheer range of his work was impressive and everything he did was imbued with honesty, humor and humanity.

He never courted publicity and the man himself remains something of an enigma, but he let his work speak for him. In 1972, a short while before his acting career finished and he disappeared from public view, he proved that he still had the power to move an audience when he gave an extempore recital from *Hamlet* during a routine press conference at MGM. It was a speech he had first learned by heart as a callow youth almost 40 years before: "Without missing a word or proper inflection," wrote one witness, "he continued through Fortinbras' monologue to its end, interpreting it so adroitly that, even in the pragmatic atmosphere of the conference room, his listeners were moved with sorrow for Shakespeare's 'sweet prince.'"[5]

Publicity still of O'Brien for *The Web* (1947).

Appendix
Edmond O'Brien's Credits Across All Media

Filmography

The Hunchback of Notre Dame. 1939. Director: William Dieterle. Screenplay: Sonya Levien, Bruno Frank, adapted from the novel *Notre Dame de Paris* by Victor Hugo. Starring Charles Laughton, Maureen O'Hara, Cedric Hardwicke, Edmond O'Brien (as Pierre Gringoire), Thomas Mitchell, Harry Davenport, Walter Hampden. RKO.

A Girl, a Guy and a Gob. 1941. Director: Richard Wallace. Screenplay: Frank Ryan, Bert Granet. Cast: Lucille Ball, Edmond O'Brien (as Stephen Herrick), George Murphy, George Cleveland, Henry Travers, Franklin Pangborn, Marguerite Churchill. RKO.

Parachute Battalion. 1941. Director: Leslie Goodwins. Screenplay: John Twist, Major John Hugh Fite. Cast: Robert Preston, Nancy Kelly, Edmond O'Brien (as Bill Burke), Harry Carey, Buddy Ebsen, Paul Kelly, Richard Cromwell. RKO.

Obliging Young Lady. 1942. Director: Richard Wallace. Screenplay: Frank Ryan, Bert Granet. Cast: Joan Carroll, Ruth Warrick, Edmond O'Brien (as "Red" Reddy, aka Prof. Stanley), Eve Arden, Franklin Pangborn, Marjorie Gateson, John Miljan. RKO.

Powder Town. 1942. Director: Rowland V. Lee. Screenplay: David Boehm, John Twist, Vicky Baum, Grace Norton, from the novel by Max Brand. Cast: Victor McLaglen, Edmond O'Brien (as J. Quincy "Penji" Pennant), June Havoc, Eddie Foy, Jr., Damian O'Flynn, Mary Gordon. RKO.

The Amazing Mrs. Holliday. 1943. Director: Bruce Manning, Frank Shaw, Jean Renoir (the latter uncredited). Screenplay: Frank Ryan, John Jacoby, adapted from a story by Sonya Levien. Cast: Deanna Durbin, Edmond O'Brien (as Tom Holliday), Frieda Inescort, Barry Fitzgerald, Harry Davenport, Arthur Treacher, Grant Mitchell. Universal.

Winged Victory. 1944. Director: George Cukor. Screenplay: Moss Hart, from his own play. Cast: Lon McCallister, Jeanne Crain, Edmond O'Brien (as Irving Miller), Jane Ball, Don Taylor, Judy Holliday, Jo-Carroll Dennison. 20th Century–Fox.

The Killers. 1946. Director: Robert Siodmak. Screenplay: Anthony Veiller, John Huston (latter uncredited). Cast: Burt Lancaster, Edmond O'Brien (as Jim Reardon), Ava Gardner, Albert Dekker, Sam Levene, Virginia Christine, Charles McGraw. Universal.

The Web. 1947. Director: Michael Gordon. Screenplay: William Bowers, Bertram Millhauser. Cast: Edmond O'Brien (as Bob Regan), Vincent Price, Ella Raines, William Bendix, Maria Palmer, John Abbott, Fritz Leiber. Universal.

A Double Life. 1947. Director: George Cukor. Screenplay: Ruth Gordon, Garson Kanin. Cast: Ronald Colman, Shelley Winters, Signe Hasso, Edmond O'Brien (as Bill Friend), Millard Mitchell, Ray Collins, Philip Loeb. Universal.

Another Part of the Forest. 1948. Director: Michael Gordon. Screenplay: Vladimir Pozner, adapted from the play by Lillian Hellman. Cast: Fredric March, Florence Eldridge, Ann Blyth, Dan Duryea, Edmond O'Brien (as Ben Hubbard), John Dall, Betsy Blair. Universal.

Fighter Squadron. 1948. Director: Raoul Walsh. Screenplay: Seton I. Miller, Martin Rackin. Cast: Edmond O'Brien (as Major Ed Hardin), Robert Stack, John Rodney, Tom D'Andrea, Henry Hull, Walter Reed, Sheppard Strudwick. Warner Brothers.

Task Force. 1948. Director & Screenplay: Delmer Daves. Cast: Gary Cooper, Walter Brennan, Jane Wyatt. Warner Brothers. O'Brien provided the radio voice announcing the Japanese attack on Pearl Harbor.

White Heat. 1949. Director: Raoul Walsh. Screenplay: Ivan Goff, Ben Roberts, from a story by Virginia Kellogg. Cast: James Cagney, Edmond O'Brien (as Hank Fallon), Virginia Mayo, Margaret Wycherly, Steve Cochran, John Archer, Fred Clark. Warner Brothers.

Backfire. 1950. Director: Vincent Sherman. Screenplay: Larry Marcus, Ivan Goff, Ben Roberts. Cast: Gordon MacRae, Virginia Mayo, Edmond O'Brien (as Steve Connelly), Dane Clark, Viveca Lindfors, Ed Begley, Sheila Stevens. Warner Brothers.

D.O.A. 1950. Director: Rudolph Maté. Screenplay: Russell Rouse, Clarence Green. Cast: Edmond O'Brien (as Frank Bigelow), Luther Adler, Pamela Britton, William Ching, Beverly Garland, Neville Brand, Lynn Baggett. United Artists.

711 Ocean Drive. 1950. Director: Joseph M. Newman. Screenplay: Richard English, Francis Swan. Cast: Edmond O'Brien (as Mal Granger), Joanne Dru, Otto Kruger, Barry Kelley, Dorothy Patrick, Don Porter, Howard St. John. Columbia.

The Admiral Was a Lady. 1950. Director: Albert S. Rogell. Screenplay: Sidney

Salkow, Johnny O'Dea. Cast: Edmond O'Brien (as Jimmy Stevens), Wanda Hendrix, Rudy Vallee, Johnny Sands, Steve Brodie, Richard Erdman, Hillary Brooke. Roxbury Productions.

Between Midnight and Dawn. 1950. Director: Gordon Douglas. Screenplay: Eugene Ling. Story: Gerald Drayson Adams, Leo Katcher. Cast: Mark Stevens, Edmond O'Brien (as Officer Dan Purvis), Gale Storm, Donald Buka, Gale Robbins, Anthony Ross, Roland Winters. Columbia.

The Redhead and the Cowboy. 1951. Director: Leslie Fenton. Screenplay: Jonathan Latimer, Liam O'Brien. Cast: Glenn Ford, Rhonda Fleming, Edmond O'Brien (as Major Dunn Jeffers), Alan Reed, Maurice Ankrum, Perry Ivins. Paramount.

Two of a Kind. 1951. Director: Harry Levin. Screenplay: Lawrence Kimble, James Gunn. Cast: Edmond O'Brien (as Michael "Lefty" Farrell), Lizabeth Scott, Terry Moore, Alexander Knox, Griff Barnett, Virginia Brissac, Robert Anderson. Columbia.

Warpath. 1951. Director: Byron Haskin. Screenplay: Frank Gruber, based on his novel *Broken Lance*. Cast: Edmond O'Brien (as John Vickers), Forrest Tucker, Dean Jagger, Harry Carey, Jr., Wallace Ford, Polly Bergen, Paul Fix. Paramount.

Silver City aka ***High Vermilion.*** 1951. Director: Byron Haskin. Screenplay: Frank Gruber, adapted from the novel *High Vermilion* by Luke Short. Cast: Yvonne de Carlo, Edmond O'Brien (as Larkin Moffatt), Edgar Buchanan, Barry Fitzgerald, Richard Arlen, Gladys George, Laura Elliott. Paramount. (DVD)

The Greatest Show on Earth. 1952. Director: Cecil B. DeMille. Screenplay: Fredric M. Frank, Theodore St. John, Frank Cavett, Barre Lyndon. Cast: Charlton Heston, Betty Hutton, Cornel Wilde, James Stewart, Gloria Grahame, Dorothy Lamour, Lyle Bettger, Edmond O'Brien (as Midway Barker). Paramount (DVD).

Screen Snapshots: Hollywood on the Ball. 1952. Director & Screenplay: Ralph Straub. With Joe E. Brown, Doris Day, Bob Hope, Roy Rogers, Mickey Rooney. In this short about a charity baseball game, O'Brien and the other cast members are seen as themselves. Columbia.

Denver and Rio Grande. 1952. Director: Byron Haskin. Screenplay: Frank Gruber. Cast: Edmond O'Brien (as Jim Vesser), Sterling Hayden, Dean Jagger, Laura Elliott, J. Carrol Naish, Zasu Pitts, Paul Fix. Paramount (DVD).

The Turning Point. 1952. Director: William Dieterle. Screenplay: Warren Duff, from the novel *Storm in the City* by Horace McCoy. Cast: William Holden, Edmond O'Brien (as John Conroy), Alexis Smith, Tom Tully, Ed Begley, Ray Teal, Ted de Corsia. Paramount (DVD Italy).

The Hitch-Hiker. 1953. Director: Ida Lupino. Screenplay: Collier Young, Ida Lupino; adapted by Robert Joseph from a story by Dainel Mainwaring. Cast: Edmond O'Brien (as Roy Collins), Frank Lovejoy, William Talman, Jose Torvay, Sam Hayes, Wendell Niles, Jean del Val. RKO (DVD).

Man in the Dark. 1953. Director: Lew Landers. Screenplay: George Bricker,

Jack Leonard, William Sackheim. Story: Tom Van Dycke, Henry Altimus. Cast: Edmond O'Brien (as Steve Rawley), Audrey Totter, Ted de Corsia, Horace McMahon, Nick Dennis, Dayton Lummis. Columbia (Blu-ray only).

Cow Country. 1953. Director: Lesley Selander. Screenplay: Adele Buffington, adapted by Thomas W. Blackburn from a novel by Curtis Bishop. Cast: Edmond O'Brien (as Ben Anthony), Helen Westcott, Robert Lowery, Barton MacLane, Peggie Castle, Robert Barrat. Allied Artists (DVD).

Julius Caesar. 1953. Director & Screenplay: Joseph L. Mankiewicz; adapted from the play by William Shakespeare. Cast: Marlon Brando, John Gielgud, James Mason, Louis Calhern, Deborah Kerr, Greer Garson, Edmond O'Brien (as Casca). MGM (DVD).

China Venture. 1953. Director: Don Siegel. Screenplay: George Worthing Yates, Richard Collins. Cast: Edmond O'Brien (as Captain Matt Reardon), Barry Sullivan, Jocelyn Brando, Richard Loo, Leo Gordon, Lee Strasberg. Columbia.

The Bigamist. 1953. Director: Ida Lupino. Screenplay: Collier Young. Story: Lawrence B. Marcus, Lou Schor. Cast: Edmond O'Brien (as Harry Graham), Ida Lupino, Joan Fontaine, Edmund Gwenn, Jane Darwell, Lillian Fontaine, George Lee. Filmakers (DVD).

The Shanghai Story. 1954. Director: Frank Lloyd. Screenplay: Steve Fisher, Seton I. Miller. Story: Lester Yard. Cast: Edmond O'Brien (as Dr. Dan Maynard), Ruth Roman, Richard Jaeckel, Barry Kelley, Whit Bissell, Basil Ruysdael, Marvin Miller. Republic (DVD).

Shield for Murder. 1954. Director: Howard W. Koch, Edmond O'Brien. Screenplay: Richard Alan Simmons, John C. Higgins; adapted by Simmons from the novel by William P. McGivern. Cast: Edmond O'Brien (as Detective Lt. Barney Nolan), Marla English, John Agar, Emile Meyer, Carolyn Jones, Claude Akins, Larry Ryle. United Artists (DVD).

The Barefoot Contessa. 1954. Director & Screenplay: Joseph L. Mankiewicz. Cast: Humphrey Bogart, Ava Gardner, Edmond O'Brien (as Oscar Muldoon), Marius Goring, Valentina Cortese, Rossano Brazzi, Warren Stevens. United Artists (DVD).

Pete Kelly's Blues. 1955. Director: Jack Webb. Screenplay: Richard L. Breen. Cast: Jack Webb, Edmond O'Brien (as Fran McCarg), Peggy Lee, Janet Leigh, Lee Marvin, Ella Fitzgerald, Andy Devine. Mark VII Limited (DVD).

1984. 1956. Director: Michael Anderson. Screenplay: William P. Templeton, Ralph Bettinson, adapted from the novel by George Orwell. Cast: Michael Redgrave, Edmond O'Brien (as Winston Smith of the Outer Party), Jan Sterling, David Kossoff, Mervyn Johns, Donald Pleasence, Ronan O'Casey. Columbia (DVD).

D–Day, the Sixth of June. 1956. Director: Henry Koster. Screenplay: Ivan Moffatt, Harry Brown, adapted from the novel by Lionel Shapiro. Cast: Robert Taylor, Dana Wynter, Richard Todd, Edmond O'Brien (as Lt. Col. Alexander Timmer), John Williams, Jerry Paris, Richard Stapley. 20th Century–Fox (DVD).

A Cry in the Night. 1956. Director: Frank Tuttle. Screenplay: David Dortort, based on the novel by Whit Masterson. Cast: Edmond O'Brien (as Capt. John Taggart), Brian Donlevy, Natalie Wood, Raymond Burr, Richard Anderson, Irene Hervey, Anthony Caruso, George J. Lewis. Warner Bros (DVD).

The Rack. 1956. Director: Arnold Laven. Screenplay: Stewart Stern, adapted from the TV play by Rod Serling. Cast: Paul Newman, Walter Pidgeon, Edmond O'Brien (as Lt. Col. Frank Wasnick), Anne Francis, Lee Marvin, Cloris Leachman, Wendell Corey. MGM (DVD).

The Girl Can't Help It. 1956. Director: Frank Tashlin. Screenplay: Frank Tashlin, Herbert Baker, adapted from *Do Re Mi* by Garson Kanin. Cast: Jayne Mansfield, Tom Ewell, Edmond O'Brien (as Marty "Fats" Murdock), John Emery, Julie London, Ray Anthony, Little Richard. 20th Century–Fox (DVD).

The Big Land. 1957. Director: Gordon Douglas. Screenplay: David Dortort, Martin Rackin, adapted from the novel *Buffalo Grass* by Frank Gruber. Cast: Alan Ladd, Virginia Mayo, Edmond O'Brien (as Joe Jagger), Anthony Caruso, Julie Bishop, John Qualen. Jaguar Productions (DVD).

Stopover Tokyo. 1957. Director: Richard L. Breen. Screenplay: Richard L. Breen, Walter Reisch, adapted from the novel *Right You Are, Mr. Moto* by John P. Marquand. Cast: Robert Wagner, Joan Collins, Edmond O'Brien (as George Underwood), Ken Scott, Larry Keating, Reiko Oyama. 20th Century–Fox (DVD).

The World Was His Jury. 1957. Director: Fred F. Sears. Screenplay: Herbert Abbott Spiro. Cast: Edmond O'Brien (as David Carson), Mona Freeman, Karin Booth, Robert McQueeney, Paul Birch, John Berardino, Dick Cutting. Columbia (DVD).

Sing Boy Sing. 1958. Director: Henry Ephron. Screenplay: Claude Binyon, adapted from the teleplay "The Singing Idol" by Paul Monash. Cast: Tommy Sands, Edmond O'Brien (as Joseph Sharkey), John McIntire, Nick Adams, Lili Gentle, Josephine Hutchinson, Diane Jergens. 20th Century–Fox (DVD).

Up Periscope. 1959. Director: Gordon Douglas. Screenplay: Richard Landau, adapted from the novel by Robb White. Cast: James Garner, Edmond O'Brien (as Commander Paul Stevenson), Alan Hale, Jr., Carleton Carpenter, Frank Gifford, Andra Martin. Warner Bros (DVD).

L'Ambiteuse. Also known as ***The Ambitious Ones***; ***The Climbers***; ***The Dispossessed***; ***The Restless and the Damned.*** 1959. Director: Yves Allegret. Screenplay: Joy Cavill, Rene Wheeler, W.P. Lipscomb, Lee Robinson, based on the novel *Manganese* by Francois Ponthier, Cast: Edmond O'Brien (as Mike Buchanan), Andrea Parisy, Richard Basehart, Nicole Berger, Nigel Lovell, Reg Lye, Jean Marchat. Silver Films.

The Last Voyage. 1960. Director & Screenplay: Andrew L. Stone. Cast: Robert Stack, Dorothy Malone, George Sanders, Edmond O'Brien (as Second Engineer Walsh), Woody Strode, George Furness, Jack Kruschen. Andrew L. Stone Productions, MGM (DVD).

The Third Voice. 1960. Director & Screenplay: Hubert Cornfield, adapted from the novel *All the Way* by Charles Williams. Cast: Edmond O'Brien (as The Voice), Laraine Day, Julie London, George Eldredge, Tom Hernandez, Abel Franco, Olga San Juan. 20th Century–Fox (DVD Spain).

The Great Imposter. 1961. Director: Robert Mulligan. Screenplay: Liam O'Brien, based on the novel by Robert Chrichton. Cast: Tony Curtis, Frank Gorshin, Gary Merrill, Edmond O'Brien (as Captain Glover), Arthur O'Connell, Karl Malden, Raymond Massey. Universal (DVD).

Moon Pilot. 1962. Director: James Neilson. Screenplay: Maurice Tombragel, adapted from the novel *Starfire* by Robert Buckner. Cast: Tom Tryon, Brian Keith, Edmond O'Brien (as "Mac" McClosky), Dany Saval, Tommy Kirk, Kent Smith, Simon Scott. Walt Disney Productions (DVD).

The Man Who Shot Liberty Valance. 1962. Director: John Ford. Screenplay: James Warner Bellah, Willis Goldbeck. Cast: James Stewart, John Wayne, Vera Miles, Lee Marvin, Edmond O'Brien (as Dutton Peabody), Andy Devine, Jeanette Nolan. Paramount (DVD).

Birdman of Alcatraz. 1962. Director: John Frankenheimer. Screenplay: Guy Trosper, adapted from the book by Thomas E. Gaddis. Cast: Burt Lancaster, Karl Malden, Thelma Ritter, Edmond O'Brien (as Tom Gaddis), Betty Field, Neville Brand, Hugh Marlowe. United Artists (DVD).

The Longest Day. 1962. Director: Ken Annakin, Andrew Marton, Bernhard Wicki, Gerd Oswald. Screenplay: Cornelius Ryan, Romain Gary, James Jones, David Pursall, Jack Seddon; adapted from the book by Cornelius Ryan. Cast: John Wayne, Robert Mitchum, Henry Fonda, Robert Ryan, Rod Steiger, Richard Burton, Edmond O'Brien (as General Raymond D. Barton). 20th Century–Fox (DVD).

Seven Days in May. 1964. Director: John Frankenheimer. Screenplay: Rod Serling, adapted from the novel by Fletcher Knebel & Charles W. Bailey II. Cast: Kirk Douglas, Burt Lancaster, Fredric March, Ava Gardner, Martin Balsam, Edmond O'Brien (as Senator Raymond Clark), George Macready. Paramount (DVD).

Rio Conchos. 1964. Director: Gordon Douglas. Screenplay: Clair Huffaker, Joseph Landon. Cast: Richard Boone, Stuart Whitman, Edmond O'Brien (as Col. Theron Pardee), Tony Franciosa, Wende Wagner, Warner Anderson, Jim Brown. 20th Century–Fox (DVD).

Sylvia. 1965. Director: Gordon Douglas. Screenplay: Sidney Boehm, Howard Fast; adapted from the novel by E.V. Cunningham. Cast: Carroll Baker, George Maharis, Peter Lawford, Joanne Dru, Ann Sothern, Viveca Lindfors, Edmond O'Brien (as Oscar Stewart). Paramount.

Synanon. 1965. Director: Richard Quine. Screenplay: Ian Bernard, S. Lee Pogostin. Cast: Edmond O'Brien (as Chuck Diderich), Chuck Connors, Stella Stevens, Alex Cord, Eartha Kitt, Richard Conte, Barbara Luna. Columbia (DVD).

Fantastic Voyage. 1966. Director: Richard Fleischer. Screenplay: Harry Kleiner; adapted by David Duncan from a story by Jerome Bixby & Otto Klement. Cast: Stephen Boyd, Raquel Welch, Edmond O'Brien (as General

Carter), Donald Pleasence, Arthur Kennedy, Arthur O'Connell, William Redfield. 20th Century–Fox (DVD).

The Viscount. 1967. Director: Maurice Cloche. Screenplay: Georges Farel, from the novel by Jean Bruce. Cast: Kerwin Mathews, Sylvia Sorrente, Fernando Rey, Edmond O'Brien (as Ricco Barone [only in some versions]). Criterion Film.

Peau d'Espion aka ***How to Commit a Murder.*** 1967. Screenplay & Director: Edouard Molinaro, adapted by Jacques Robert from his own novel. Cast: Louis Jourdan, Senta Berger, Edmond O'Brien (as Sphax), Bernard Blier, Maurice Garrel, Fabrizio Capucci. Eichberg Film, Franca Film.

The Wild Bunch. 1969. Director: Sam Peckinpah. Screenplay: Walon Green, Sam Peckinpah. Cast: William Holden, Ernest Borgnine, Robert Ryan, Edmond O'Brien (as Freddie Sykes), Warren Oates, Jaime Sanchez, Ben Johnson. Warner Brothers/Seven Arts (DVD).

The Love God? 1969. Director & Screenplay: Nat Hiken. Cast: Don Knotts, Anne Francis, Edmond O'Brien (as Osborn Tremaine), James Gregory, Maureen Arthur, Maggie Mancuso. Universal (DVD).

Dream No Evil. 1970. Director & Screenplay: John Hayes. Cast: Edmond O'Brien (as Timothy McDonald), Brooke Mills, Marc Lawrence, Paul Prokop, Arthur Franz. Clover Films (DVD).

They Only Kill Their Masters. 1972. Director: James Goldstone. Screenplay: Lane Slate. Cast: James Garner, Katharine Ross, Hal Holbrook, Harry Guardino, June Allyson, Tom Ewell, Edmond O'Brien (as George). MGM (DVD).

The Other Side of the Wind (unfinished). 1972. Director: Orson Welles. Screenplay: Orson Welles, Oja Kodar. Cast: John Huston, Peter Bogdanovich, Lilli Palmer, Edmond O'Brien (Pat), Mercedes McCambridge, Cameron Mitchell, Paul Stewart. Royal Road Entertainment.

Lucky Luciano. 1973. Director: Francesco Rosi. Screenplay: Jerome Chodorov, Tonino Guera, Lino Ianuzzi, Francesco Rosi. Cast: Gian Maria Volonte, Vincent Gardenia, Silverio Blasi, Magda Konopka, Edmond O'Brien (Commissioner Harry J. Anslinger), Rod Steiger. Harbor Productions/Les Filmes de la Boete/Vides Cinematografica.

The Irish: A Storm of Strangers. 1974. National Communication Foundation documentary film about the arrival of Irish settlers in the U.S. Director: Chris Jenkyns. Cast: Edmond O'Brien (Narrator). National Communication Foundation/Elaine Attis, Paul Attias, MacMillan Films.[1]

99 and 44/100% Dead aka ***Call Harry Crown.*** 1974. Director: John Frankenheimer. Screenplay: Robert Dillon. Cast: Richard Harris, Edmond O'Brien (Uncle Frank), Bradford Dillman, Ann Turkel, Chuck Connors, Constance Ford. 20th Century–Fox (DVD).

Theater

Lady Godiva. Comedy drama by Laurence Langner, circa August 1932, Westport Playhouse, Westchester. O'Brien played Attendant.

Hamlet. Tragedy by William Shakespeare. Circa 1934, Morningside Heights. O'Brien played Horatio.

Othello. Tragedy by William Shakespeare. Circa 1934, Morningside Heights. O'Brien played Othello.

The Admirable Crichton. Drama by J.M. Barrie. Circa 1935. O'Brien played William Crichton.[2]

I'll Leave It to You. Comedy by Noël Coward. Heckscher Theater, Manhattan, April 15 to 18, 1935.[3]

The Command to Love. Comedy by Rudolf Lother & Fritz Gottwald, Urban Playhouse, Waverly Terrace Auditorium, Yonkers, New York, June 15 to June 20, 1936.[4]

The Bat. Mystery melodrama by Mary Roberts Rinehart & Avery Hopwood, Urban Playhouse, Waverly Terrace Auditorium, Yonkers, New York, June 22 to 24, 1936. O'Brien played Brooks Bailey.[5]

Meet the Wife. Comedy by Lynn Starling, Urban Playhouse, Waverly Terrace Auditorium, Yonkers, New York, June 29 to July 3, 1936.[6]

Best Years. Tragedy by Raymond Van Sickle. Urban Playhouse, Waverly Terrace Auditorium, Yonkers, New York, July 6 to July 10, 1936.[7]

Daughters of Atreus Classical drama by Robert Turner. 44th Street Theater, New York, October 14, 1936, to October 23, 1936. O'Brien played Pylades.

Hamlet. Tragedy by William Shakespeare. 1936 to January 1937, Empire Theater, New York. January to February 1937, St. James' Theater, New York. O'Brien played Second Gravedigger (replacement).

Busman's Honeymoon. Mystery-comedy by Dorothy Sayers. Westchester Playhouse, Mount Kisco, July 12 to 19, 1937. O'Brien played Gardener.[8]

The Star-Wagon. Drama by Maxwell Anderson. Empire Theater, New York, September 29, 1937, to April 1938. O'Brien played Paul Reiger.

Julius Caesar. Historical drama by William Shakespeare. National Theater, New York, May 13 to May 28, 1938, and tour. O'Brien played Marc Antony (replacement).

Fools' Hill. Satiric drama by Robert Wetzel. Westport County Playhouse, Connecticut, June 27 to July 2, 1938; Westchester Playhouse, Lawrence Farms, Mount Kisco, New York.[9]

The Inner Light. Drama by Hugo Osergo. Westport County Playhouse, Connecticut, July 25 to 30, 1938.

Susanna and the Elders. Religious satire by Lawrence Langner & Armina Marshall, Westport County Playhouse, Connecticut, August 1, 1938.

Henry IV, Part 1. Historical drama by William Shakespeare. St. James' Theater, New York, January 30, to April 1939. O'Brien played Henry, Prince of Wales.

Five Kings. Historical drama by Orson Welles. Colonial Theater, Boston, February 27, 1939.

Parnell. Historical drama by John Van Druten. Tour, circa May 1939. O'Brien played Timothy Healy.

Family Portrait. Religious drama by Lenore Coffee & William Joyce Cowen. Tour, circa May 1939.

Lilliom. Drama by Ferenc Molnar. Washington, D.C., and tour, circa May 1939. O'Brien played Lilliom.

Bury the Dead. Drama by Irwin Shaw. Royal Alexander Theater, Toronto, Canada, May 18, 1939. O'Brien acted and directed.

Leave Her to Heaven. Drama by John Van Druten. Robert Ewen. Longacre Theater, New York, February 27, 1940, to March 9, 1940.

Romeo and Juliet. Drama by William Shakespeare. 51st Street Theater, May to June 8, 1940. O'Brien played Mercutio.

Winged Victory. A play with music by Moss Hart, 44th Street Theater, New York, November 20, 1943, to May 20, 1944, and tour 1944 to 1945. O'Brien played Irving Miller.

I've Got Sixpence. Drama by John Van Druten, Walnut Theater, Philadelphia, November 12 to 25, 1952; Ethel Barrymore Theater, New York, December 2 to December 20, 1952. O'Brien played Peter Tyndall.

Radio

The March of Time. CBS News current affairs documentary series. Circa 1936 to 1938. O'Brien played various roles.

The Shadow. Syndicated mystery with Orson Welles. In various episodes (circa 1938), O'Brien played various roles.

The Mercury Theater. CBS drama adaptations. "A Tale of Two Cities" by Charles Dickens, with Orson Welles, Ray Collins, Martin Gabel, Edmond O'Brien, July 25, 1938. "The Thirty-Nine Steps" by John Buchan, with Orson Welles, Ray Collins, Eustace Wyatt, Edmond O'Brien, Edgar Barrier, Dan Seymour (Announcer), Music by Bernard Herrmann, August 1, 1938. "I'm a Fool," "The Open Window" and "My Little Boy," by Saki, with Orson Welles, Edgar Barrier, Ray Collins, Anna Stafford, Betty Garde, Edmond O'Brien, August 8, 1938. "The Count of Monte Cristo" by Alexandre Dumas, with Orson Welles, George Coulouris, Edgar Barrier, Edmond O'Brien, August 29, 1938. "The Man Who Was Thursday" by G.K. Chesterton, with Orson Welles, George Coulouris, Edgar Barrier, Joseph Cotten, Edmond O'Brien; music by Bernard Herrmann, September 5, 1938. "The Immortal Sherlock Holmes" by Arthur Conan Doyle, with Orson Welles, Eustace Wyatt, Brenda Forbes, Mary Taylor, Edmond O'Brien, September 25, 1938. "Around the World in Eighty Days" by Jules Verne, with Orson Welles (Host), Ray Collins (Narrator), Stefan Schnabel, Arlene Francis, William Alland, Edmond O'Brien; music by Bernard Herrmann, October 23, 1938. "Heart of Darkness" by Joseph Conrad and "Life with Father" by Clarence Day, Edgar Barrier, Frank Readick, Edmond O'Brien, Ray Collins (Narrator), George Coulouris, Mary Wickes, Mildred Natwick,

Edmond O'Brien, Orson Welles (Host), November 6, 1938. "The Pickwick Papers" by Charles Dickens, with Alfred Shirley, Ray Collins, Elliott Reid, Mary Wickes, Edmond O'Brien, November 20, 1938.

Graphic Preview. WGN–Mutual Network (Chicago); dramatized previews of features in the forthcoming edition of the *Chicago Sunday Tribune Coloroto Graphic Section*, April 1, 1938. O'Brien narrated.[10]

Curtain Time. WGN–Mutual Network religious drama. "The First Easter" by Robert Johnstone, April 15, 1938.[11]

Mrs. Wiggs of the Cabbage Patch. NBC comedy drama series, circa 1938. O'Brien played a supporting role.

Great Plays. Blue Network drama. "Camille" by Alexandre Dumas, with Jane Cowl, George Gaul, Edmond O'Brien, Brooks Atkinson (host), March 12, 1939. "Edward II" by Christopher Marlowe, with Edmond O'Brien, Alfred Shirley, Florence Malone, Raymond Edward Johnson, November 5, 1939. O'Brien played Edward II. "Volpone" by Ben Jonson, with Edmond O'Brien, Rex O'Malley, Carl Benton Reid, Harry Mesteyer, December 3, 1939. O'Brien played Volpone.[12] "Ruy Blas" by Victor Hugo, with Edmond O'Brien, Kay Strozzi, January 21, 1940.

Adventure in Reading. NBC biographical drama. "Leo Tolstoy" by Helen Walpole, Margaret Leaf, with Carl Benton Reid, Mary Michael, Ellen Marr, Edmond O'Brien, March 27, 1939. "Wilkie Collins" with Harriet Sterling, Burford Hampden, Harold Vermilyea, Edmond O'Brien, May 29, 1939.

The Shadow of Fu Manchu. Syndicated Radio Attractions; adapted from the story by Sax Rohmer. "The Insidious Dr. Fu Manchu" with Edmond O'Brien, Ted Osbourne, Paula Winslowe, May 8, 1939. O'Brien played Inspector Rymer.

Arch Oboler's Plays. Blue Network drama. "Crazytown" by Arch Oboler, with Edmond O'Brien, John Brown, Charlotte Manson, Paul Stewart, Betty King, May 20, 1939. O'Brien played Captain Vittora. "Immortal Gentleman," June 17, 1939. "The Word" with Edmond O'Brien, Helen Mack, October 4, 1939.

Aunt Jenny's Real-Life Stories. CBS human interest drama series, circa 1938 to 1939. O'Brien played various roles.

Kay Kyser's That's Right You're Wrong. WHN Network (New York) variety show; live broadcast from the stage of the Criterion Theater, New York; O'Brien and other guests were introduced over the microphone, December 9, 1939.[13]

A Visit from St. Nicholas. Syndicated broadcast of poem by Clement Clarke Moore, from London Terrace Apartments, Old Bridge, New York, December 24, 1939. O'Brien was a reader.[14]

Radio Guild Drama. "The Most Tragic Brutus" by Walter C. Hackett, with Edmond O'Brien, Henry Hull, Jr., February 10, 1940. O'Brien played John Wilkes Booth.[15]

Fight for Freedom. Syndicated political discussion and current affairs program broadcast on WOR and WCMA in New York on behalf of the Fight for

Freedom Committee, April 25, 1941, to June 1942. O'Brien provided various voices, including Adolf Hitler.

Treasury Star Parade. Treasury Department; syndicated, with Vaughan Monroe and His Orchestra, The Five V's, Edmond O'Brien, 1942. O'Brien was the guest host.

Hello Americans. CBS drama series. "Would Immediate Freedom for India Hasten or Retard Victory?" Stories of South American revolutionaries and conquistadors: "Pizarro: El Conquistador," "Simon Bolivar: El Liberador" and "Jose de San Martin," with Orson Welles, Pedro de Cordoba, Ray Collins, Edmond O'Brien; music by Bernard Herrmann, November 22, 1942. O'Brien played various roles.

Contact. AFRS drama broadcast on WKAT (Fort Lauderdale and Miami), "Rule of Evidence" a tale of the supernatural by Alonzo Deen Cole, March 17, 1943.[16] "Appointment" by Norman Corwin, with Pvt. Edmond O'Brien, Pvt. Harold Barrow, Pvt. Harold Nemetz, Pvt. Robert Crawford, April 7, 1943.[17]

Work Shop. AFRS drama; series of experimental plays broadcast over WKAT (South Florida), "Rope" by Patrick Hamilton, adapted by Sgt. Draper Lewis, with Pvt. Edmond O'Brien, Morgan Farley, March 25, 1943. O'Brien played Rupert Cadell.[18]

War Town. AFRS Syndicated Community Chests. "On with the Show," the story of the USO, with Jackson Beck (announcer), James F. Koch, July 13, 1944.[19] "Ex-Soldier" with Pvt. Edmond O'Brien, Peggy Conklin, July 16, 1944. O'Brien played Ned Martin.[20] "Sergeant Joe" and "A Visiting Nurse Story" with Sgt. Edmond O'Brien, Jon Gart, Peggy Conklin, 1945. O'Brien played Joe Carney.

Hollywood Showtime. Drama broadcast on WSAI. "Marriage of Inconvenience" with Edmond O'Brien, Lurene Tuttle, June 10, 1945.[21]

AFRS Entertainment. AFRS Variety show, with the Tommy Dorsey Orchestra, July 8, 1945. O'Brien was a guest.

Lux Radio Theater. CBS drama. "The Canterville Ghost," based on the novella by Oscar Wilde, with Charles Laughton, Edmond O'Brien, June 18, 1945. O'Brien played Cuffy Williams. "The Amazing Mrs. Holliday" with Gene Tierney, Edmond O'Brien, Walter Brennan, March 4, 1946. O'Brien played Tom Holliday. "The Web" by William Bowers, with Ella Raines, Edmond O'Brien, Vincent Price, Maria Palmer, September 29, 1947. O'Brien played Bob Regan. "Key Largo" by Maxwell Anderson, with Edward G. Robinson, Claire Trevor, Edmond O'Brien, Dan Seymour, Frances Robinson, November 28, 1949. O'Brien played Frank McCloud. "Flamingo Road" with Jane Wyman, David Brian, Edmond O'Brien, October 2, 1950. O'Brien played Sheriff Titus Semple/ "The Star" by Katherine Albert, Dale Eunson, with Ida Lupino, Edmond O'Brien, Sherry Jackson, Dan Riss, April 19, 1954. "The Treasure of the Sierra Madre" with Edmond O'Brien, Walter Brennan, Lamont Johnson, Don Diamond, February 15, 1955. O'Brien played Fred C. Dobbs.

The Fourth Estate. Syndicated NBC crime drama. "The Tip Off" with Mark Hellinger (host), Jack Adams, Edmond O'Brien, June 27, 1946.

This Is Hollywood. CBS variety drama show. "Temptation" with Merle Oberon, Edmond O'Brien, March 1, 1947. O'Brien played Nigel Armine.[22] "The Killers" with Burt Lancaster, Edmond O'Brien, April 19, 1947. O'Brien played Jim Reardon.

Betty and Bob. NBC drama series, with Arlene Francis, Everett Sloane, Agnes Moorehead, Ray Collins, Edmond O'Brien, June 15, 1947.

Suspense. CBS mystery drama series. "The Argyle Album" by Cyril Enfield, with Edmond O'Brien, Hans Conried, Lurene Tuttle, Joseph Kearns (announcer), September 4, 1947. O'Brien played Harry Mitchell. "The Blind Spot" by Lois Eby & John C. Fleming, with Edmond O'Brien, Jeff Corey, Bud Widom, Bill Alley, May 1, 1948. O'Brien played Eric Strange. "Muddy Track" by Bob Shelly & Buckley Angel, with Edmond O'Brien, Ann Blyth, November 11, 1948. O'Brien played Harry Clark. "Ordeal in Donner Pass" by Arthur Ross, with Edmond O'Brien, Charlotte Lawrence, Joseph Kearns, November 2, 1953. O'Brien played Patrick Breen.

Mutual Family Theater. Mutual drama. "Robin Hood" by Arthur Sawyer, with Edmond O'Brien, William Conrad, Edgar Barrier, Lillian Buyeff, Ed Begley, July 27, 1949. O'Brien played Robin of Loxley. "The Man Without a Country" by Edward Everett Hale, with Edmond O'Brien, Ed Begley, Carleton Young, Virginia Eiler, Lizabeth Scott (host), June 7, 1950. O'Brien played Lt. Philip Nolan. "Stopwatch Finale" by Father Timothy J. Mulvey, with Edmond O'Brien, John Larch, Tudor Owen, Grace Kelly (hostess), September 1, 1954. "Act of Contrition" by John T. Kelly, with Gene Raymond (host), Edmond O'Brien, Virginia Gregg, Margaret Brayton, Lawrence Dobkin, April 20, 1955. O'Brien played Ralph Stokes. "The Visitor" with Edmond O'Brien, Dorothy Warenskjold, January 18, 1956.[23] "Nightmare at Noon" by John T. Kelly, with Ralph Edwards (host), Edmond O'Brien, Charlotte Lawrence, Jack Kruschen, May 1, 1957. O'Brien played Cliff.

Hallmark Playhouse. CBS drama. "O'Halloran's Luck" by Stephen Vincent Benet, with Edmond O'Brien, Dan O'Herlihy, James Hilton (host), October 28, 1948. O'Brien played O'Halloran. "Two Years Before the Mast" by Richard Henry Dana, with Edmond O'Brien, Lurene Tuttle, Ted de Corsia, Parley Baer, April 26, 1951. O'Brien played Richard Henry Dana.

Escape. CBS mystery adventure series. "The Country of the Blind" by H.G. Wells, with Edmond O'Brien, Berry Kroeger, Peggy Webber, Harry Bartell, March 20, 1949. O'Brien played Nunez.

NBC University Theater. NBC Drama. "The History of Henry Esmond, Esq." by William Makepeace Thackeray, with Edmond O'Brien, Donald Morrison, Doris Lloyd, Grey Stafford, March 27, 1949. O'Brien played Henry Esmond.

Night Beat. NBC crime drama series audition show. "The Ted Carter Murder Case" by Larry Marcus, with Edmond O'Brien, Betty Moran, Jack Kruschen, Anne Stone, May 19, 1949. O'Brien played Hank Mitchell.

Proudly We Hail. AFRS Syndicated drama, "Take a Letter, Miss Devlow" June 15, 1949. O'Brien played Joe Cooper.

Skippy Hollywood Theater. CBS drama. "The Minister's Angel" with Edmond O'Brien, Francis X. Bushman, October 13, 1949. O'Brien played Security Officer.[24] "A Poltergeist for Harry" with Edmond O'Brien, June 15, 1950. O'Brien played Harry, a bookie.

Screen Director's Playhouse. NBC drama anthology. "The Big Lift" with Edmond O'Brien, Betty Lou Gerson, Byron Kane, Edward Marr, January 18, 1951. O'Brien played T/Sgt. Danny MacCullough.

Yours Truly, Johnny Dollar. CBS detective series, February 3, 1950, to July 2, 1952. O'Brien played *Johnny Dollar.* Partial list: "The Murder of Loyal B. Martin" with Irene Tedrow, Ted de Corsia, John Dehner, February 3, 1950. "The S.S. *Malay Trader*" with Elliott Reid, Lillian Buyeff, February 10, 1950. "How the Gravedigger's Spades Came Close to Being Trumps" with Peggy Webber, Parley Baer, Hugh Thomas, February 17, 1950. "Archeologist" with Virginia Gregg, Jay Novello, Ed Begley, February 24, 1950. "The Alec Jefferson Matter" with Michael Ann Barrett, Edwin Max, Tony Barrett, March 7, 1950. "The Eighty-Five Little Minks" with Gloria Blondell, Hans Conried, March 14, 1950. "Stuart Palmer, the Man Who Wrote Himself to Death" with Lurene Tuttle, Bill Bouchey, March 21, 1950. "The Missing Masterpiece" with Charles McGraw, Walter Burke, March 23, 1950. "The Story of the Big Red Schoolhouse" with Elliott Reid, Clay Post, April 4, 1950. "The Dead First Helpers" with Joe Forte, Junius Matthews, April 11, 1950. "The Story of the 10.08" with Jeanne Bates, Ted de Corsia, April 18, 1950. "The Search for Policy Holder Pearl Carassa" with Hy Averback, Martha Wentworth, April 25, 1950. "The Abel Tackett Matter" with Maria Palmer, Dan O'Herlihy, May 2, 1950. "The Harold Trandem Matter" with Edwin Max, Raymond Burr, May 9, 1950. "The Sidney Rykoff Matter" with Howard McNear, John McIntire, May 16, 1950. "The Earl Chadwick Matter" with Virginia Gregg, Walter Owen, May 23, 1950. "The Port Au Prince Story" with Byron Kane, Ted de Corsia, May 30, 1950. "The Caligio Diamond Matter" with Jane Webb, June 8, 1950. "The Arrowcraft Matter" with Jeanette Nolan, June 15, 1950. "The London Matter" with Wally Maher, June 22, 1950. "The Barbara James Matter" with Jack Moyles, June 29, 1950. "The Belo Horizonte Railroad Matter" with Francis X. Bushman, July 6, 1950. "The Calgary Matter" with Ted Osbourne, July 13, 1950. "The Henry J. Unger Matter" with Raymond Burr, July 20, 1950. "The Blood River Matter" with William Conrad, August 3, 1950. "The Hartford Alliance Matter" with Raymond Burr, August 10, 1950. "The Mickey McQueen Matter" with Ben Wright, August 17, 1950. "The Trans-Pacific Import-Export Company, South China Branch" with Hal March, August 24, 1950. "The Virginia Beach Matter" with Bob Sweeney, August 31, 1950. "The Howard Caldwell Matter" with Jeanne Bates, September 30, 1950. "The Richard Splain Matter" with Jack Kruschen, October 7, 1950. "The Yankee Pride Matter" October 14, 1950. "The Jack Madigan Matter" October 21, 1950. "The Joan Sebastian Matter" October 28, 1950. "The Queen Anne Pistols Matter" November 4, 1950. "The Adam Kegg Matter" November 11, 1950. "The Nora Faulkner Matter" November 18, 1950. "The Woodward Manila Matter" November 25, 1950. "The Leland Blackbourne Matter" December 16, 1950. "The Port O' Call Matter"

January 13, 1951. "The David Rocky Matter" January 20, 1951. "The Jarvis Wilder Matter" February 24, 1951. "The Celia Woodstock Matter" March 3, 1951. "The Stanley Springs Matter" March 10, 1951. "The Byron Hayes Matter" March 24, 1951. "The Jackie Cleaver Story" March 31, 1951. "The Edward French Matter" April 7, 1951. "The Willard South Matter" April 21, 1951. "The Month End Matter" April 28, 1951. "The Lillis Bond Matter" May 26, 1951. "The Sodeberry, Maine Matter" June 2, 1951. "The George Farmer Matter" June 9, 1951. "The Arthur Boldrick Matter" June 6, 1951. "The Malcolm Wish, M.D. Matter" June 16, 1951. "The Hatchet House Theft Matter" June 27, 1951. "The Alonzo Chapman Matter" July 4, 1951. "The Fairway Matter" July 11. 1951. "The Horace Lockhart Matter" August 1, 1951. "The Lucky Costa Matter" August 15, 1951. "The Leland Case Matter" August 22, 1951. "The Cuban Jewel Matter" September 19, 1951. "The Protection Matter" September 22, 1951. "The Douglas Taylor Matter" October 6, 1951. "The Millard Ward Matter" October 13, 1951. "The Tollhurst Theft Matter" October 27, 1951. "The Hannibal Murphy Matter" November 3, 1951. "The Baskerville Matter" November 10, 1951. "The Youngstown Credit Group Matter" December 8, 1951. "The Alma Scott Matter" December 29, 1951. "The Amelia Hartwell Matter" with John McIntire, July 2, 1952.

The Quiz Kids. NBC quiz show, with Felix Adler, Joe Kelly (host), July 1950. O'Brien was a guest.

The Miracle of America. CBS patriotic drama series. "Freedom of Speech" with Edmond O'Brien, Howard Duff, August 22, 1950.

Hollywood Star Playhouse. CBS drama. "Death in the Desert" with Edmond O'Brien, Jeff Alexander Orchestra, October 23, 1950. "Avalanche" with Edmond O'Brien, Wendell Niles (host), August 10, 1952. O'Brien played Mountain Guide.

Hollywood Marathon. Syndicated 14-hour charity appeal on behalf of the City of Hope Cancer Fund, with Margaret Whiting, Spike Jones, Lena Horne et al., September 1951. O'Brien was a guest.[25]

Philip Morris Playhouse. CBS drama. "Blind Alley" aka "Homecoming" by Wyllis Cooper, with Edmond O'Brien, Olga San Joan, April 5, 1951. O'Brien played Hal Wilson. "711 Ocean Drive" with Edmond O'Brien, Tippy Stringer, January 20, 1952. O'Brien played Mal Granger.

The Martin and Lewis Show. NBC comedy variety show, with Ginger Rogers, Jean Peters, Connee Boswell, December 16, 1952. O'Brien was a guest.[26]

Cavalcade of America. NBC drama. "Barbed Wire Christmas" by Warner Law, with Edmond O'Brien, Kermit Murdoch, Dan Ocko, Nelson Olmsted, December 16, 1952. O'Brien played Sergeant Bert Petersen.

Bud's Bandwagon. AFRS record show, with Bud Widom, Doris Day,, circa 1953. O'Brien was a guest interviewee.

Hollywood Story. NBC drama series. "The Life Story of Richard Dix" starring Edmond O'Brien, November 1, 1953. O'Brien played Richard Dix.

Hollywood Calling. NBC variety-interview series; George Fisher interviews the stars, with Ronald Colman, Jack Benny, Edmond O'Brien, circa 1953. O'Brien was a guest interviewee.

The Standard Hour. NBC. Classical music. "I Am an American Day" patriotic broadcast, "I Am an American" with Carmen Dragon & Orchestra, from the War Memorial Opera House, San Francisco, September 12, 1954. O'Brien was the narrator.

House Party. WCCO Minneapolis, Minnesota, variety show, with Connee Boswell, Edith Head, November 3, 1954. O'Brien was a guest.[27] Introduced by Art Linkletter, with Margaret Whiting, May 16, 1958.[28]

Kraft Music Hall. CBS variety show, presented by Rudy Vallee, with Les Baxter, Janet Leigh, Debra Paget, May 14, 1955. O'Brien was a guest.[29]

Amos n' Andy Music Hall. CBS comedy variety series, June 5, 1955. O'Brien was a guest.[30]

Academy Awards Program. NBC live broadcast from the Century Theater, New York, and the Pantages Theater in Hollywood, with Harry Belafonte, Jane Powell, James Cagney, Edmond O'Brien, *et al.*, March 21, 1956.

Across the Blue Pacific. AFRS Music variety show for the Navy, "Ship's Log" January 7, 1958. O'Brien was a guest.[31]

Note: The Edmond O'Brien Collection, *consisting of 105 programs, including some of those listed above and many episodes of* Yours Truly, Johnny Dollar, *is available in three different formats from the Old Time Radio Catalog: https://www.otrcat.com/p/edmond-obrien.*

Television

Easy Does It. NBC variety show, with Johnny Andrews, Francey Lane, July 17, 1950. O'Brien was a guest.[32]

The Peter Lind Hayes Show. NBC variety show, with guests Edmond O'Brien and Olga San Juan, December 14, 1950.

The Milton Berle Show. NBC variety show, with Constance Moore, Georgie Price, March 27, 1951. O'Brien was a guest.

Pulitzer Prize Playhouse. "Icebound" by Owen Davis, with Edmond O'Brien, Elmer Davis, Charles Dingle, Nina Foch, April 13, 1951. O'Brien played Ben Jordan.

Lux Video Theater. CBS drama. "Hit and Run" by Mac Shoub, with Edmond O'Brien, Christopher Barbieri, Andrew Bernard, April 23, 1951. O'Brien played Hal. "A Matter of Life" by Mac Shoub, with Edmond O'Brien, Celia Johnson, Dickie Moore, September 24, 1951. O'Brien played Mr. Protis. "Ceylon Treasure" by David Goodis, with Edmond O'Brien, Audrey Meadows, Marie Riva, Stefan Stoubel, January 14, 1952. O'Brien played Rorsford. "Lady of Suspicion" (aka "We'll Never Be Free") by Will La Jolla, Ellis Marcus, with Edmond O'Brien, Ray Bennett, Faith Domergue, November 12, 1952. O'Brien played Mike Dixon. "Five Star Final" by Louis Weitzenkorn, with Edmond O'Brien, Mae Clarke, Ken Christy, November 11, 1954. O'Brien played Randall. "A Bell for Adano" by John Hersey, with James Mason (host), Edmond O'Brien, Charles Bronson, February 10, 1955. O'Brien played Major Jepelo. "To Have and Have Not" by William Faulkner, with Edmond O'Brien, Beverly Garland, John Qualen, January 17, 1957. O'Brien played Harry "Steve" Morgan.

Hollywood Marathon. Syndicated 14-hour charity appeal on behalf of the City of Hope Cancer Fund, with Margaret Whiting, Spike Jones, Lena Horne, Edmond O'Brien *et al.*, September 1951.[33]

Texaco Star Theater. NBC variety show, with Vivian Blaine, Edmond O'Brien, Louis Jordan, Milton Berle (host), November 20, 1951.

The Kate Smith Evening Hour. NBC variety talk show, with Kate Smith (host), Edmond O'Brien, Olga San Juan, Ralph Flanagan & Orchestra, Peggy Ryan, Ray MacDonald, December 26, 1951.

Robert Montgomery Presents. "Ricochet" by Adrian Spies, with Edmond O'Brien, Patricia Benoit, Dorothy Hart, January 12, 1953.

Ford Television Theater. NBC drama. "To Any Soldier" by Robert Hardy Andrews, with Edmond O'Brien, Stanley Clements, Johnny Duncan, April 2, 1953. "Charlie C Company" by Steve Fisher, William Chamberlain, with Edmond O'Brien, Kerwin Mathews, Robert Strauss, December 9, 1954. O'Brien played Capt. Joyce.

Schlitz Playhouse. CBS comedy drama. "The Long Shot" by Ellery Queen, with Edmond O'Brien, Douglas Kennedy, Patrick O'Neal, October 9, 1953. O'Brien played Capt. Simpson. "Lineman's Luck" by S.N. Savage, with Edmond O'Brien, Margaret Field, William Bishop, November 6, 1953. "The Net Draws Tight" by Walter C. Brown, Don Martin, with Edmond O'Brien, Skip Homeier, Paul Bryar, October 8, 1954. O'Brien played Rick Saunders. "Tower Room 14-A" by Raymond Chandler, with Edmond O'Brien, Ruta Lee, Richard Jaeckel, January 11, 1957. "The Town That Slept with the Lights On" by Liam O'Brien, with Edmond O'Brien, Diane Brewster, Robert Middleton, May 16, 1958. O'Brien played Jim Reardon.

Climax! CBS Drama. "An Error in Chemistry" by William Faulkner, with William Lundigan (host), Edmond O'Brien, Lon Chaney, Tommy Ivo, December 2, 1954. O'Brien played Joel Flint. "Figures in Clay" by Jerry Davis, Howard Leeds, with Edmond O'Brien, Lloyd Bridges, Henry Hull, May 31, 1956. O'Brien played Leo Waldek.

The Bob Hope Show. NBC comedy show, with Dorothy Lamour, Edmond O'Brien, Sheldon Leonard, May 11, 1954.

Holiday. Travelogue telefilm shown on Midwest stations, with Ida Lupino, Joan Fontaine, Edmond O'Brien, August 20, 1954. O'Brien was one of the narrators.[34] "Tibet" shown as part of *Trio*, February 27, 1956. O'Brien narrated.[35]

The Henry Fonda Show. "The Dark Stranger" by Betty Ulius, Joel Morcott, with Edmond O'Brien, Joanne Woodward, Evelyn Ankers, January 8, 1955. O'Brien played Ray Ericson. "End of Flight" by W. Somerset Maugham, with Edmond O'Brien, Marguerite Chapman, Bobby Dominguez, October 29, 1955.

Hollywood's Best. KRCA variety interview show on which O'Brien twice guested: (1) with Ruth Roman, Katy Jurado, Paul Gilbert, Rose Marie, January 22, 1955.[36] (2) with Ginger Rogers, Harry Mimmo, September 13, 1955.[37]

Stage 7. CBS drama. "Debt of Honor" by Cornell Woolrich, with Edmond O'Brien, Charles Bronson, Kasey Rogers, February 20, 1955. O'Brien played Clinton Sturges.

The Red Skelton Hour. CBS comedy. February 22, 1955: O'Brien was a grizzled old prospector in a sketch with Skelton. "*Look* Magazine Movie Awards Show" with Irving Berlin, Judy Garland, Walt Disney *et al.*, March 8, 1955. O'Brien was a guest.

The 27th Annual Academy Awards. NBC live broadcast, with Humphrey Bogart *et al.*, March 30, 1955. O'Brien was the recipient of the Best Supporting Actor Academy Award for *The Barefoot Contessa*.

Damon Runyon Theater. CBS comedy drama. "Old Em's Kentucky Home" by Jerry Davis, Martin Ragaway, with Edmond O'Brien, Donald Woods, Fay Baker, May 28, 1955. O'Brien played Duke Martin.

Thank Your Lucky Stars. WNDR (New York) astrology show, "Mysteries of the Zodiac" with special guest Edmond O'Brien, Jim McKechnie, Alan Wilder, September 11, 1955.[38]

Playhouse '56. NBC drama. "The Heart's a Forgotten Hotel" by Arnold Schulman, with Edmond O'Brien, Sylvia Sidney, Cliff Tatum, October 25, 1955. O'Brien played Sidney.

The Ed Sullivan Show. CBS variety show, with Susan Hayward, James Wong Howe, Edmond O'Brien, March 4, 1956.

The 28th Annual Academy Awards. NBC, March 21, 1956. O'Brien presented the award for Best Supporting Actress to Jo Van Fleet.

Screen Directors Playhouse. NBC drama. "A Ticket for Thaddeus" by A.I. Bezzerides, with Edmond O'Brien, Raymond Bailey, Russ Conway, May 9, 1956. O'Brien played Thaddeus Kubaczik.

The George Gobel Show. CBS comedy show, with April Ames, January 5, 1957. Guest O'Brien sang a rock'n'roll number.

Playhouse 90. CBS drama. "The Comedian" by Ernest Lehman, with Mickey Rooney, Kim Hunter, Edmond O'Brien, Mel Torme, Constance Ford, February 14, 1957. O'Brien played Al Preston. "The Male Animal" by Helene Hanff, Elizabeth Nugent, with Edmond O'Brien, Ann Rutherford, Charles Ruggles, March 13, 1958. O'Brien played Joe Ferguson. "The Blue Men" by Alvin Boretz, with Edmond O'Brien, Eileen Heckart, Jack Warden, January 15, 1959. O'Brien played Roy Brenner.

Zane Grey Theater. CBS Western series. "A Gun Is for Killing" with Marsha Hunt, Edmond O'Brien, Robert Vaughn, October 18, 1957. O'Brien played Russ Andrews. "Lonesome Road" with Edmond O'Brien, Rita Lynn, Tol Avery, November 19, 1959. O'Brien played Marshal Ben Clark.

House Party. CBS variety show with guests Edmond O'Brien, Margaret Whiting, May 16, 1958.[39]

Appendix

Suspicion. NBC drama anthology. "Death Watch" by John Hawkins, Ward Hawkins. Cast: Edmond O'Brien, Janice Rule, Florence Marly, June 2, 1958, Director: Ray Milland. O'Brien played Sgt. Miles Odeen.

Lux Playhouse. CBS drama. "Coney Island Winter" by Halstead Welles. Cast: Edmond O'Brien, Bob Fuller, Kathleen Crowley, November 28, 1958. O'Brien played Big Jim Webber.

Laramie. NBC Western series. "The Iron Captain" by E. Jack Neuman. Cast: Edmond O'Brien, Valerie Allen, Hoagy Carmichael, October 27, 1959. O'Brien played Captain Sam Prado.

Johnny Midnight. Syndicated crime drama series distributed by MCA Television, January 3, 1960, to September 21, 1960. O'Brien played Johnny Midnight. "X Equals Murder" with Harry Townes, Viveca Lindfors, Richard Coogan, January 3, 1960; "Voice of the Dummy" with Robert H. Harris, Katherine Squire, Arthur Batanides, January 10, 1960; "The Villain of the Piece" with Adam West, John Hoyt, Yuki Shimoda, January 17, 1960; "Leading Lady" Ann Robinson, Mike Mazurki, Johnny Silver, January 24, 1960; "Once Again" with Carol Ohmart, Harry Bartell, Marc Cavell, January 31, 1960; "A Taste of Curry" with Joe Bushkin, Carl Benton Reid, Cynthia Chenault, February 7, 1960; "Mother's Boy" with Doug McClure, Robert Cornthwaite, Eleanor Audley, February 14, 1960; "Award for Murder" with John Gallaudet, Connie Hines, Lurene Tuttle, February 21, 1960; "Magic at Midnight" with Grace Field, Jacqueline Holt, Tom Palmer, February 28, 1960; "The Inner Eye" with Henry Hunter, DeForest Kelley, William Keene, March 4, 1960; "The Impresario" with Yuki Shimoda, Billy De Wolfe, Grant Richards, March 11, 1960; "Beyond Infamy" with Virginia Field, Bartlett Robinson, Olive Sturgess, March 18, 1960; "An Old-Fashioned Frame" with Virginia Gregg, Philip Pine, Chris Winters, March 25, 1960; "Slight Delay at Dimity" with Gordon Gebert, Andrea King, Carole Matthews, April 1, 1960; "The 9th Doll" with Arthur Batanides, Yuki Shimoda, Lurene Tuttle, April 8, 1960; "Death Over My Shoulder" with Barney Phillips, John Stevenson, Jean Willes, April 15, 1960; "Phantom Bribe" with Arthur Batanides, Perry Lopez, Robert Warrick, April 22, 1960; "The Tokyo Doll" with Yuki Shimoda, Philip Ahn, Reiko Sito, April 29, 1960; "Trouble on the Road" with Olga San Juan, Anthony Caruso, Alan Reed, May 5, 1960; "Registered Mail" with William Schallert, Walter Burke, Elaine Edwards, May 12, 1960; "Somebody Loves You" with Roxanne Berard, J. Pat O'Malley, Jeffrey Stone, May 19, 1960; "The Emerald Star" with Arthur Batanides, Whitney Blake, Ina Victor, May 26, 1960; "Return to Murder" with Suzy Crandall, Stephen Ellsworth, Onslow Stevens, June 2, 1960; "One Over Par" with Murray Alper, Tol Avery, Scott Douglas, June 9, 1960; "Tender Loving Care" with Norma Calderon, Stanley Clements, Tommy Cook, June 16, 1960; "A Token of Love" with Arthur Batanides, Yuki Shimoda, Carol Ohmart, June 23, 1960; "Schatzi" with Gail Robbins, Herbert Patterson, Nestor Paiva, June 30, 1960; "The Sweet-Tooth Murder" with Jean Willes, Kathie Browne, Peter Adams, July 6, 1960; "Ring of Truth" with Wilton Graff, William Swan, Grace Raynor, July 13, 1960; "Her Sister's Keeper" with Yuki Shimoda, Frances Robinson, Jacqueline de Wit, July 20, 1960; "The Single" with Charles Horvath,

Frank Albertson, Rita Lynn, July 27, 1960; "Dark Trophy" with Yuki Shimoda, James Yagi, Tsuruko Kobayashi, August 3, 1960; "Inside Man" with Helen Spring, Rand Brooks, Abbagail Shelton, August 10, 1960; "Ding-A-Ling" with Veda Ann Borg, Virginia Carroll, David Lewis, August 17, 1960; "The Switchback Murder" with Miriam Colon, Alberto Morin, Ernest Sarracino, August 24, 1960; "Pay-Off to Death" with Andrea King, Russ Conway, Virginia Gibson, August 31, 1960; "Romeo and Julie" with Stanley Clements, Lisa Montell, Ernest Sarracino, September 7, 1960; "How Tight a Web" with Parley Baer, Angela Greene, Barney Phillips, September 14, 1960; "The Whammy" with Jay Novello, Dorothy Green, Charlita Regis, September 21, 1960.

I've Got a Secret. CBS panel game show presented by Garry Moore, with Edmond O'Brien, Betsy Palmer, January 20, 1960.

Insight. CBS drama series. "Breakthrough," with Edmond O'Brien, Bettye Ackerman, Dick York, September 10, 1961. "The Seven Minute Life of James Houseworthy" with Edmond O'Brien, Bruce Davison, Jeanne Cooper, April 2, 1970. O'Brien played James Houseworthy.

The Dick Powell Theater. NBC drama. "Killer in the House" by Borden Deal, with Edmond O'Brien, Earl Holliman, Wallace Ford, October 10, 1961. O'Brien played Sid Williams.

Target: The Corruptors. ABC crime drama series. "The Invisible Government" with Stephen McNally, Robert Burton, Edmond O'Brien, Yvonne White, October 20, 1961. O'Brien played Ollie Crown.

Sam Benedict. MGM Television legal drama series shown on NBC, September 15, 1962, to March 30, 1963. O'Brien played Sam Benedict. With Richard Rust as Henry Tabor. "Hannigan" with Gene Raymond, Sandy Kenyon, Donna Douglas, September 15, 1962; "A Split Week in San Quentin" with Jack Weston, Katharine Ross, Rex Ingram, September 22, 1962; "Nor Practice Make Perfect" with Claude Rains, Linda Watkins, John Anderson, September 29, 1962; "Nothing Equals Nothing" with Nancy Kelly, Otto Kruger, Constance Ford, October 6, 1962; "Tears for a Nobody Doll" with Miyoshi Umeki, Joanna Barnes, Michael Constantine, October 13, 1962; "Twenty Aching Years" with Herschel Bernardi, Harry Townes, Paul Carr. October 20, 1962; "Maddon's Folly" with Vera Miles, Robert Lansing, Ken Renard, October 27, 1962; "Hear the Mellow Wedding Bells" with Joseph Schildkraut, Zohra Lampert, Barry Kelley, November 3, 1962; "Life Is a Lie, Love Is a Cheat" with Audrey Meadows, Joe Mantell, Ed Nelson, November 10, 1962; "The Bird of Warning" with Diana Hyland, George Tobias, Maria Palmer, November 17, 1962; "The View from an Ivory Tower" with Dan O'Herlihy, Phyllis Avery, Al Ruscio, November 24, 1962; "Everybody's Playing Polo" with Burgess Meredith, Yvonne Craig, Irene Dailey; Director: Ida Lupino, December 1, 1962; "Too Many Strangers" with Marsha Hunt, Gloria Grahame, Michael Parks, December 8, 1962; "So Various, So Beautiful" with Hazel Court, Theodore Bikel, Richard Loo, December 15, 1962; "Where There's a Will" with Geraldine Brooks, Connie Gilchrist, Norman Fell, December 22, 1962; "The Target Over the Hill" with Inger Stevens, Everett Sloane, Jacques Aubuchon, December 29, 1962; "Not

Even the Gulls Shall Weep" with Ida Lupino, Howard Duff, Karl Swenson, January 5, 1963; "The Boiling Point" with David Wayne, Gary Merrill, Abner Biberman, January 12, 1963; "Green Room, Grey Morning" with Ruth Roman, Tige Andrews, Ralph Manza, January 19, 1963; "Run Softly, Oh Softly" with Brian Keith, Lori Martin, Philip Ober; Director: Paul Henreid, January 26, 1963; "Sugar and Spice and Everything..." with Arthur O'Connell, Robert Emhardt, Yvonne Craig; Director: Ida Lupino, February 6, 1963; "Some Fires Die Slowly" with Barry Sullivan, James MacArthur, Betty Field, February 16, 1963; "Image of a Toad" with Nehemiah Persoff, Beverly Garland, Russell Collins, February 23, 1963; "Seventeen Gypsies and a Sinner Named Charlie" with Maria O'Brien, Ross Elliott, Kurt Russell, March 2, 1963; "Accomplice" with Eddie Albert, Brock Peters, Phillip Pine, March 9, 1963; "Read No Evil" with Paul Fix, Robert Lansing, Frank Sinatra, Jr., March 16, 1963; "Of Rusted Canons and Fallen Sparrows" with James Gregory, Nina Foch, Michael Strong, March 23, 1963; "Season for Vengeance" with Paul Lukas, Lou Jacobi, Gusti Huber, March 30, 1963.

The 22nd Annual Golden Globes Awards. CBS awards show, with Carroll Baker, Charles Boyer, George Cukor *et al.*, February 8, 1964. O'Brien received an award for Best Actor in a Supporting Role in a Motion Picture, *Seven Days in May*.

The Greatest Show on Earth. ABC circus drama series. "Clancy" with Jack Palance, Maggie McNamara, Jody McCrea, Edmond O'Brien, February 25, 1964. O'Brien played Mike O'Kelley.

Breaking Point. ABC drama series. "The Tides of Darkness" by Meta Rosenberg, Jean Holloway, with Edmond O'Brien, Laurie Martin, Paul Richards, March 2, 1964. O'Brien played Roger Conning.

Men in Crisis. David L. Wolper Productions (32 episodes). "Hitler vs Chamberlain" April 20, 1964. "Eisenhower vs Rommel" September 17, 1964. "Mussolini vs Selassie" September 23, 1964. "Wilson vs the Senate" September 30, 1964. "MacArthur vs Welch" October 12, 1964. "De Gaulle vs Petain" October 13, 1964. "Byrd vs Amundsen" October 15, 1964. "Mao Tse-Tung vs Chiang Kai-Shek" November 13, 1964. "Rommel vs Montgomery" December 2, 1964. "Salk vs Polio" December 4, 1964. "State vs Bruno Haupmann" December 10, 1964. "Stalin vs Trotsky" December 12, 1964. "MacArthur vs Truman" December 15, 1964. "Mitchell vs Military Tradition" December 15, 1964. "Kefauver vs the Syndicates" December 20, 1964. "Churchill vs Goering" December 23, 1964. "Windsor vs the Crown" December 23, 1964. "Hitler vs Hindenburg" January 3, 1965. "Truman vs Stalin" January 5, 1965. "Khrushchev vs Nagy" January 12, 1965. "Lindbergh vs the Atlantic" February 10, 1965. "Nasser vs Ben-Gurion" February 15, 1965. "Pershing vs Ludendorff" February 26, 1964. "Roosevelt vs Isolation" February 26, 1964. "Wets vs Drys" March 10, 1965. "Darrow vs Bryan" May 6, 1965. "Castro vs Batista" May 11, 1965. "Nautilus vs the Arctic" May 11, 1964. "Kennedy vs Khrushchev" May 12, 1965. "State vs Jimmy Walker" May 14, 1964. "Grant vs Lee" May 24, 1965. "Halsey vs Yamamoto" June 7, 1965. O'Brien was the narrator.

The Eleventh Hour. NBC drama series. "The Color of Sunset" with Ralph Bellamy, Leonard Nimoy, Edmond O'Brien. April 22, 1964. O'Brien played Buck Denholt.

Freedom Spectacular. NBC all-star show in aid of the National Advancement of Colored People, with Cannonball Adderley, Harry Belafonte, Tony Bennett, Edmond O'Brien *et al.*, May 1964.

To Slay a White Horse. Syndicated documentary about the work of Synanon Drug Rehabilitation Center, Santa Monica, California, July 19, 1964. O'Brien narrated.[40]

The Hanged Man. TV movie. Director: Don Siegel. Screenplay: Jack Laird, Stanford Whitmore, adapted from the novel *Ride the Pink Horse* by Dorothy B. Hughes. Cast: Robert Culp, Vera Miles, Edmond O'Brien, Norman Fell, Gene Raymond. Revue Studios. 1964. O'Brien played *Arnie Seeger.*

Walt Disney's Wonderful World of Color. NBC/Walt Disney Productions. Children's drama series, with Edmond O'Brien, Roger Mobley, Ray Teal. "The Adventures of Gallegher" (three episodes). "The Further Adventures of Gallegher" (three episodes): "A Case of Murder," "The Big Swindle" and "The Daily Press vs. City Hall" 1965. O'Brien played Jefferson Crowley.

The Long, Hot Summer. Twentieth Century–Fox Television/ABC drama series based on the novel by William Faulkner, with Roy Thinnes, Ruth Roman, Nancy Malone, Lana Wood. "The Homecoming" September 16, 1965. "A Time for Living" September 23, 1965. "A Stranger to the House" September 30, 1965. "The Twisted Image, Part 1" October 7, 1965. "The Twisted Image, Part 2" October 14, 1965. "Home Is a Nameless Place" October 21, 1965. "No Hiding Place" October 28, 1965. "Run, Hero, Run" November 4, 1965. "The Desperate Innocent" November 11, 1965. "Bitter Harvest" November 18, 1965. "Hunter to the Wild" November 25, 1965. "Nor Hell a Fury" December 2, 1965. "The Return of the Quicks" December 16, 1965. O'Brien played "Boss" Will Varner.

The Doomsday Flight. December 13, 1966. Director: William A. Graham. Teleplay: Rod Serling. Cast: Edmond O'Brien, Van Johnson, Ed Asner, Jack Lord. Universal Television/NBC. O'Brien played *The Man.*

The Virginian. NBC Western series. "Ah Sing Vs. Wyoming" with Charles Bickford, Sarah Lane, Edmond O'Brien, Clu Gulager, October 25, 1967. O'Brien played Thomas Manstead.

The Outsider. Universal/NBC crime drama TV movie. Director: Michael Ritchie. Screenplay: Roy Huggins. Cast: Darren McGavin, Ann Sothern, Nancy Malone, Edmond O'Brien. November 27, 1967. O'Brien played Marvin Bishop.

Flesh and Blood. Dramatic Universal TV movie. Director: Arthur Penn. Screenplay: William Hanley. Cast: Edmond O'Brien, Kim Stanley, E.G. Marshall, Suzanne Pleshette, Robert Duvall. January 26, 1968. *Harry.*

Mission: Impossible. Paramount Television/CBS crime adventure series. "The Counterfeiter," with Peter Graves, Martin Landau, Barbara Bain, Edmond O'Brien, February 4, 1968. O'Brien played Raymond Halder.

It Takes a Thief. Universal Television/ABC crime adventure series, with

Robert Wagner, Edmond O'Brien, Malachi Throne. "Rock-Bye, Bye, Baby" March 25, 1969. O'Brien played Rocky McCauley.

The Bold Ones: The Protectors. Universal Television/NBC drama series, with Leslie Nielsen, Edmond O'Brien, Hari Rhodes, Robert Drivas. "If I Should Wake Before I Die" October 29, 1969. O'Brien played Warden Millbank.

The Movie Game. NBC variety game show, with guests O'Brien, Jane Fonda, Debbie Reynolds, Edmond O'Brien, Joan Rivers, August 17, 1970.

The Intruders. Universal TV Western. Director: William Graham. Screenplay: Dean Riesner. Story: William Douglas Lansford. Cast: Anne Francis, Don Murray, Edmond O'Brien, John Saxon. O'Brien played Col. William Bodeen. (Filmed in 1967, broadcast November 10, 1970).

The Young Lawyers. Paramount Television, ABC drama series. "MacGillicuddy Always Was a Pain in the Neck" with Edmond O'Brien, Lee J. Cobb, Dabbs Greer. December 21, 1970. O'Brien played MacGillicuddy.

The Name of the Game. Universal TV, NBC science fiction series. "L.A., 2017" with Gene Barry, Edmond O'Brien, Barry Sullivan, January 15, 1971. O'Brien played Bergman.

The High Chaparral. NBC Western series. "The Hostage" with Leif Erickson, Cameron Mitchell, Linda Cristal, Edmond O'Brien, March 5, 1971. O'Brien played Morgan MacQuarie.

River of Mystery. Universal Television Movie. Director: Paul Stanley. Screenplay: Albert Rubin. Cast: Vic Morrow, Niall MacGinnis, Claude Akins, Edmond O'Brien. October 1, 1971. O'Brien played R. J. Twitchell. (Made in 1969, not released until 1971).

What's a Nice Girl Like You...? Universal TV Movie. Director: Jerry Paris. Story & Screenplay: Howard Fast. Cast: Brenda Vaccaro, Jack Warden, Roddy McDowall, Jo Anne Worley, Edmond O'Brien. December 18, 1971. O'Brien played Morton Stillman.

Cade's Country. 20th Century–Fox Television, CBS western series, "The Brothers" with Glenn Ford, Edgar Buchanan, Christopher Stone, Edmond O'Brien; January 23, 1972. O'Brien played Clint Pritchard.

Jigsaw. Universal TV Movie. Director: William A. Graham. Screenplay: Robert E. Thompson. Cast: James Wainwright, Vera Miles, Andrew Duggan, Edmond O'Brien. March 26, 1972. O'Brien played Detective Ed Burtelson.

The Streets of San Francisco. Warner Brothers Television, ABC crime drama series. "The Thirty-Year Pin" with Karl Malden, Michael Douglas, Edmond O'Brien. September 23, 1972. O'Brien played Officer Gus Charnovski.

McMillan & Wife. Universal Television, NBC crime drama series. "Cop of the Year" with Rock Hudson, Susan St. James, Nancy Walker, Edmond O'Brien; November 19, 1972. O'Brien played Mr. Fontaine.

The New Temperatures Rising Show. Ashton Productions, ABC comedy series. "Super Doc" with Cleavon Little, Joan Van Ark, Reva Rose, Edmond O'Brien. March 20, 1973. O'Brien played Dr. Banning.

Isn't It Shocking? ABC mystery movie. Director: John Badham. Screenplay: Lana Slate. Cast: Alan Alda, Louise Lasser, Edmond O'Brien, Lloyd Nolan, Will Geer. October 2, 1973. O'Brien played Justin Oates.

Police Story. David Gerber Productions, NBC crime series. "Chain of Command" with Stuart Whitman, Edmond O'Brien, Charles McGraw. January 8, 1974. O'Brien played Chief Frank Modeer.

Juicio de Socrates. Series of five historical television dramas for Mexican television *Noticias de la Historia.* Director: Raul Araiza. Cast: Edmond O'Brien, Dorothy Sinclair, Telis Zotos. Telesistema Mexicano. 1974. O'Brien played Socrates.

The 50th Annual Academy Awards. ABC awards ceremony hosted by Bob Hope, with Bette Davis, Fred Astaire, Greer Garson *et al.* O'Brien appeared on stage with numerous other past Academy Awards winners, April 3, 1978.

Recordings

My Beloved: A Collection of Poetic Masterpieces. "A Blue Valentine," "Three Sonnets," Mercury A-1016: "Annabel Lee," Mercury A-1017: "High Flight," Mercury A-1018, (10" 78rpm records), July 20, 1946. *Reader.*

My Beloved: A Collection of Poetic Masterpieces. "A Blue Valentine," by Joyce Kilmer; "Annabel Lee," by Edgar Allan Poe; Three Sonnets—"How Do I Love Thee," by Elizabeth Barrett Browning—"The Hill," by Rupert Brooke—Renouncement," by Alice Meynell; "The Windy Nights,"—"If I Had Loved You More,"—"Atonement," by Aline Murray Kilmer; Three Sonnets—"High Flight,"- by John Gillespie Magee, Jr., "Safety," by Rupert Brooke—"The Dead," by Rupert Brooke; "My Last Duchess," by Robert Browning. *Reader.* Mercury 10" LP Reissue, MG-25013, July 15, 1950. Reissued on CD by NAXOS NS1206 (2013) and available digitally.

Julius Caesar. MGM Cast recording EP K204 (45 rpm); MGM E3033 (33⅓ rpm), August 29, 1953. *Casca.* Also released in the UK as ***Highlights from the MGM Film Soundtrack of William Shakespeare's Julius Caesar*** EMI/Music for Pleasure MFP 2122 circa 1962.

Hail, America! RCA Custom Records RR3M-1429: "I Am an American" (Carmen Dragon, Elizabeth Ellen Evans, Adrian Michaelis) *Narrator.* Circa 1955.

Pete Kelly's Blues. Film soundtrack with narrative by Jack Webb. RCA Victor LPM-1126, 1955.

The Red Badge of Courage by Stephen Crane. Caedmon Records TC—1040, July 29, 1957. Narrator. Digitally available.

The Girl Can't Help It. Film Soundtrack. "Rock Around the Rock Pile" performed by Ray Anthony & His Orchestra; *vocal.* Capitol Records 7" EP EAP 1–823 (UK) 1956. Almost full soundtrack reissued (minus two tracks) as a picture disc by All Round Trading PD 1050 2008 (Denmark).

Sing Boy Sing. Film Soundtrack, by Tommy Sands. Features stills from the film. Capitol Records T 929, 1958.

Radio Greats Volume 5. Yours Truly, Johnny Dollar/Sam Spade. O'Brien and Howard Duff depicted on the cover. Side 1: "The Amelia Harwell Matter" LP Radio RG 105/ 41291. Circa 1974.

Classic Programs from the Golden Age of Radio: Yours Truly, Johnny Dollar. O'Brien is depicted on the cover. Four episodes; No.2 stars O'Brien: "The Dead First Helpers Matter" Cassette issued by The Audio File of Glendale, Illinois: No. YT 2401. Circa 1976.

The History of Henry Esmond, Esq. by William Makepeace Thackeray. NBC University Theater, March 27, 1949. *Henry Esmond.* Saland Publishing, 2010 (Digital).

Chapter Notes

Chapter 1

1. United States. Census Bureau. *James O'Brien*, Washington, GPO, 1910.
2. "O'Brien—Descendants of the High King." *Ireland Calling*, http://ireland-calling.com/irish-names-obrien/.
3. Connellan, Owen, translator. *The Annals of Ireland Translated from the Original Irish of the Four Masters*. Dublin, Bryan Geraghty, 1846.
4. "New York City Marriage Records, 1829–1940: James O'Brien and Agnes Baldwin, Nov. 23, 1898, Manhattan, New York." *FamilySearch*, https://familysearch.org/ark:/61903/1:1:24ZD-KCW.
5. Braggioti, Mary. "Close-Up." *New York Evening Post*, 2 Dec. 1943, p. 12.
6. Ireland Civil Registration Indexes, 1845–1958, Marriages entry for Michael Baldwin; citing Fermoy, 1871, vol. 4, p. 937, General Register Office, Custom House, Dublin: Family Search (https://familysearch.org/ark:/61903/1:1:FYSN-H2Z).
7. "Irish Surname—Tobin." *Ireland Roots*, http://irelandroots.com/tobin.htm.
8. Braggioti, Mary. "Close-Up." *New York Evening Post*, 2 Dec. 1943, p. 12.
9. United States. Census Bureau. Washington, GPO, 1910, 1920, 1930.
10. "Edmond O'Brien Home for 'Flesh and Blood.'" *Schenectady Gazette*, 28 Jan. 1968, p. 7.
11. Hopper, Hedda. "Fishing Relaxation of Edmond O'Brien." *Valley Morning Star*, 6 May 1963, p. 10.
12. Hopper, Hedda. "Edmond O'Brien Feels Better When He Is on the Move." *The Kansas City Times*, 11 March 1965, p. 38.
13. "Edmond O'Brien Home for 'Flesh and Blood.'" *Schenectady Gazette*, 28 Jan. 1968, p. 7.
14. Soanes, Wood. "Curtain Call: Edmond O'Brien Got Easy Start in His Stage Career." *Oakland Tribune*, 31 Oct. 1950, p. 19.
15. "Irishmen of Note in American Life." *The Advocate*, 15 Dec. 1945, p. 4.
16. Oliver, Myrna. "Obituaries: Liam O'Brien: Movie Writer, TV Producer." *The Los Angeles Times*, 26 March 1996, p. 33.
17. Scheuer, Steven H. "Edmond O'Brien Wanted to Act." *Citizen Reporter*, 15 Feb. 1960, p. 9.
18. Program for *John van Druten*'s I've Got Sixpence at the Shubert Theater, New Haven. Playbill, 1952.
19. Scott, John L. "O'Brien Fell Flat in Debut." *The Los Angeles Times*, 16 Dec. 1956, p. 119.
20. Braggioti, Mary. "Close-Up: to His New Air Base on 44th Street." *New York Evening Post*, 2 Dec. 1943, p. 18.
21. "Edmond O'Brien." *Film Dope*, 1991, pp. 46–49.
22. Kane, Patrice M. Email. Received by Derek Sculthorpe, 25 July 2016.
23. Hopper, Hedda. "Edmond O'Brien Feels Better When He Is on the Move." *The Kansas City Times*, 11 March 1965, p. 38.
24. "Stage Player Learns New Tricks in Films." *The Montreal Gazette*, 28 Dec. 1939, p. 3.
25. Garrett, Betty. *Betty Garrett & Other Songs: A Life of Stage and Screen*. Madison Books, 1999.
26. Anderson, Nancy. "Yesterday's Stars Today: O'Brien Brilliant in Conversation." *Lodi News-Sentinel*, 20 Oct. 1972, p. 7.
27. "The Prince Hal of 'King Henry IV.'" *The New York Sun*, 25 Feb. 1939, p. 29.
28. Anderson, Nancy. "Yesterday's Stars Today: O'Brien Brilliant in Conversation." *Lodi News-Sentinel*, 20 Oct. 1972, p. 7.
29. Sheaffer, Lew. "Concerning the Activities of Amateur and Semi-Professional

Groups: The Little Theaters." *The Brooklyn Daily Eagle*, 14 April 1935, p. E9.
  30. Hopper, Hedda. "Edmond O'Brien Feels Better When He Is on the Move." *The Kansas City Times*, 11 March 1965, p. 38.
  31. "Players Forgot That Columbus 'No Spika Da Eengleesh' at All." *The Jackson Sun*, 15 Feb. 1951, p. 9.

Chapter 2

  1. "The Prince Hal of 'King Henry IV.'" *The New York Sun*, 25 Feb. 1939, p. 29.
  2. "In Leading Role: Herbert Duffy to Play Lead in Mystery Drama 'The Bat' Next Week." *The Herald Statesman*, 20 June 1936, p. 14.
  3. "Urban Playhouse Audience Is Amused by 'Meet the Wife.'" *The Herald Statesman*, 30 June 1936, p. 14.
  4. "Audience Thrills and Chills Mark 'The Bat' Presentation." *The Herald Statesman*, 23 June 1936, p. 9.
  5. Mason Brown, John. "Two on the Aisle: Robert Turney's 'Daughters of Atreus' at the 44th St." *New York Post*, 15 Oct. 1936, p. 21.
  6. "The Prince Hal of 'King Henry IV.'" *The New York Sun*, 25 Feb. 1939, p. 29.
  7. Anderson, Nancy. "Yesterday's Stars Today: O'Brien Brilliant in Conversation." *Lodi News-Sentinel*, 20 Oct. 1972, p. 7.
  8. "'Brush Up Your Shakespeare' Says Film Actor Edmond O'Brien." *The Montreal Gazette*, 18 July 1951, p. 9.
  9. "Westport to Stage New Langner Play." *Wilton Bulletin*, 28 July 1938, p. 8.
  10. Oderman, Stuart. *Lillian Gish: A Life on Stage & Screen*. McFarland, 2000.
  11. Francis, Robert. "The Theater: 'The Star Wagon' at the Empire an Old Story Well Presented with Burgess Meredith, Russell Collins, Lillian Gish." *The Brooklyn Daily Eagle*, 30 Sept 1937, p. 23.
  12. Johnson, Erskine. "Edmond O'Brien One Who Doesn't Mock Television." *The North Adams Transcript*, 23 Oct. 1965, p. 12.
  13. The Play's the Thing" *The Yale Daily News*, January 21, 1938, 2; "Mercury Theater's Vital Productions Win Praise," *The Pittsburgh Press*, 22 Feb. 1938, p. 15.
  14. Fisher Parry, Florence. "On with the Show: Nixon's Production Is 'Spot News' Drama." *The Pittsburgh Press*, 1 March 1938, p. 10.
  15. Cohen, Harold V. "Orson Welles Brings An Exciting 'Julius Caesar' to the Nixon." *Pittsburgh Post-Gazette*, 1 March 1938, p. 12.
  16. Scheuer, Steven H. "TV Keynotes: Edmond O'Brien Wanted to Act." *Citizen Register*, 15 Feb. 1960, p. 9.
  17. Hopper, Hedda. "Hollywood: Weekend of a Century." *The Times*, 24 June 1942, p. 5.
  18. "Road 'Caesar' Ends Tour with 'Bury Dead.'" *Variety*, 18 May 1938, p. 47.
  19. "Fool's Hill at Mt Kisco Playhouse." *Dobbs Ferry Register*, 24 June 1938, p. 6.
  20. "Woman Who Hires and Fires Actors Makes Stage Debut." *Hartford Courant*, 3 Aug. 1938, p. 6.
  21. "Play Centered About Blind Presented at Mount Kisco." *The Daily News*, 26 July 1938, p. 3.
  22. Thomas, Bob. "Hollywood." *The Miami News*, 15 July 1945, p. 13.
  23. "Plays on B'way: Henry IV (Part 1)." *Variety*, 1 Feb. 1939, p. 50.
  24. Wolfert, Ira. "Shakespeare Now Termed Six Per Cent Will." *The Miami News*, 12 Feb. 1939, p. 42.
  25. Pollack, Arthur. "The Theaters: Maurice Evans, Playing Falstaff in Shakespeare's 'Henry IV' Adds a Bright New Portrait to His Choice Collection." *The Brooklyn Daily Eagle*, 31 Jan. 1939, p. 7.
  26. "Seven Weeks More for 'Henry IV.'" *The New York Post*, 13 Feb. 1939, p. 8.
  27. "Winner's Not Scared of That Jinx." *The Singapore Free Press*, 8 Oct. 1955, p. 17.
  28. Mason Brown, John. "Two on the Aisle: Maurice Evans Fine Playing of Sir John." *New York Post*, 22 March 1939, p. 22.
  29. Lockridge, Richard. "The New Play: Maurice Evans Revives 'Henry IV, Part I' at the St James Theater." *The New York Sun*, 31 Jan. 1939, p. 18.
  30. Fidler, Jimmie. "Hollywood Roundup." *The Evening Standard*, 17 April 1939, p. 24.
  31. "Locust Valley Lists 3 Tryouts; Spa, Long Beach, New Hope, Skeds: Dimond at Long Beach." *Variety*, 21 June 1939, p. 48.
  32. O'Hara, Maureen.*'Tis Herself: An Autobiography*. Simon & Schuster, 2005.
  33. Walker, Paul. "Previews." *Harrisburg Telegraph*, 28 Dec. 1939, p. 5.
  34. David, George L. "'Hunchback' Scores as Film Masterpiece." *Democrat & Chronicle*, 31 Dec. 1939, p. 22.
  35. Schallert, Edwin. "'Hunchback' Absorbing Spectacular Offering." *The Los Angeles Times*, 15 Dec. 1939, p. 44.
  36. Jewel, Richard. "RKO Film Grosses 1931–51." *Historical Journal of Film, Radio and Television*, vol. 14, no. 1, 1994, p. 56.
  37. Higham, Charles. *Charles Laughton: An Intimate Biography*. Doubleday, 1976.
  38. Carroll, Harrison. "In Hollywood." *The Daily Journal*, 29 Aug. 1939, p. 4.
  39. "Re-Signs O'Brien," *BoxOffice*, 11 Nov. 1939, p. 112.
  40. Pollack, Arthur. "The Theater: Ruth

Chatterton Here in Van Druten Play." *The Brooklyn Daily Eagle*, 28 Feb. 1940, p. 8.
  41. Lockridge, Richard. "The New Play: Ruth Chatterton Returns in 'Leave Her to Heaven' at the Longacre." *The New York Sun*, 28 Feb. 1940, p. 18.
  42. Quick, Dorothy. "What's New in New York." *The East Hampton Star*, 21 March 1940, p. 4.
  43. Barron, Mark. "Broadway: Youth and Experience Vie in Writing: Ruth Chatterton Returns." *Buffalo Courier-Express*, 3 March 1940, p. 13.
  44. Ziegler, Philip. *Olivier*. MacLehose Press, 2013.
  45. Arthur Pollock "Amusements: Olivier and Leigh Meet Shakespeare" *The Brooklyn Daily Eagle*, May 10, 1940, 21.
  46. Watts, Jr., Richard. "Vivien Leigh, Laurence Olivier, Fail to Click in Bard's Romance." *The Pittsburgh Press*, 19 May 1940.
  47. Wolfert, Ira. "Distinguished Actors Unable to Save Two Broadway Shows." *Great Falls Tribune*, 27 May 1940, p. 4.
  48. Wilde, Cornel. Television interview with Skip E. Lowe, 1987.
  49. Vickers, Hugo. *Vivien Leigh*. Hamish Hamilton, 1988).

Chapter 3

  1. "Laraine Day Wins 'Future Star' Ballot." *Motion Picture Daily*, 8 Aug. 1941, p. 6.
  2. "Critics of U.S. Vote 'Chips' Best Picture." *Motion Picture Daily*, 27 Feb. 1940, p. 9.
  3. Cohn, Herbert. "The Sound Track." *The Brooklyn Daily Eagle*, 27 April 1941, p. 46.
  4. "Harold Lloyd Has Added Many New Personalities to Screendom." *The Salt Lake Tribune*, 4 Jan. 1941, p. 20.
  5. McCaffrey, Donald W. *Three Classic Silent Screen Comedies Starring Harold Lloyd*. Fairleigh Dickinson University Press, 1976.
  6. *Good Housekeeping*, vol. 140, 1955, p. 199.
  7. Brownlow, Kevin. *The Parade's Gone By*. University of California Press, 1968.
  8. "Lloyd Film, Laugh Riot." *Newark Courier-Gazette & Marion Enterprise*, 17 April 1941, p. 12.
  9. Lawson, Edna W. "Lloyd's Touch Put on Comedy." *Honolulu Star-Advertiser*, 5 March 1941, p. 4.
  10. Brady Kathleen. *Lucille*. Billboard Books, 2001.
  11. "Let's Hear from You: Bole Seeks Audience Recruit on 'A Girl, a Guy and a Gob.'" *Motion Picture Herald*, 22 March 1941, p. 63.
  12. Church, Roy A., and Andrew Godley, editors. *The Emergence of Modern Marketing*. Frank Cass, 2003.
  13. "Para. Drops Spanish Films, Signs Latin-American Star." *Motion Picture Daily*, 25 Sept. 1940, p. 4.
  14. "Screen Stars." *Cazenovia Republican*, 24 Oct. 1940, p. 3.
  15. Fidler, Jimmie. "In Hollywood." *The Los Angeles Times*, 9 Dec. 1941, p. 49.
  16. "In Camp." *Motion Picture Herald*, 23 Aug. 1941, p. 11.
  17. "'Parachute Battalion' Opens." *Motion Picture Herald*, 23 Aug. 1941, p. 18.
  18. "Variety Club Notes: Tent No. 24 Charlotte." *Showmen's Trade Review*, 30 Aug. 1941, p. 24.
  19. "Romance for Nancy and Ed Negotiates Rough Course." *The Pittsburgh Press*, 6 April 1941, p. 22.
  20. "Lovely Nancy Kelly Returns to Mother." *San Bernardino Sun*, 21 June 1941, p. 2.
  21. Casey, Tom. "Nancy Kelly's Strange Marriage Pact." *Hollywood*, June 1941, p. 23.
  22. "Nancy Kelly Marries O'Brien After Dinner." *The Morning News*, 20 Feb. 1941, p. 2.
  23. "Actress Nancy Kelly Married." *St. Louis Post-Dispatch*, 19 Feb. 1941, p. 9.
  24. Graham, Sheilah. "Joan Leslie Draws $300 a Week, Once Couldn't Get $50." *Buffalo Courier-Express*, 8 July 1941, p. 22.
  25. "Hollywood Round and Round." *Pittsburgh Post-Gazette*, 27 June 1941, p. 2.
  26. "Actress Files Suit to Obtain Freedom." *San Bernardino Sun*, 7 Jan. 1942, p. 19.
  27. "Nancy Kelly Files Suit for Divorce." *The Pittsburgh Press*, 6 Jan. 1942, p. 24.
  28. "Divorces Tardy Date." *San Bernardino Sun*, 3 Feb. 1942, p. 2.
  29. Fidler, Jimmie. "Actress Revives Divorce Suit." *The Los Angeles Times*, 31 Dec. 1941, p. 16.
  30. "Nancy Kelly Alimony Fought." *Los Angeles Times*, 22 Jan. 1942, p. 10.
  31. "Coburn Starred." *Variety*, 7 May 1941, p. 4.
  32. "Filmdom News Reel." *Buffalo Courier-Express*, 15 June 1941, p. 5.
  33. Cohen, Harold V. "The Drama Desk: News from Hollywood." *Pittsburgh Post-Gazette*, 18 Feb. 1942, p. 4.
  34. "Actress Gets Even; Ducks Fellow Actor," *The Indianapolis Star*, 25 Jan. 1942, p. 4.
  35. Wells, J. N. "What the Picture Did for Me: RKO Radio: Obliging Young Lady." *Motion Picture Herald*, 18 July 1942, p. 53.
  36. "Program Notes from the Studios." *Showmen's Trade Review*, 31 Jan. 1942, p. 38.

37. Thomas, Bob. "I Said It and I'm Glad: Film Stars Name Worst Picture." *The Evening Independent*, 25 Aug. 1948, p. 9.
38. Renoir, Jean. *Renoir on Renoir: Interviews, Essays & Remarks*. Cambridge University Press, 1989.

Chapter 4

1. Dixon, Hugh. "Hollywood: Notes for a Column." *Pittsburgh Post-Gazette*, 24 July 1942, p. 21.
2. Schallert, Edwin. "Warners to Pair Brent, Brenda Marshall Again." *The Los Angeles Times*, 23 May 1942, p. 9.
3. "Michele Morgan Married." *The Philadelphia Inquirer*, 17 Sept. 1942, p. 17.
4. Fidler, Jimmie. "In Hollywood." *Battle Creek Enquirer*, 10 March 1942, p. 4.
5. Kilgallen, Dorothy. "Voice of Broadway: Gossip in Gotham." *Shamokin News-Dispatch*, 21 March 1942, p. 27.
6. Coons, Robbin. "Hollywood." *News-Journal*, 19 Oct. 1942, p. 2.
7. "Hollywood Here and There." *The Philadelphia Inquirer*, 17 Aug. 1942, p. 11.
8. York, Cal. "Cal York's Inside Stuff." *Photoplay*, Aug. 1942, p. 10.
9. York, Cal. "Cal York's Inside Stuff." *Photoplay*, Oct. 1942, p. 15.
10. Parsons, Louella O. "Bob Hope Seeks to Cut Movie Output; Wants More Time to Entertain Men in Camps." *The Fresno Bee the Republican*, 21 Oct. 1942, p. 7.
11. Davis, Walt. "Candidly Yours." *Modern Screen*, Dec. 1942, p. 48.
12. Dixon, Hugh. "Hollywood." *Pittsburgh Post-Gazette*, 11 Dec. 1942, p. 19.
13. Kilgallen, Dorothy. "Down Hollywood Way." *News-Journal*, 26 June 1943, p. 2.
14. "Films' O'Brien and Luke Lea Pals at Beach," *The Miami News*, April 23, 1943, 10.
15. "Army Air Force Show," *The Miami News*, April 3, 1943, 8.
16. Thomas, Bob. "In Hollywood." *News-Journal*, 3 May 1945, p. 13.
17. Vernon, Scott. "TV Profile: 'Sam Benedict' Role Means Lots of Homework for Eddie." *Hartford Courant*, 28 April 1963, p. 136.
18. Francis, Robert. "Candid Close-Ups: Edmond O'Brien's Brooklyn Flier Is Top-Flight in 'Winged Victory.'" *The Brooklyn Daily Eagle*, 12 Dec. 1943, p. 34.
19. Thomas, Bob. "Million Dollar Cast Now a Thing of the Past." *Binghampton Press*, 17 Nov. 1953, p. 20.
20. Nichols, Lewis. "The Play in Review: 'Winged Victory.'" *The New York Times*, 22 Nov. 1943, p. 63.
21. Thomas, Bob. "Million Dollar Cast Now a Thing of the Past." *Binghampton Press*, 17 Nov. 1953, p. 20.
22. Francis, Robert. "Candid Close-Ups: Edmond O'Brien's Brooklyn Flier Is Top-Flight in 'Winged Victory.'" *The Brooklyn Daily Eagle*, 12 Dec. 1943, p. 34.
23. Cesari, Ernesto. *Mario Lanza: An American Tragedy*. Baskerville Publishing, 2004.
24. Handsaker, Gene. "Sights and Sounds from Hollywood." *The Leader-Republican*, 14 April 1951, p. 4.
25. Garrett, Betty, and Dorothy Kilgallen. "Voice of Broadway: Broadway Bulletin." *Pittsburgh Post-Gazette*, 1 Oct. 1943, p. 25. Duke, Doris. "Hollywood." *Star Tribune*, 24 March 1945, p. 4. Andrews, Lois, and Dorothy Kilgallen. "On Broadway: Gossip in Gotham." *Pittsburgh Post-Gazette*, 20 March 1945, p. 18.
26. "Snapshots of Hollywood." *Democrat and Chronicle*, 31 March 1945, p. 9.
27. Nigh, Jane, and Dixon, Hugh.. "Hollywood: Around the Town." *Pittsburgh Post-Gazette*, 10 Nov. 1945, p. 16. Albritton, Louise, and Hedda Hopper. "Hollywood." *The Indiana Gazette*, 31 Jan. 1946, p. 13.
28. Lyons, Leonard. "The Lyons Den." *Endicott Daily Bulletin*, 23 March 1944, p. 4.
29. Gorham, Ken. "Town Hall Theater, Middleburg, Vermont: What the Picture Did for Me." *Motion Picture Herald*, 24 Feb. 1945, p. 62.
30. W. E. J. M., "Review of the Theater: Shea's Great Lakes." *Buffalo Courier-Express*, 19 Jan. 1945, p. 18.
31. "Learned About Brooklyn from the Army." *The Brooklyn Daily Eagle*, 11 Feb. 1944, p. 27.
32. Graham, Sheilah. "In Hollywood Today." *The Indianapolis Star*, 11 June 1945, p. 4.

Chapter 5

1. Hopper, Hedda. "Non-Stop Edmond O'Brien." *The Detroit Press*, 9 March 1965, p. 17.
2. Cassidy, Claudia. "'Porgy and Bess' Returns Tomorrow." *Chicago Tribune*, 3 Dec. 1944, p. 68.
3. "Radio News Pictures Programs Radio Listings: Edmund O'Brien in Drama; WEAF 10:30; Neutrality Topic of Radio Focus on WABC." *The Central New Jersey Homes News*, 14 Oct. 1939, p. 5.
4. "Radio: Two Programs Based on Life of Lincoln to Be Broadcast Tonight on NBC

and CBS." *The Central New Jersey Homes News*, 10 Feb. 1940, p. 3.
  5. Lyons, Leonard. "Broadway Notes: The Lyons Den." *The Pittsburgh Post-Gazette*, 31 Dec. 1941, p. 18.
  6. "Soldier Show." *The Miami News*, 7 April 1943, p. 8.
  7. "Ambitious Radio Show." *The Miami News*, 25 March 1943, p. 18.
  8. "Edmond O'Brien on 'War Town' Broadcast." *The Plain Speaker*, 13 July 1944, p. 6.
  9. Johnson, Erskine. "In Hollywood: Edmond O'Brien Tough Only in Studio Scenes." *San Bernardino Sun*, 2 Dec. 1950, p. 4.
  10. Steinhauser, Si. "Theater Owners Seek Hearings on Television." *The Pittsburgh Press*, 11 July 1950, p. 34.
  11. Johnson, Erskine. "In Hollywood: Edmond O'Brien Only Tough in Studio Scenes." *San Bernardino Sun*, 2 Dec. 1950, p. 4.
  12. Sterling, Christopher H. *Encyclopedia of Radio*. Routledge, 2004.
  13. Cox, Jim. *American Radio Networks: A History*. McFarland, 2009.
  14. Terrace, Vincent. *The Encyclopedia of Television Pilots 1937–2012*. McFarland, 2013.
  15. Ames, Walter. "Compulsory Wanderlust Grips Ed O'Brien; Pantomime Quiz Back on TV Screen Tonight." *The Los Angeles Times*, 4 July 1952, p. 42.
  16. Salmaggi, Bob. "Man of Many Faces O'Brien Enjoys Himself in New Detective Series." *The Corpus Christi Caller-Times*, 10 April 1960, p. 28.
  17. Terrace, Vincent. *The Encyclopedia of Television Pilots 1937–2012*. McFarland, 2013.
  18. "Radio." *The Pittsburgh Press*, 23 Jan. 1949, p. 52.
  19. "Hollywood—(NC)." *North Country Edition of Our Sunday Visitor*, 29 Aug. 1954, p. 7A.
  20. "Radio Theater." *The Miami News*, 19 April 1954.
  21. Handsaker, Gene. "Sights and Sounds from Hollywood." *The Leader-Republican*, 14 April 1951, p. 4.
  22. Scheuer, Steven. "TV Keynotes: Edmond O'Brien Wanted to Act." *Citizen Reporter*, 15 Feb. 1960, p. 9.
  23. Sleeve Notes. *Hail, America!*, RCA Custom LP, 1954.
  24. "Edmond O'Brien Dies." *The Bryan Times*, 7 May 1985, p. 3.
  25. "Reviews and Ratings of New Popular Albums: Spoken Word: The Red Badge of Courage." *Billboard*, 29 July 1957, p. 32.
  26. The *Edmond O'Brien Collection* consisting of 105 programs including many episodes of *Yours Truly, Johnny Dollar*, is available in three different formats from the Old Time Radio Catalog: See OTRCAT.com https://www.otrcat.com/p/edmond-obrien.

Chapter 6

  1. "Film Contract Prohibits Plays." *The Philadelphia Inquirer*, 22 Aug. 1943, p. 11.
  2. Cohen, Harold V. "The Drama Desk: Observation Post." *Pittsburgh Post-Gazette*, 26 Feb. 1943, p. 10.
  3. Lait, Jr., Jack. "Hollywood." *The Brooklyn Daily Eagle*, 4 Nov. 1946, p. 14.
  4. Wilson, Earl. "It Happened Last Night: Clothes Make the Man—and Stars, in Hollywood." *New York Post*, 13 Jan. 1950, p. 17.
  5. Connelly, Lyn. "Peeks at the Stars." *The Vestal News*, 10 Oct. 1951, p. 7.
  6. Fishgall, Larry. *Against Type: The Biography of Burt Lancaster*. Simon & Schuster, 1995
  7. Fishgall, Larry. *Against Type: The Biography of Burt Lancaster*. Simon & Schuster, 1995
  8. Bishop, Jim. *The Mark Hellinger Story: A Biography of Broadway and Hollywood*. Appleton-Century-Crofts, 1952.
  9. "Hellinger Visits Key Towns to Ballyhoo 'The Killers.'" *Motion Picture Herald*, 24 Aug. 1946, p. 44.
  10. Manners, Dorothy. "Starlets Named for Remake of 'Stage Door' Claire Trevor to do Robert Montgomery Play." *The Cincinnati Enquirer*, 23 Aug. 1946, p. 15.
  11. Hopper, Hedda. "Looking at Hollywood: Sitting It Out." *Harrisburg Telegraph*, 21 May 1947, p. 8.
  12. "TCM Notes *Ivy* (1947)." *Turner Classic Movies*, http://www.tcm.com/tcmdb/title/79611/Ivy/notes.html.
  13. "Powell Plans 2-Year Leave from MGM Lot." *The Bee*, 28 July 1947, p. 14.
  14. "Early Day Song in Madera Film: 'The Web' Tonight." *Madera Tribune*, 4 Oct. 1947, p. 4.
  15. "'The Web' Brilliantly-acted Melodrama Packed with Surprises." *Independent Exhibitors Film Bulletin*, 9 June 1947, p. 17.
  16. "A Double Life U-I-Kanin—Distinguished Entertainment." *Motion Picture Herald*, 3 Jan. 1948, p. 4001.
  17. "Box Office Slant: A Double Life." *Showmen's Trade Review*, 3 Jan. 1948, p. 15.
  18. "Women ... as Edmond O'Brien sees them." Advert in unnamed film magazine in pile of cuttings, circa 1947, p. 14.

Chapter 7

1. "Spinsters Call Edmond O'Brien Most Magnetic" *The Los Angeles Times*, December 27, 1949, 23; "Actor Edmond O'Brien Named Most Magnetic." *The Brooklyn Daily Eagle*, 27 Dec. 1949, p. 12.
2. "Top Ten Stars of Tomorrow." *Motion Picture Herald*, 30 Aug. 1947, p. 12.
3. "Janitor's Girl, 8, Steals Show in Comedy." *Democrat & Chronicle*, 7 Aug. 1951, p. 12.
4. "Briefs from the Lots." *Variety*, 4 June 1947. p. 7.
5. Hopper, Hedda. "Looking at Hollywood." *The Los Angeles Times*, 27 Nov. 1947, p. 19.
6. Parsons, Louella O. "In Hollywood With." *Albany New York Times-Union*, 15 April 1951, p. B-11.
7. Lyons, Leonard. "In the Lyons Den." *Endicott Daily Bulletin*, 5 Jan. 1948, p. 4.
8. Paris, Michael. *From the Wright Brothers to Top Gun: Aviation, Nationalism and Popular Cinema*. Manchester University Press, 1995.
9. "Film at Playhouse Shows Actual Scenes of Combat." *Tampa Bay Times*, 5 Jan. 1949, p. 20.
10. Thomas, Bob. "Show to Aid Victims of Floods Planned in Hollywood." *Lubbock Evening Journal*, 9 June 1948, p. 15.
11. "'Chute Leap for Movie Shot in 2 Locations." *The Post-Standard*, 17 Jan. 1949, p. 8.
12. "Scene Too Realistic; Wrestling Actor Hurt." *San Bernardino Sun*, 11 July 1948, p. 14.
13. Fristoe, Roger. "Notes; Fighter Squadron (1948)." *Tampa Bay Times*, http://www.tcm.com/tcmdb/title/1663/Fighter-Squadron/articles.html.
14. "Odd Fan Gift." *Democrat & Chronicle*, 9 Jan. 1949, p. 66.
15. Hopper, Hedda. "Hollywood." *Hartford Courant*, 18 Aug. 1948, p. 16.
16. "Reported Romancing." *The Brownsville Herald*, 28 Aug. 1946, p. 14.
17. Knudsen, Peggy, and Dixon, Hugh.. "Hollywood Movie Memos." *Pittsburgh Post-Gazette*, 5 Nov. 1946, p. 18. Mauree, Mike, and Dorothy Kilgallen. "Voice of Broadway." *Toledo Blade*, 16 Dec. 1946, p. 31. Carter, Helena, and Dixon, Hugh. "Hollywood: The Monday Wash." *Pittsburgh Post-Gazette*, 24 March 1947, p. 15.
18. Lait, Jr., Jack. "Hollywood: Romantic Roundup." *The Brooklyn Daily Eagle*, 24 March 1947, p. 4.
19. Totter, Audrey, and Dixon, Hugh. "Hollywood; Around the Town." *Pittsburgh Post-Gazette*, 9 April 1947, p. 13. Caulfield, Joan, and Dixon, Hugh. "Hollywood." *Pittsburgh Post-Gazette*, 3 May 1947, p. 18.
20. Skolsky, Sidney. "Hollywood Is My Beat: Tintyped: Edmond O'Brien Tough Shakespearean." *New York Post*, 26 Oct. 1953, p. E14.
21. "Olga San Juan of Flatbush, Talked, Talked and Pleaded." *The Brooklyn Daily Eagle*, 6 Oct. 1946, p. 29.
22. Sheaffer, Louis. "Curtain Time: Olga San Juan Glad She Went to Those Two Parties." *The Brooklyn Daily Eagle*, 4 Dec. 1951, p. 18.
23. "Olga San Juan of Flatbush, Talked, Talked and Pleaded." *The Brooklyn Daily Eagle*, 6 Oct. 1946, p. 29.
24. Sheaffer, Louis. "Curtain Time: Olga San Juan Glad She Went to Those Two Parties." *The Brooklyn Daily Eagle*, 4 Dec. 1951, p. 18.
25. Sheaffer, Louis. "Curtain Time: Olga San Juan Glad She Went to Those Two Parties." *The Brooklyn Daily Eagle*, 4 Dec. 1951, p. 18.
26. Skolsky, Sidney. "Hollywood Is My Beat: Tintyped: Edmond O'Brien Tough Shakespearean." *New York Post*, 26 Oct. 1953, p. E14.
27. San Juan, Olga. "Why I Fell in Love with Eddie." *Screenland*, June 1951, p. 46.
28. "Movies' O'Brien and Olga San Juan Wed." *San Bernardino Sun*, 27 Sept. 1948, p. 1. "California, County Marriages, 1850–1952." database with images, *Family Search*, 28 Nov. 2014, https://familysearch.org/ark:/61903/1:1:K8KT-1WH. James Alfred O'Brien in entry for Edmond Joseph O'Brien and Olga Mercedes San Juan, 26 Sep 1948; citing Los Angeles, California, United States, county courthouses, California; FHL microfilm 2,116,805.
29. "Rudely Shocked." *Lansing State Journal*, 30 Jan. 1949, p. 30.
30. Bower, Helen. "Star Gazing: In Judging, the Heart Can't Be Counted Out." *Detroit Free Press*, 19 Feb. 1949, p. 15.
31. Lee Carroll. "Geraldine Brooks: Making Every Minute Count." *Screenland*, Sept. 1948, p. 64.

Chapter 8

1. "Edmond O'Brien Gets Warner Brothers Job." *The Central New Jersey Home News*, 23 May 1948, p. 24.
2. "AFI Catalog of Feature Films: Backfire." *AFI*, http://www.afi.com/members/catalog/DetailView.aspx?s=&Movie=26213.
3. "'Backfire' Run-of-the-mill Mystery Meller." *Film Bulletin*, 30 Jan. 1950, p. 12.

4. Sherman, Vincent. *Studio Affairs: My Life as a Film Director.* University of Kentucky Press, 1996.
5. *Time* quoted in Halliwell, Leslie, *Halliwell's Film Guide.* Guild Publishing Ltd, 1983.
6. Crowther, Bosley. "The Screen in Review: James Cagney Back as Gangster in 'White Heat.' Thriller Now at the Strand." *The New York Times,* 3 Sept. 1949, p. 51.
7. Cohen, Harold V. "New Film: James Cagney in 'White Heat' Comes to Stanley." *Pittsburgh Post-Gazette,* 10 Sept. 1949, p. 22.
8. Freeland, Michael. *James Cagney.* W. H. Allen, 1974.
9. Cagney, James. "In Hollywood: Cagney Puts Axiom Before Public 'Crime Doesn't Pay.'" *Plattsburgh Press-Republican,* 27 Aug. 1949, p. 5.
10. Gerhard, Inez. "Star Dust: Stage Screen Radio." *The Boyden Reporter,* 23 June 1949, p. 4.
11. "Unexpected Realism." *Showmen's Trade Review,* 4 June 1949, p. 30.
12. Robinson, Johnny. "Clark Finally Draws a Comedy Role in Hollywood." *Lewiston Evening Journal,* 4 Aug. 1949, p. 17.
13. Scott, Vernon. "TV Profile: 'Sam Benedict' Role Means Lots of Homework for Eddie." *Hartford Courant,* 28 April 1963, p. 136.
14. Graham, Sheilah. "Hollywood." *Pittsburgh Post-Gazette,* 12 Sept. 1949, p. 10.
15. Hopper, Hedda. "Facts on Garbo-James Mason Picture." *Toledo Blade,* 7 Sept. 1949, p. 40.
16. "Star Stage Drama Aimed at O'Brien." *Los Angeles Times,* 10 Jan. 1950, p. 25.
17. Hopper, Hedda. "Gene Fowler Will Write William O'Dwyer Story." *Los Angeles Times,* 6 Oct. 1950, p. 36.
18. Meil, Eila. *Casting Might-Have-Beens: A Film by Film Directory of Roles Given to Others.* McFarland, 2005.
19. Mattheis, Paul. *The 12 O'Clock High Log Book: The Unofficial History of the Novel, Motion Picture and TV Series.* McFarland, 2005.
20. Graham, Sheilah. "News and Views from Hollywood Notebook." *Ottawa Citizen,* 15 July 1950, p. 30.
21. Schallert, Edwin. "Next Berle Picture Set; Glamour Queen Resumes; Van Upp Buys 'Jughead.'" *The Los Angeles Times,* 1 May 1950, p. 47.
22. Schallert, Edwin. "O'Brien Urges 'Pachuco.'" *The Los Angeles Times,* 17 Jan. 1950, p. A7.
23. Schallert, Edwin. "Mitchell Likely Cap'n Andy; Preston to Star as Heavy with Rooney." *The Los Angeles Times,* 22 Aug. 1950, p. 35.
24. Hopper, Hedda. "Frank Seltzer Coaxes O'Brien, Mary Cummings." *The Los Angeles Times,* 6 Sept. 1950, p. 39.
25. Hopper, Hedda. "'Riviera Story' Airs at Two French Stations." *The Los Angeles Times,* 16 Nov. 1949, p. 42.
26. Sheaffer, Lew. "Big Top Draws H'wood, Astaire's Next, 'Detective Story' Sale—Other Film News." *The Brooklyn Daily Eagle,* 16 July 1949, p. 12.
27. Dawson, Jim. *Nervous Man Nervous: Jim McNeely and the Rise of the Honking Tenor Sax.* McFarland, 1995.
28. "In Hollywood." *The Independent Record,* 13 Nov. 1949, p. 8.
29. Gerhard, Inez. "Star Dust: Stage Screen Radio." *Cape Vincent Eagle,* 30 April 1950, p. 7.
30. Aaker, Everett *Encyclopedia of Early Television Crime Fighters* (Jefferson, NC: McFarland & Co, Inc., 2006), 226; Del Vecchio, Deborah *Beverly Garland Her Life & Career* (Jefferson, NC: McFarland & Co, Inc., 2012), 25.
31. Hare, William. *L. A. Noir: Nine Dark Visions of the City of Angels.* McFarland, 2004.
32. Alfred, Tom. "The Screen Scene." *California Eagle,* 12 Dec. 1949, p. 18.

Chapter 9

1. Bower, Helen. "Star Gazing: Track Is Safer Place If You Have to Bet." *Detroit Free Press,* 13 Aug. 1950, p. 26.
2. Johnson, Erskine. "In Hollywood: Not Bugsy, but—." *San Bernardino Sun,* 26 May 1950, p. 4.
3. Macpherson, Virginia. "Film Newcomer Stages Command Preview of Epic for Congress." *Madera Tribune,* 13 July 1950, p. 7.
4. "Powerful Film on Gambling at the Village." *Desert Sun,* 21 July 1950, p. 7.
5. Marsh, Marilyn. "In Hollywood: Hollywood Exposes Crooks in Pendergast Story." *Tampa Bay Times,* 25 Aug. 1950, p. 27.
6. Parsons, Louella O. "In Hollywood With." *Albany New York Times-Union,* 15 April 1951, p. B-11.
7. "711 Ocean Drive: OK Gambling Expose Melodrama." *Film Bulletin,* 25 Sept. 1950, p. 8.
8. Gerhard, Inez. "Star Dust: Stage Screen Radio." *Cape Vincent Eagle,* 17 July 1950, p. 3.
9. Macpherson, Virginia. "Film Newcomer Stages Command Preview of Epic for Congress." *Madera Tribune,* 13 July 1950, p. 7.

10. Corby, Jane. "Screenings: Film Exposing Gambling Racket, '711 Ocean Drive' at NY Paramount." *The Brooklyn Daily Eagle*, 20 July 1950, p. 5.
11. Johnson, Erskine. "In Hollywood: Best Notices." *San Bernardino Sun*, 19 Aug. 1950, p. 4.
12. "Illinois Day Vies with O'Brien Day at Fair Today." *Chicago Tribune*, 21 July 1950, p. 26.
13. "Columbia: Cohn Bolsters Studio with New Inde Manpower." *Film Bulletin*, 12 Feb. 1951, p. 11.
14. Parsons, Louella O. "Hollywood Overlooks Talented San Juan, Olga. Lolly Opines." *Albuquerque Journal*, 15 April 1951, p. 8.
15. Parsons, Louella O. "Gene Markey Returns from Abroad; Sells Novel." *Daily Times*, 2 Feb. 1951, p. 39.
16. Marsh, Marilyn. "In Hollywood: Hollywood Exposes Crooks in Pendergast Story." *Tampa Bay Times*, 25 Aug. 1950, p. 27.
17. Johnson, Erskine. "In Hollywood: Movie Layoff May Help Judy Garland." *The Gastonia Gazette*, 23 Feb. 1951, p. 2.
18. "Draft Dodger, Actor in Brawl." *Madera Tribune*, 7 Sept. 1951, p. 1.
19. "All Silent After Fight in Hollywood." *The Akron Beacon Journal*, 8 Sept. 1951, p. 7.
20. Parsons, Louella O. "Hollywood." *The Daily Times*, 30 May 1950, p. 23.
21. Gwynn, Edith. "Hollywood: Bitter Pill for 'Curley' Crosby." *The Cincinnati Enquirer*, 13 Jan. 1950, p. 14.
22. Gwynn, Edith. "Hollywood: Rumor That Mayer May Fire Ava Gardner." *The Cincinnati Enquirer*, 22 May 1950, p. 8.
23. Thomas, Bob. "Hollywood: Edmond O'Brien Seeks Change of Pace." *The Ithaca Journal*, 14 March 1950, p. 7.
24. "The Admiral Was a Lady (Songs)." *Variety*, 10 May 1950, p. 6.

Chapter 10

1. "Edmond O'Brien." *Lancaster Eagle-Gazette*, 29 March 1950, p. 4.
2. Graham, Sheilah. "Pair of Veterans Eyed as Team." *The Tampa Times*, 24 Feb. 1950, p. 29.
3. "Storm for 'Prowl Car.'" *Tampa Bay Times*, 1 April 1950, p. 30.
4. "Prowl Car." *Hollywood Reporter*, 21 Feb. 1950, p. 3.
5. "Kibitzing Cops Aid Director." *Elmira Star-Gazette*, 18 May 1950, p. 33.
6. Bowers, Lynn. "What Hollywood Itself Is Talking About!" *Screenland*, June 1950, p. 51.
7. "British Censors Quickly Reform America's Films." *Buffalo Evening News*, 8 April 1950, p. 7.
8. "O'Brien in 'Two of a Kind.'" *The Los Angeles Times*, 29 Oct. 1950, p. 108.
9. "Town Hall Theater Friday & Saturday 'Two of a Kind.'" *The Journal & Republican*, 13 March 1952, p. 9.
10. Scott, John L. "Wald, Krasna Will Star Mitchum in 'Cowpoke'; Celli Tests for Julie." *The Los Angeles Times*, 14 Sept. 1950, p. 66.
11. Schallert, Edwin. "Quinn Will Package Episode Film, Sloane Picked as Gaucho Aide." *The Los Angeles Times*, 29 Sept. 1951, p. 16.
12. Hopper, Hedda. "'Farewell to Master' Named for Anne Baxter." *The Los Angeles Times*, 29 April 1950, p. 8.

Chapter 11

1. "O'Brien Starred in 'Warpath.'" *Lansing State Journal*, 12 Oct. 1950, p. 24.
2. "Train Shortage Minor Detail." *Elmira Star-Gazette*, 12 Oct. 1950, p. 39.
3. "Hollywood Group to Work on Film in Billings Area." *Great Falls Tribune*, 19 Aug. 1950, p. 4.
4. Handsaker, Gene. "Moon's Shining Tonight on Rod Redwing." *The Salt Lake Tribune*, 29 April 1951, p. 80.
5. Gwynn, Edith. "Hollywood: Everybody's Going Thataway, It Would Seem." *The Cincinnati Enquirer*, 25 Sept. 1950, p. 15.
6. "Miles City Girl Declines Offer of Chance in Movies." *Great Falls Tribune*, 19 Sept. 1950, p. 4.
7. MacLeod, Hope. "Crime Pays for Actor O'Brien." *The Akron Beacon Journal*, 1 Sept. 1951, p. 9.
8. Johnson, Erskine. "In Hollywood: Something Fishy Going on Around 'Pagan Love Song' Set." *Plattsburgh Press-Republican*, 10 July 1950, p. 8.
9. Johnson, Erskine. "Film Shows for Television: Title Change." *San Bernardino Sun*, 23 June 1950, p. 5.
10. "Indians Don't Wear Traditional Dress." *Cumberland Sunday Times*, 4 June 1950, p. 22.
11. Haskin, Byron. *The Director's Guild of America*. University of California Press, 1984.
12. "O'Brien Stands Out as a Saddle Star." *The Daily Chronicle*, 24 Aug. 1951, p. 5.
13. Thomas, Bob. "In Hollywood: Glenn Ford, Edmond O'Brien and Rhonda Fleming." *The Ottawa Journal*, 26 May 1950, p. 31.
14. Eichelman, Fred. "Divine Intervention in the Life of Rhonda Fleming." *Life Supernatural*, 2013.
15. "National Pre-Selling: Copley Fabrics, Inc." *Motion Picture Daily*, 31 March 1951, p. 3.

16. "Six on Sets Give Par. Bright Hopes for Future." *Film Bulletin*, 23 May 1951, p. 22.
17. "O'Brien Lets Double Take a 95-foot Dive." *Covina Argus*, 25 Jan. 1952, p. 16.
18. "Actor Falls Off Log." *The Pittsburg Press*, 8 May 1951.
19. Carroll, Harrison. "Alan Ladd Jockeys for New Contract." *The News-Messenger*, 19 May 1951, p. 4.
20. "'Silver City' Well-Made Technicolor Western." *Film Bulletin*, 8 Oct. 1951, p. 8.
21. Haskin, Byron. *The Director's Guild of America*. University of California Press, 1984.
22. Heffernan, Harold. "John Gilbert Was Most 'Colorgenic.'" *The Star Press*, 5 Aug. 1951, p. 14.
23. Hopper, Hedda. "Roger Edens Becomes Producer for 'Jumbo.'" *The Los Angeles Times*, 25 July 1951, p. 11.
24. Haskin, Byron. *The Director's Guild of America*. University of California Press, 1984.
25. *New York Times*, 29 July 1951 article cited by the AFI Catalog of Feature Films.
26. "Utah Governor to Attend 'Rio' Bow." *Motion Picture Daily*, 6 May 1952, p. 5.
27. "10,000 See 'Denver' Premiere Fete." *Motion Picture Daily*, 5 May 1952, p. 5.
28. "Top Grossers of 1952." *Variety*, 7 Jan. 1953, p. 61.
29. Gwynn, Edith. "Hollywood." *Pottsdown Mercury*, 17 July 1951, p. 4.
30. Parsons, Louella O. "Monday Morning Gossip of the Nation." *The Philadelphia Inquirer*, 29 Sept. 1952, p. 15.
31. "Film: 'Cow Country' Is Barren." *Catholic Weekly*, 18 March 1954, p. 14.
32. Handsaker, Gene. "All Is Color at Big Conference." *Oakland Tribune*, 14 Aug. 1956, p. 25.
33. Hopper, Hedda. "Hollywood and Vine." *The Times*, 5 March 1956, p. 15.
34. "Roles in Bunches: O'Brien Always Has Choice Selections." *Arizona Republic*, 5 Aug. 1956, p. 38.
35. Hopper, Hedda. "'Rio Bravo' Getting John Ford Regulars." *Los Angeles Times*, 8 April 1950, p. 10.
36. Lait, Jr., Jack. "'Slaughter Trail' in Bumpy Ride Around Howard da Silva." *The Brooklyn Daily Eagle*, 24 May 1951, p. 13.
37. Mell, Eila. *Casting Might-Have-Beens: A Film-By-Film Directory of Those Considered for Roles Given to Others*. McFarland, 2013.

Chapter 12

1. Schallert, Edwin. "Pidgeon, O'Hara Duet Now Being Programmed." *The Los Angeles Times*, 20 July 1942, p. 30.
2. "Learned About Brooklyn from the Army." *The Brooklyn Daily Eagle*, 11 Feb. 1945, p. 27.
3. Schallert, Edwin. *Los Angeles Times*, 29 July 1948, p. 23.
4. Dixon, Hugh., "Hollywood: Around the Town." *Pittsburgh Post-Gazette*, 30 Sept. 1948, p. 19.
5. Dixon, Hugh., "Hollywood: The Monday Wash." *Pittsburgh Post-Gazette*, 15 March 1948, p. 16.
6. Graham, Sheilah. "Hollywood." *Pittsburgh Post-Gazette*, 16 June 1949, p. 7.
7. "Edmond O'Brien a Hit." *The Brooklyn Daily Eagle*, 18 Sept. 1949, p. 29.
8. Manso, Peter. *Brando: The Biography*. Hyperion, 1994.
9. "MacMurray, Claire Trevor Border Bound." *The Los Angeles Times*, 13 Feb. 1950, p. 31.
10. Gaver, Jack. "Musical 'Paint Your Wagon' Continues New Casting Trend." *The Brooklyn Daily Eagle*, 16 Sept. 1951, p. 29.
11. Hopper, Hedda. "George Seaton Takes Radio Team's Story." *The Los Angeles Times*, 13 March 1951, p. 32.
12. Johnson, Erskine. "In Hollywood: Tallulah Aims Remarks at Movie Actress Bette Davis." *The San Bernardino Sun*, 13 Dec. 1950, p. 4.
13. Hopper, Hedda. "Animation Headliners: Disney Cooking Up Plans for 2 More Features." *The Salt Lake Tribune*, 27 Nov. 1950, p. 23.
14. "Busy Van Druten Thrives on Overwork." *The Philadelphia Inquirer*, 16 Nov. 1952, p. 24.
15. Hopper, Hedda. "Donnybrook Battler's Roles Prepared for Granger." *Buffalo Courier-Express*, 23 Oct. 1952, p. 10.
16. "On the Stages: I've Got Sixpence." *The Philadelphia Enquirer*, 23 Nov. 1952, p. 103.
17. Sherman, George. "Last Night's Play: A Confused Pattern." *The Yale Daily News*, 13 Nov. 1952, p. 8.
18. Atkinson, Brooks. "Broadway: Van Druten Small Play Unfit for Big Themes." *The Cincinnati Press*, 4 Dec. 1952, p. 12.
19. Sheaffer, Louis. "Theaters: Van Druten Play Muddled Story of Love and Religion." *The Brooklyn Daily Eagle*, 3 Dec. 1952, p. 14.
20. Martin, Linton. "The Call Boy's Chat: Observation Vs Action in New Plays Poles Apart." *The Philadelphia Inquirer*, 23 Nov. 1952, p. 27.
21. "Nothing Like the Stage, O'Brien Tells Youngsters." *The Courier News*, 5 Jan. 1957, p. 2.

Chapter 13

1. Cohen, Harold V. "The New Films: 'The Turning Point' Comes to the Stanley; 'The Steel Trap' to the Harris." *Pittsburgh Post-Gazette*, 1 Nov. 1952, p. 18.
2. "Glamor Days of U.S. Gangsters Gone, Says O'Brien." *Hartford Courant*, 6 May 1951, p. 31.
3. Allen, Jay. "Behind the Scenes of Film Production; Studio Size-Ups: Columbia: Plenty of Flat and 3D Product Planned for April." *Film Bulletin*, 23 March 1953, p. 11.
4. Johnson, Erskine. "In Hollywood; Actor Claims Screen Plots, Techniques Make Fans Lazy." *San Bernardino Sun*, 7 July 1953, p. 3.
5. Scheuer, Philip K. "Ex-Star House Peters Ends 23-Year Silence; Marjorie Lawrence Due." *The Los Angeles Times*, 25 Aug. 1951, p. 9.
6. "Top Grossers of 1952." *Variety*, 7 Jan. 1953, p. 61.
7. Lyons, Leonard. "The Lyons Den." *The Times*, 10 June 1953, p. 20.
8. Denton, Charles. "O'Brien Back to Shakespeare." *Democrat & Chronicle*, 15 Sept. 1952, p. 22.
9. "Brilliant: By Our Film Critic." *The Sydney Morning Herald*, 9 May 1953, p. 2.
10. "Well-Intentioned Bigamist." *The Times*, 7 Dec. 1953, p. 12.
11. "Edmond O'Brien 'Surprise' Reviews for Part in Caesar." *The Tampa Tribune*, 28 June 1953, p. 56.
12. Mangan, Richard. *Gielgud's Letters*. Weidenfeld & Nicholson, 2004.1
13. Mason, James *Before I Forget* (London: Hamish Hamilton, 1981), 89.
14. Morley, Sheridan. *John Gielgud: The Official Biography*. Simon & Schuster, 2010.
15. "Falcons to Tour U.S." *Oakland Tribune*, 13 Dec. 1953, p. 90.
16. Dauth, Brian. *Joseph L. Mankiewicz: Interviews (Conversations with Filmmakers)*. University of Mississippi Press, 2008.
17. Mankiewicz, Joseph L. interviewed by Michel Climent in the documentary *All About Mankiewicz*, directed by Luc Berard, Janus Films, 1983.
18. Hopper, Hedda. "Andrews and Crain Going to Africa for Duel." *The Los Angeles Times*, 17 June 1953, p. 61.
19. Kelleher, Ron. "Special Student Price Attracts College Crowd to 'Julius Caesar.'" *The Pony Express*, 7 May 1954, p. 1.
20. Adams, Cindy. *Sunday Herald*, 12 March 1961, p. 26.
21. Schallert, Edwin. "Schary Pens Original; Hayworth Return Near; Big Bard Venture Looms." *The Los Angeles Times*, 7 Dec. 1953, p. 53.
22. Hopper, Hedda. "Looking at Hollywood: Granger Is Taking Over 'King's Thief' Star Role." *Chicago Tribune*, 4 April 1953, p. 12.
23. MacLeod, Hope. "Crime Pays for Actor O'Brien." *The Akron Beacon Journal*, 1 Sept. 1951, p. 9.

Chapter 14

1. Donati, William. *Ida Lupino: A Biography*. University of Kentucky Press, 1996.
2. "Fred MacMurray Moves to Swashbuckling Roles." *Arizona Republic*, 30 July 1952, p. 20.
3. "Miss Lupino on Movie Location at Long Point." *Hollywood Riviera Tribune*, 17 July 1952, p. 1.
4. Manners, Dorothy. "Louella Parsons." *The Philadelphia Inquirer*, 21 July 1952, p. 15.
5. "Taking Orders from a Gal Is Ok Is she's Ida Lupino." *Toledo Blade*, 17 May 1953, p. 4.
6. "Taking Orders from a Gal Is Ok Is she's Ida Lupino." *Toledo Blade*, 17 May 1953, p. 4.
7. Handsaker, Gene. "Hollywood: Ida as Director Makes Set Feel Like Home, Actors Say." *Newport Daily News*, 22 Aug. 1953, p. 13.
8. "'The Hitch-Hiker' Exciting Suspense Meller." *Film Bulletin*, 9 Feb. 1953, p. 14.
9. Hopper, Hedda. "Hedda Hopper's Hollywood: Six Major Stars to Play in 'Three Coins' by 20th." *Buffalo Courier-Express*, 26 June 1953, p. 6.
10. Hastie, Amelie. *BFI Classics: The Bigamist*. Palgrave Macmillan, 2009.
11. Johnson, Erskine. "The Hollywood Parade." *The Town Talk*, 31 Aug. 1953, p. 20.
12. "Ida Lupino and The Bigamist." *The Freeport Facts*, 23 July 1953, p. 12.
13. Graham, Sheilah. "News from Hollywood: Film About Louis IV Has Claudette Colbert in Role of Marquise." *Buffalo Evening News*, 9 July 1953, p. 34.
14. "Independents: Disney Plans New Series Circuit Topper Backs Film Unit." *Film Bulletin*, 22 March 1954, p. 15.
15. "Tregaskis Gets New Assignment." *Pittsburgh Post-Gazette*, 17 March 1953, p. 14.
16. Bogdanovitch, Peter. *Who the Devil Made It?* Alfred A. Knopf, 1997.
17. Johnson, Erskine. "Star Dust," *The Times-Standard*, 24 June 1954, p. 2.
18. Meil, Eila. *Casting Might-Have-Beens: A Film by Film Directory of Roles Given to Others*. McFarland, 2005.

19. Graham, Sheilah. "In Hollywood: Party Puts Frankie in Mood." *Honolulu Star-Bulletin*, 30 May 1952, p. 10.
20. "Monogram Signs O'Brien." *Motion Picture Daily*, 27 May 1952, p. 2.
21. Graham, Sheilah. "Hollywood Today: Huge Birthday Party Proves Filmdom Really Loves Lucy." *Arizona Daily Star*, 12 Aug. 1953, p. 17.

Chapter 15

1. Hopper, Hedda. "Hollywood: Ed O'Brien to Direct, Star in 'The Murder.'" *Buffalo Courier-Express*, 15 Jan. 1952, p. 6.
2. Parsons, Louella O. "News of Hollywood." *Albany New York Times-Union*, 22 April 1952, p. 10.
3. "O'Brien to Direct," *Buffalo Courier-Express*, May 4, 1952, 30-D.
4. Hopper, Hedda. "Edmond O'Brien Will Direct 'Shiner.'" *The Los Angeles Times*, 11 Sept. 1951, p. B7.
5. Heffernan, Harold. "Hollywood." *The Star Press*, 5 Aug. 1951. p. 17.
6. Hopper, Hedda. "Hollywood." *Courier-Post*, 15 Nov. 1951, p. 41.
7. Hopper, Hedda. "Hedda Hopper's Hollywood: Metro Grabs Lollobrigida for 'Swordsmen of Siena.'" *Buffalo Courier-Express*, 13 Nov. 1954, p. 15. Graham, Sheilah. "In Hollywood: Franchot Tone Writing a Play." *The Tampa Times*, 2 July 1951, p. 11.
8. Scott, Vernon. "Group of Top Stars Form Own Producing Company." *The Schenectady Gazette*, 25 Nov. 1954, p. 7.
9. Johnson, Erskine. "The Hollywood Parade." *The Town Talk*, 31 Aug. 1953, p. 20.
10. Agar, John & Van Savage, L. C. *On the Good Ship Hollywood* (Albany, GA: Bear Manor Media, 2007), 45;"Maria Solves Slap Problem for O'Brien." *The Star Press*, 18 July 1954, p. 15.
11. "Black-Haired." [Caption under picture] *Long Beach Independent*, 26 May 1954, p. 15.
12. McMahon, M. J. "Talking of Films: Shield for Murder." *The Australian Women's Weekly*, 16 May 1956, p. 62.
13. Macek, Carl. "Shield for Murder (1954)." in *Film Noir*. Secker & Warburg, 1980.
14. Schallert, Edwin. "Jeanne Crain, Donna Reed Wanted as Costars; Naish Smooth Gangster." *The Los Angeles Times*, 13 July 1954, p. 55.
15. Parsons, Louella O. "Danny Kaye Among Friends Making Picture in Britain." *The Milwaukee Sentinel*, 4 Nov. 1952, p. 6.
16. Gwynn, Edith. "Hollywood." *The Pottsdown Mercury*, 12 Feb. 1953, p. 25.
17. Parsons, Louella O. "Jackie Cooper, Jr. Skips First Chance at Movie to Star in School Play." *Albuquerque Journal*, 4 Nov. 1952, p. 21.
18. Johnson, Erskine. "Hollywood Gossip Heard Here and There." *Plattsburgh Press-Republican*, 24 Feb. 1954, p. 11.
19. Graham, Sheilah. "News from Hollywood: Evelyn Keyes Finally Receives Chance to Sing in Movies." *Buffalo Evening News*, 3 Dec. 1954, p. 58.
20. Wilson, Earl. "On Broadway: Blue Monday." *The Des Moines Register*, 27 Dec. 1954, p. 2.
21. "Actor-Narrator Scott Gets 'Eve' Chance; New Career on for Hickman." *The Los Angeles Times*, 19 Jan. 1957, p. 21.
22. "Film of Mexican Legend." *The Times*, 5 April 1954, p. 5.
23. "Film Reviews: The Shanghai Story." *Variety*, 29 Sept. 1954, p. 16.

Chapter 16

1. Bacon, James. "Ed O'Brien Shrugs Off Star Billing." *Press*, 2 March 1963, p. 9.
2. Mankiewicz, Joseph L. *American Film Vol. 3*. American Film Institute, 1977.
3. Dauth, Brian. *Joseph L. Mankiewicz: Interviews (Conversations with Filmmakers)*. University of Mississippi Press, 2008.
4. Thomas, Bob. "Edmond O'Brien: Academy Award Winner Says Process Is War of Nerves." *Geneva Daily Times*, 21 April 1955, p. 22.
5. Hyams, Joe. "The Legend of Bogie—3: Bogart and Tracy Refused to Give Top Billing." *Star Gazette*, 26 Aug. 1966, p. 10.
6. Thomas, Bob. "Edmond O'Brien Tells of Oscar." *The Central New Jersey Home News*, 15 April 1955, p. 15.
7. "Ed's Easy Subjects: O'Brien, Ruth and Roman Films." *The Pittsburgh Press*, 23 July 1965, p. 20.
8. Angel Fernandez-Santos "El Actor Edmond O'Brien, uno de los grandes 'secundarios' de Hollywood, murio en Los Angeles" *El Pais*, May 11, 1985, 1. (Author's Translation)
9. Gardern, Ava, with Peter Evans, *Ava Gardner: The Secret Conversations*. Simon & Schuster, 2014.
10. Parsons, Louella O. "Louella's Movie Go Round: Aldo Ray Signs for Lead in Warner's Great New War Story, 'Battle Cry.'" *Albuquerque Journal*, 18 Jan. 1954.
11. Schallert, Edwin. "Nick the Greek Story Intrigues Stellar Duo." *The Los Angeles Times*, 11 March 1954, p. 45.
12. "'Barefoot Contessa' in World Premiere

at Capitol." *The Brooklyn Daily Eagle*, 31 Aug. 1954, p. 6.
13. Crowther, Bosley. "The Screen in Review: 'The Barefoot Contessa' Arrives at Capitol." *The New York Times*, 30 Sept. 1954, p. 58.
14. "'Barefoot Contessa' Gets a Seventh Capitol Week." *The Brooklyn Daily Eagle*, 8 Nov. 1954, p. 4.
15. Truffaut, Francois. *The Films in My Life*. Simon & Schuster, 1978.
16. Schallert, Edwin. "Writer Davis Becomes Director; Tandy, Cronyn going on Platford Tour." *Los Angeles Times*, 26 Feb. 1954, p. 39.
17. Hopper, Hedda. "Mature and Simmons Co-Star in 'Desiree.'" *Los Angeles Times*, 12 March 1954, p. 32.
18. Schallert, Edwin. "Victor Mature Stars Opposite Simmons; Wald Seeks New Hayward Deal." *Los Angeles Times*, 10 July 1952, p. 39.
19. Hopper, Hedda. "Hollywood: Dinah Shore Is Hoping Mate Can Visit New York." *Buffalo Courier-Express*, 11 Jan. 1954, p. 10.
20. Schallert, Edwin. "O'Briens Blend Efforts for Comedy Film; Cameron Sells Screenplay." *The Los Angeles Times*, 14 Jan. 1954, p. 67.
21. O'Brien, Bridget. "The Big Night Dad Brought Home an Oscar." *The Los Angeles Times*, 10 April 1988, p. 699.

Chapter 17

1. "O'Brien's Quiet Man at Home." *Chicago Tribune*, 28 April 1963, p. 320.
2. "Actors on Holiday Get into Picture." *The Sunday Herald*, 18 May 1947, p. 5.
3. Bowers, Lynn. "What Hollywood Itself Is Talking About." *Screenland*, Nov. 1948, p. 67.
4. Heffernan, Harold. "A Look into Movieland: Millie Perkins Likes Hollywood, Will Stay." *Herald Statesman*, 21 Oct. 1958, p. 23.
5. Hackett, Walter. "Hackett in Hollywood: Actor Edmond O'Brien Hits a Starring Stride." *Lansing State Journal*, 14 Dec. 1952, p. 40.
6. Parsons, Louella O. "One Oscar Made a Difference." *The Milwaukee Sentinel*, 25 March 1956, p. 21.
7. "Mr. O'Brien's Dream Home; Built It Himself, with Olga's Aid." *Oakland Tribune*, 18 Dec. 1950, p. 31.
8. Ames, Walter. "Comedy Hour Renewed for 1951–52 Season; Actor Plans Home-Building Video Show." *The Los Angeles Times*, 22 June 1951, p. 22.

9. "Mr. O'Brien's Dream Home; Built It Himself, with Olga's Aid." *Oakland Tribune*, 18 Dec. 1950, p. 31.
10. "O'Brien's Quiet Man at Home." *Chicago Tribune*, 28 April 1963, p. 320.
11. Skolsky, Sidney. "Hollywood Is My Beat: Tintyped: Edmond O'Brien Tough Shakespearean." *New York Post*, 26 Oct. 1953, p. E14.
12. Handsaker, Gene. "Hollywood Sights and Sounds." *Corsica Daily Sun*, 25 Feb. 1949, p. 12.
13. "Edmond O'Brien Has Private Eye for Kitchen, Too." *Chicago Tribune*, 3 Feb. 1961, p. 40.
14. Torme, Mel. *It Wasn't All Velvet*. Robson Books Ltd., 1989.
15. Solsky, Sidney. "Hollywood Is My Beat: Tintyped: Edmond O'Brien Tough Shakespearean." *New York Post*, 26 Oct. 1953, p. E14.
16. San Juan, Olga. "Why I Fell in Love with Eddie." *Screenland*, June 1951, p. 68.
17. Solsky, Sidney. "Hollywood Is My Beat: Tintyped: Edmond O'Brien Tough Shakespearean." *New York Post*, 26 Oct. 1953, p. E14.
18. Handsaker, Gene. "Hollywood Sights and Sounds." *Corsica Daily Sun*, 25 Feb. 1949, p. 12.
19. Johnson, Erskine. "In Hollywood: Maureen O'Hara Will Be Deglamorized in Next Role." *San Bernardino Sun*, 6 July 1950, p. 4.
20. "Actors Can't Afford Bad Memories." *The World's News*, Sydney, 30 Dec. 1950, p. 23.
21. "Players Superstitious? No, They Call It Merely Idiosyncratic." *The Salt Lake Tribune*, 21 Jan. 1941, p. 14.
22. "Mysteries of Zodiac." *The Post-Standard*, 11 Sept. 1952, p. 92.
23. Heffernan, Harold. "A Look into Movieland: Millie Perkins Likes Hollywood, Will Stay." *Herald Statesman*, 21 Oct. 1958, p. 23.
24. Svensrud, Lois. "Good News: Ice Skating." *Modern Screen*, March 1940. p. 54.
25. "'They Blew It,' Mutters L. A. Fan." *The San Bernardino County Sun*, 4 Oct. 1962, p. 43.
26. "The Case of O'Brien vs. O'Brien." *TV Guide*, 27 Oct. 1961, p. 17.
27. Carroll, Harrison. "Wayne Discusses Work on Latest Picture." *Plattsburgh Press-Republican*, 29 April 1957, p. 11.
28. Finnigan, Joe. "Diamonds Are Standbys: Amazing Hollywood Gifts." 25 Dec. 1958, p. 22.
29. Parsons, Louella O. "In Hollywood: Robert Stack Gives Dramatic Performance." *Albany New York Times-Union*, 2 Oct. 1956,

p. 10. "In Hollywood." *Vidette-Messenger of Porter County*, 20 Nov. 1956, p. 4.
30. San Juan, Olga. "Why I Fell in Love with Eddie." *Screenland*, June 1951, p. 68.
31. San Juan, Olga. "Why I Fell in Love with Eddie." *Screenland*, June 1951, p. 69.
32. "Liens Against Berkeley, O'Brien." *Motion Picture Herald*, 4 Dec. 1943, p. 42.
33. Johnson, Erskine. "New Private Eye Gimmick." *The Central New Jersey Home News*, 2 March 1960, p. 18.
34. "Fashion News from Van Heusen." *U. of B. Spectrum*, 25 Feb. 1955, p. 7.
35. "Voglin Corp." *Film Report*, 26 May 1952, p. 98.
36. Carroll, Harrison. "Behind the Scenes in Hollywood." *The Wilkes-Barre Record*, 5 Nov. 1947, p. 24.
37. Hackett, Walt. "Hackett in Hollywood: 'King Solomon's Mines' One of Best for Year." *Lansing State Journal*, 3 Dec. 1950, p. 42.
38. San Juan, Olga. "Why I Fell in Love with Eddie." *Screenland*, June 1951, p. 68.
39. Johnson, Erskine. "The Movie World." *The Eugene Guard*, 4 June 1953, p. 17.
40. Walt Hackett, "Hackett in Hollywood: 'King Solomon's Mines' One of Best for Year." *Lansing State Journal*, 3 Dec. 1950, p. 42.
41. "Births: Actress San Juan, Olga." *The St Louis Star and Times*, 6 April 1949, p. 7.
42. San Juan, Olga. "Why I Fell in Love with Eddie." *Screenland*, June 1951, p. 68.
43. "No Midnight Snacks for Johnny." *TV Guide*, 2 July 1960, p. 21.
44. Parsons, Louella O. "Keeping Up with Hollywood." *Courier-Post*, 8 March 1951, p. 26.
45. O'Brien, Edmond. "Edmond O'Brien Reduced 60 Pounds in 90 Days." *Tampa Bay Times*, 23 Aug. 1959, p. 26.
46. Hopper, Hedda. "Cyd Charisse Named for 'Silk Stockings'; In Tribute." *The Los Angeles Times*, 2 April 1956, p. 64.
47. "B'nai B'rith Honors 11 Southlanders." *The Los Angeles Times*, 9 Feb. 1955, p. 64.
48. Carroll, Harrison. "Edmond O'Brien Is Off-Screen Hero Too." *Lancaster Eagle-Gazette*, 11 Jan. 1950, p. 6.
49. "The Case of O'Brien vs. O'Brien." *TV Guide*, 27 Oct. 1961, p. 17.
50. Manners, Dorothy. "Irish Eddie Knows His Shakespeare." *Los Angeles Examiner*, 26 April 1953, p. 23.
51. "The Case of O'Brien vs. O'Brien." *TV Guide*, 27 Oct. 1961, p. 17.
52. "Capitol: Edmond O'Brien Appears in Lively Film Showing on Local Theater Screens." *Shamokin News-Dispatch*, 12 Dec. 1949, p. 9.

Chapter 18

1. Gwynn, Edith. "Hollywood: Celeste Holm and Jessica Tandy Busy on Broadway." *The Cincinnati Enquirer*, 2 Oct. 1950, p. 13.
2. Johnson, Erskine. "In Hollywood: Clooney-Mitchell Combine Proves Error of Old Agents." *San Bernardino Sun*, 3 June 1953, p. 5.
3. Hopper, Hedda. "Looking at Hollywood: Joanne Dru in Film with a 'Meek' Hero." *Chicago Tribune*, 23 Dec. 1953, p. 39.
4. Johnson, Erskine. "The Hollywood Parade." *The Town Talk*, 22 March 1954, p. 18.
5. Ames, Walter. "Hedley Fan Mail Makes Him Wonder; Edmond O'Brien Sought for Role." *The Los Angeles Times*, 24 Nov. 1954, p. 16.
6. Graham, Sheilah. "Gadabout's Diary: Dean, Jerry Broadway Axe During Judy's Party." *The Deseret News*, 30 July 1958, p. 13.
7. Ames, Walter. "Championship Fight 'Blacked Out' on Radio, Video Repeat Due for O'Brien TV Starrer." *The Los Angeles Times*, 14 Nov. 1951, p. 26.
8. "'Ports of Call' Series Cues Filmakers' Entry into TV Pix." *The Billboard*, 12 Sept. 1953, p. 8.
9. Humphrey, Hal. "L. A. Video Fans Prefer Movies, Poll Reveals." *Oakland Tribune*, 4 March 1954, p. 28.
10. "TV Key: 9:00pm Ch. 2—Playhouse of Stars. 'The Long Shot.'" *The Brooklyn Daily Eagle*, 9 Oct. 1953, p. 25.
11. "TV Reviews." *Time*, vol. 64, 1954, p. 36.
12. Ivo, Tommy. "Email subject line." Received by Derek Sculthorpe, 28 Oct. 2017.
13. Clements, Bob. "Television: 'Today' Started 8th Video Year Today." *Daily Bulletin, Endicott*, 14 Jan. 1959, p. 20.
14. "Speaking of Television: Hope Stanza Hit by Old Time." *The Long Island Star-Journal*, 17 Jan. 1959, p. 10.
15. Adams, Cindy. *Sunday Herald*, 12 March 1961, p. 26.
16. Handsaker, Gene. "Sights and Sounds from Hollywood." *The Leader-Republican*, 14 April 1951, p. 4.
17. "Nothing Like Stage, O'Brien Tells Youngsters." *The Courier News*, 5 Jan. 1957, p. 2.
18. "John Crosby Radio and Television: From Little Screen to Big." *The Marion Star*, 10 Aug. 1959, p. 5.
19. Smith, Cecil. "The TV Scene: O'Brien Brothers Team Up for Play." *The Los Angeles Times*, 16 May 1958, p. 33.
20. "TV Scout: 'Parade' Features Jazz." *The Pittsburgh Press*, 28 Nov. 1958, p. 37.

21. Seydor, Paul. *Peckinpah: The Western Films—A Reconsideration*. University of Illinois Press, 1999.

Chapter 19

1. "The Cornet Player and the Racketeer; Rituals of Defiance on the Screen." *The Times*, 26 Sept. 1955, p. 4.
2. "Hollywood Film Shop." *The Morning Call*, 10 Jan. 1956, p. 23.
3. "It's a New Experience." *The Singapore Free Press*, 28 July 1955, p. 17.
4. Watts, Stephen. "Orwell That Ends Well? Letters to the editor." *The Times*, 10 March 1956, p. 7.
5. Carroll, Harrison. "Behind the Hollywood Scene." *The Day*, 20 June 1955, p. 22.
6. "O'Briens May Team in Britain." *The Los Angeles Times*, 11 June 1956, p. A6.
7. "The Remarkable Mr. Pennypacker—New Theatre." *Theatre World*, Aug. 1955, p. 20.
8. Carroll, Harrison. "Behind the Scenes in Hollywood." *The Dispatch*, 12 July 1955, p. 8.
9. "O'Brien Options New British Subject." *The Los Angeles Times*, 18 July 1955, p. 62.
10. Hanauker, Joan. "Edmond O'Brien Takes Westerns or Shakespeare." *Corsica Daily Sun*, 29 Aug. 1956, p. 7.
11. Strachan, Alan. *Secret Dreams: A Biography of Michael Redgrave*. Weidenfeld & Nicholson, 2004.
12. Manners, Dorothy. "Movie About Little League Program Strikes Snag." *The Call-Leader*, 5 Aug. 1955, p. 7.
13. Heffernan, Harold. "A Look into Movieland: Millie Perkins Likes Hollywood, Will Stay." *Herald Statesman*, 21 Oct. 1958, p. 23.
14. Graham, Sheilah. "Roz Russell Schedules Play, Movie." *Indianapolis Star*, 29 July 1955, p. 14.
15. Schallert, Edwin. "Cliff Robertson Wins Plum Crawford Lead, Lance Fuller Starred: Edmond O'Brien to Do 'Oedipus Rex.'" *The Los Angeles Times*, 18 Aug. 1955, p. 79.
16. Johnson, Erskine. "Hollywood Today: Movies-TV-Radio." *Park City Daily News*, 1 March 1960, p. 1.
17. Cohen, Harold V. "The New Films: 'D-Day the Sixth of June' at Harris; 'Sea Shall Not Have Them' at Studio." *Pittsburgh Post-Gazette*, 31 May 1956, p. 12.
18. "The Arts: 'The Bad Seed' Reaches the Screen." *The Times*, 27 Aug. 1956, p. 6.
19. "Actress Has Many Talents." *Rocky Mountain Telegram*, 24 June 1956, p. 14.
20. "Weighty Challenge Pares Off Actors." *Sunday Journal & Star*, 16 Sept. 1956, p. 43.
21. "Natalie Feasts on Set." *The Courier News*, 5 Jan. 1957, p. 2.
22. Schallert, Edwin. "Wald Programs Comedy 'Kiss Them for Me'; Ladd Eyes O'Brien Film." *The Los Angeles Times*, 11 Sept. 1956, p. 26.
23. Schallert, Edwin. "Ladd Buys Novelette for Abbe Lane; Compo Vote Yuletide Event." *The Los Angeles Times*, 19 Oct. 1956, p. 47.
24. Scott, John L. "O'Brien Fell Flat on Debut." *The Los Angeles Times*, 16 Dec. 1956, p. 119.
25. Carroll, Harrison. "Behind the Scenes in Hollywood." *Plattsburgh Press-Republican*, 26 Nov. 1956, p. 8.
26. "AA to Produce 7 Films in 4 Months." *Motion Picture Daily*, 24 April 1956, p. 4.
27. Connolly, Mike. "Mike Connolly Says: 'King' Cole Gets Fabulous Offer for Las Vegas Show." *Quad-City Times*, 6 July 1956, p. 24.
28. Hopper, Hedda. "Cyd Charisse, Leslie Caron in Cast of Film 'Les Girls.'" *Star-Gazette*, 25 March 1956, p. 34.
29. Hopper, Hedda. "Hunter to Star in Film of War Time Rangers." *Chicago Tribune*, 17 Jan. 1957, p. 28.
30. Thomas, Bob. "Star Fears TV Inroads." *Lansing State Journal*, 2 Oct. 1956, p. 12.
31. Boyle, Hal. "Hal Boyle Speaks Up." *Vidette-Messenger of Porter County*, 22 March 1957, p. 4.
32. Collins, Joan. *Past Imperfect: An Autobiography*. New York, Berkley Books, 1985.
33. Ishii, Kenneth. "Japanese Women Enhance Mystery with Kimono." *Corsica Daily Sun*, 6 June 1957, p. 23.
34. "'Stopover Tokyo' Star Hit by Blank." *Oakland Tribune*, 15 Oct. 1957, p. 25.
35. "Ken Scott Hurt in Film Scene." *The Los Angeles Times*, 15 June 1957, p. 3.
36. "A Film Insecurely Based: Stopover Tokyo." *The Times*, 29 Nov. 1957, p. 5.
37. "Edmond Gets Steamed Up on Japan Set." *Oakland Tribune*, 20 Nov. 1957, p. 37.
38. Winsten, Arthur. "Reviewing Stand: 'The World Was His Jury' at the Brooklyn Fox." *New York Post*, 20 March 1958, p. 35.
39. Nash, Alanna. *The Colonel: The Extraordinary Story of Colonel Tom Parker and Elvis Presley*. New York, Simon & Schuster, 2003.
40. Thomas, Bob. "Edmond O'Brien Declares Tahiti Isn't Paradise." *The Jackson Sun*, 15 Jan. 1959, p. 21.
41. Baker, Ainslee. "Films with Ainslee Baker: The Restless and the Damned." *The Australian Women's Weekly*, 1 April 1959, p. 65.

42. Scheuer, Philip K. "'Party Girl' Film Throwback to 30s." *The Los Angeles Times*, 27 Nov. 1958, p. 103.
43. Thomas, Bob. "Edmond O'Brien Declares Tahiti Isn't Paradise." *The Jackson Sun*, 15 Jan. 1959, p. 21.
44. Finnigan, Joe. "Movie Wives Find Gems in Stockings." *The Tennessean*, 26 Dec. 1958, p. 32.
45. Hopper, Hedda. "Hedda Hopper's Hollywood: 3 Actresses Selected for Wald Movie." *Buffalo Courier-Express*, 2 Feb. 1959, p. 8.
46. Smith, Cecil. "TV Scene: O'Brien Brothers Team Up for Play." *The Los Angeles Times*, 16 May 1958, p. 33.
47. Scott, John L. "Alan Young Named for 'Time Machine.'" *The Los Angeles Times*, 18 May 1959, p. 90.
48. Garner, James, with Jon Winokur, *The Garner Files: A Memoir*. Simon & Schuster, 2012.

Chapter 20

1. "Edmond O'Brien's Ordeal—Star's Slimming Feat Lands Him Fat Role." *Schenectady Gazette*, 22 Aug. 1959, p. 6.
2. Williams, Bob. "On the Air," *New York Post*, 15 March 1960, p. 59.
3. Olpe, Marie. "Edmond O'Brien Stars as 'Johnny Midnight.'" *Greenfield Recorder-Gazette*, 27 Feb. 1960, p. 1.
4. Moore, John. "Edmond O'Brien Is Nice Guy, Like a Neighbor." *Binghampton Press*, 16 Feb. 1960, p. 28.
5. Scheuer, Steven H. "TV Notes: 'Clock-Watchers' Pilot for Series." *Citizen Register*, 2 June 1959, p. 17.
6. Lowry, Cynthia. "Radio-TV: Lawyer Program to Show Hero Losing a Few Cases." *Hattiesburg American*, 24 Aug. 1962, p. 10.
7. Marvin, Murray. "A Look at TV: Show to Star 3 O'Briens—One a Double." *The Philadelphia Inquirer*, 1 March 1963, p. 28.
8. Thomas, Bob. "From Hollywood: Edmond O'Brien Stays on Go with New Video Series." *Ocala Star-Banner*, 28 Oct. 1962, p. 21.
9. *Time* cited in Hal Erickson, *Encyclopedia of Television Law Shows: Factual & Fictional Series About Judges, Lawyers & the Courtroom, 1948–2008*. McFarland, 2009.
10. Witbeck, Charles. "TV Keynotes: Faulkner Story Basis of Long Hot Summer." *Daily News*, 9 Oct. 1965, p. 3.
11. "But Career Profitable Stardom Still Eludes Edmond O'Brien." *The Victoria Advocate*, 31 Oct. 1965, p. 24.
12. Denton, Charles. "Cops-and-Robbers Series Not for Edmond O'Brien." *St Petersburg Times*, 26 April 1956, p. 63.
13. Du Brow, Rick. "No Smiles: Television Seems to Equate Serious Drama with a Single Note of Misery." *The Town Talk*, 29 Jan. 1968, p. 19.
14. "O'Brien Finally Gets a Break." *Boston Sunday Herald Traveler*, 21 Jan. 1968, p. 7.
15. "Serling Regrets 'Doomsday,'" *Daily News*, May 30, 1971, 14.
16. Monahan, Kaspar. "Readers Aid Casting of 'Airport'; 100 Movie Editors Asked to Name Stars for Roles." *The Pittsburgh Press*, 21 Aug. 1968, p. 43.
17. "National Collegiate Football Championship at Stake in Orange Bend Saturday Evening." *Rome News-Tribune*, 31 Dec. 1971, p. 9.
18. Apikian, Nevart. "O'Brien Starring in Faulkner Epic." *The Post Standard*, 1965, p. 18.
19. Penton, Edgar. "Long, Hot Summer Very Fine Weather for Veteran Actor O'Brien." *Showtime, The Florence Times Tri-Cities Daily*, 10 Oct. 1965, p. 7.
20. Penton, Edgar. "Long, Hot Summer Very Fine Weather for Veteran Actor O'Brien." *Showtime, The Florence Times Tri-Cities Daily*, 10 Oct. 1965, p. 7.
21. Gardell, Kay. "Distaff Side Complains Manly Men Missing from TV Milieu." *The Los Angeles Times*, 10 Aug. 1965, p. 55.
22. "Why Did Edmond O'Brien Give Up Acting?" *Honolulu Star-Bulletin*, 27 Feb. 1966, p. 103.
23. Wingreen, Jason. "Interview by Stephen Bowie Part Two." *The Classic TV History Blog*, 21 May 2010. https://classictvhistory.wordpress.com/tag/edmond-obrien/.

Chapter 21

1. Lyons, Leonard. "The Lyons Den: Chaplin Likes Role of a Clown in a Nazi Concentration Camp." *Lawrence World-Journal*, 24 Aug. 1962, p. 4.
2. Heffernan, Harold. "Ile de France Has Finale in Big Technicolor Setting." *The Pittsburgh Press*, 27 Sept. 1959, p. 57.
3. Stack, Robert, with Mark Evans, *Straight Shooting*. Macmillan Publishing Co., Inc., 1980.
4. Connolly, Mike. *The Philadelphia Inquirer*. 14 May 1959, p. 29.
5. Oviatt, Ray. "On the Aisle; Suspense Film Gets Unusual Treatment." *The Blade*, 26 Feb. 1960, p. 17.
6. Berns, Samuel D. "Reviews: The Third Voice 20th-Fox-Cinemascope." *Motion Picture Daily*, 26 Jan. 1960, p. 7.

7. Cohen, Harold V. "The New Films: Edmond O'Brien in 'The 3rd Voice' Comes to Harris." *Pittsburgh Post-Gazette*, 21 May 1960, p. 6.
8. Hopper, Hedda. "Edmond O'Brien to Star in 'The Voice.'" *Los Angeles Times*, 26 Sept. 1959, p. 12.
9. Hopper, Hedda. "Looking at Hollywood: New Deal for O'Brien." *The Odessa American*, 18 Dec. 1960, p. 55.
10. Hopper, Hedda. "'Sons and Lovers' Is Rated Among '60s Top Films.'" *Buffalo Courier-Express*, 2 Jan. 1961, p. 8.
11. Thomas, Bob. "Edmond O'Brien Turns Director with Gusto." *Pittsburgh Post-Gazette*, 14 March 1961, p. 12.
12. Thomas, Bob. "Director O'Brien Enlivens Films." *The Milwaukee Sentinel*, 29 March 1961, p. 19.
13. Thomas, Bob. "Director O'Brien Enlivens Films." *The Milwaukee Sentinel*, 29 March 1961, p. 19.
14. Wilson, Liza. "Is Stella Stevens?" *Pittsburgh Post-Gazette*, 28 May 1961, p. 7.
15. Johnson, Erskine. "Edmond O'Brien Turns to Role of a Director." *The Tuscaloosa News*, 30 April 1961, p. 36.
16. Hunter, Jeffrey. "Actor's Choice." *Films & Filming*, April 1962, p. 17.
17. Johnson, Erskine. "Edmond O'Brien Turns to Role of a Director." *The Tuscaloosa News*, 30 April 1961, p. 36.
18. Thomas, Bob. "Edmond O'Brien Turns Director with Gusto." *Pittsburgh Post-Gazette*, 14 March 1961, p. 12.
19. "O'Brien Readies 'Touch.'" *Motion Picture Daily*, 20 Dec. 1960, p. 2.
20. Scheuer, Philip K. "Shulman Readies Two Stage Plays." *The Los Angeles Times*, 29 April 1960, p. 42.
21. Hopper, Hedda. "Hollywood." *Tucson Daily Citizen*, 7 April 1960, p. 15.
22. Parsons, Louella O. "Glenn Ford to Make Three Films in Italy." *The Indianapolis Star*, 26 May 1960, p. 41.
23. Connolly, Mike. "In Hollywood: Darins 'Vant to Be Alone.'" *Pittsburgh Post-Gazette*, 29 Jan. 1961, p. 6.
24. Hopper, Hedda. "Looking at Hollywood." *The Odessa American*, 15 Feb. 1962, p. 7.
25. Hopper, Hedda. "Looking at Hollywood: Marilyn, Cyd Charisse, Dean Martin to Team." *Chicago Tribune*, 4 April 1962, p. 40.
26. Turner, Adrian. *The Making of David Lean's Lawrence of Arabia*. Dragon's World, 1994.
27. "The Exhibitor Has His Say About Pictures: Buena Vista Moon Pilot (BV)." *Boxoffice*, 22 Oct. 1962, p. 172.
28. Cohen, Karl F. *Forbidden Animation: Censored Cartoons and Blacklisted Animators in America*. McFarland, 2004.
29. "Feature Reviews: The Man Who Shot Liberty Vallance." *Boxoffice*, 16 April 1962, p. 2621.
30. "Mr. Edmond O'Brien." *The Times*, 13 May 1985, p. 14.
31. Parsons, Louella O. "New '1-Way Passage' Discussed as Musical." *The Indianapolis Star*, 8 Sept. 1961, p. 2.
32. McBride, Joseph. *Searching for John Ford: A Life*. St Martin's Press, 2001.
33. Hopper, Hedda. "Hollywood and Vine." *The Times*, Shreveport, Louisiana, 16 April 1962, p. 17.
34. Letter from Edmond O'Brien to John Ford, Feb. 22, 1962, cited in Scott Allen Nollen's *Three Bad Men: John Ford, John Wayne, Ward Bond*. McFarland, 2013.
35. McInery, Lee. "The New Films: 'The Man Who Shot Liberty Valance'—Stanley." *Pittsburgh Post-Gazette*, 4 May 1962, p. 11.
36. "Feature Reviews: The Man Who Shot Liberty Vallance." *Boxoffice*, 16 April 1962, p. 2621.
37. Gaddis, Martha. "Eugenean Visits 'Birdman' Set." *The Eugene Guard*, 23 Feb. 1961, p. 20.
38. Henriksen, Margot A. *Dr. Strangelove's America: Society and Culture in the Atomic Age*. University of California Press, 1997.
39. Armstrong, Stephen B. *Pictures About Extremes: The Films of John Frankenheimer*. McFarland, 2007.
40. Albert, Don. "Eddie O'Brien Getting Back into Film Swing After TV Shipwreck." *The Los Angeles Times*, 16 June 1963, p. 74.

Chapter 22

1. Witbeck, Charles. "TV Keynotes: Faulkner Story Basis of 'Long Hot Summer.'" *Daily News*, 9 Oct. 1965, p. 3.
2. Hopper, Hedda. "Actor Edmond O'Brien Debuted in Connecticut." *Hartford Courant*, 13 March 1965, p. 20.
3. Carroll, Harrison. "In Hollywood." *Vidette-Messenger of Porter County*, 9 May 1964, p. 4.
4. "Ailing O'Brien Withdraws from Film." *Arizona Daily Star*, 30 April 1964, p. 2.
5. Hopper, Hedda. "O'Brien Functions Best When Busy." *The Los Angeles Times*, 9 March 1965, p. 61.
6. "O'Brien Considers Play." *The Los Angeles Times*, 22 March 1963, p. 82.
7. Hopper, Hedda. "Peter O'Toole Will Attend Oscar Show." *The Los Angeles Times*, 21 March 1963, p. 66.

8. Hopper, Hedda. "In Hollywood." *The Los Angeles Times*, 21 Oct. 1964, p. 84.
9. Parsons, Louella. "Best of Hollywood." *The Philadelphia Inquirer*, 31 Dec. 1964, p. 6.
10. "Plays Role with Feeling: O'Brien Admires Man He Portrays." *Buffalo Courier-Express*, 26 Nov. 1964, p. 7.
11. Knickerbocker, Paine. "Edmond O'Brien's Approach to Synanon." *San Francisco Chronicle*, 5 May 1965, p. 19.
12. Van Gelder, Lawrence. "Charles Dederich, 83, Synanon Founder, Dies." *The New York Times*, 4 March 1997, p. 39.
13. "O'Brien Signs for 'Synanon.'" *Buffalo Courier-Express*, 11 Oct. 1964, p. 6.
14. "Plays Role with Feeling: O'Brien Admires Man He Portrays." *Buffalo Courier-Express*, 26 Nov. 1964, p. 7.
15.{en Thomas, Bob. "Director Has Reasons for His Film on Rehabilitating Dope Addicts." *Post-Journal*, 5 Sept. 1964, p. 15.
16. "Film Drama About Drug Addiction and Its Treatment." *The Times*, 20 Jan. 1966, p. 17.
17. "Synanon." *Variety*, 31 Dec. 1964, p. 32.
18. Milner, Tom. "MFB." quoted in Halliwell, Leslie, *Halliwell's Film Guide*. Guild Publishing Ltd, 1983.
19. "Special." *Independent Press-Telegram*, 19 July 1964, p. 145.
20. Coats, Patricia. "TV View: Victor Borge Wins Ticket for Best Commercial." *Democrat and Chronicle*, 3 March 1963, p. 70.
21. "Rights Purchased." *The Los Angeles Times*, 8 May 1963, p. 81.
22. Scheuer, Philip K. "'Hawaii's Direction by George Roy Hill." *The Los Angeles Times*, 27 April 1964, p. 68.
23. "May Play Pilate." *The Los Angeles Times*, 12 Feb. 1963, p. 57.
24. Parsons, Louella O. "Louella Parsons in Hollywood: O'Brien, Loren Will Be Teamed Up." *Albany New York Times-Union*, 15 March 1965, p. 8.
25. Kael, Pauline quoted in Halliwell, Leslie, *Halliwell's Film Guide*. Guild Publishing Ltd, 1983.
26. Apikian, Nevart. "O'Brien Starring in Faulkner Epic." *The Post-Standard*, 29 Sept. 1965, p. 14.
27. Kleiner, Dick. "Raquel Scores in Roller Role." *The Sumter Daily Item*, 24 Oct. 1972, p. 9.
28. "Edmond O'Brien (1915–1985)." *Crawley's Casting Calls*, http://www.crawleys castingcalls.com/index.php/component/actors/index.php?option=coc_actors&Itemid=56&id=5022&lettre=O.
29. Martin, B. "Movie Call Sheet." *The Los Angeles Times*, 6 Aug. 1965, p. 67.
30. Drew, Bernard. "Spy Thriller." *The Herald Statesman*, 15 Jan. 1970, p. 26.
31. Crowther, Bosley. "The Screen: 'The Viscount' Begins Run; European Gang Picture Heads Double Bill." *New York Times*, 11 May 1967, p. 57.
32. "Edmond O'Brien's Daughter." *The Post-Standard*. 7 July 1967, p. 23.
33. "Filmed in Brazil." *The Journal & Courier*, 3 Aug. 1968, p. 42.
34. Borgnine, Ernest. *Ernie: The Autobiography*. Citadel, 2008.
35. Thomas, Bob. *Golden Boy: The Untold Story of William Holden*. Weidenfeld & Nicolson, 1983.
36. Bennett, Colin. "New Films: Ballet of Bullets in Blood Red." *The Age*, 1 Dec. 1969, p. 2.
37. Judith Crist quoted in Halliwell, Leslie. *Halliwell's Film Guide*. Guild Publishing Ltd, 1983.
38. "Film of Distinction: 'The Wild Bunch' Powerful Comment on Western Violence." *Film Bulletin*. Wax Publications, vol. 38, 1969.
39. Everitt, David. *King of the Half Hour: Nat Hiken and the Golden Age of TV Comedy*. Syracuse University Press, 2001.
40. Knapp, Dan. "Stage Notes: Pearl Bailey Set in 'Dolly' at Greek." *The Los Angeles Times*, 26 Nov. 1969, p. 61.

Chapter 23

1. "O'Briens Plan Santa Film." *The Los Angeles Times*, 6 July 1970, p. E17.
2. Haber, Joyce. "Patty Emoted for Emmy Cameras." *The Los Angeles Times*, 17 June 1970, p. 87.
3. Karp, Joseph. *Orson Welles's Last Movie: The Making of the Other Side of the World*. St. Martin's Press, 2015.
4. McBride, Joseph. *Whatever Happened to Orson Welles? A Portrait of an Independent Career*. The University Press of Kentucky Press, 2006.
5. Karp, Joseph. *Orson Welles's Last Movie: The Making of the Other Side of the World*. St. Martin's Press, 2015.
6. Karp, Joseph. *Orson Welles's Last Movie: The Making of the Other Side of the World*. St. Martin's Press, 2015.
7. "Actor Edmond O'Brien Stricken." *The Los Angeles Times*, 1 Sept. 1971, p. 34.
8. "TV Movies." *The Ithaca Journal*, 1 Nov. 1971, p. 18.
9. Lanken, Dane. "Movie Savage Masters and a Political Feud." *The Montreal Gazette*, 9 Dec. 1972, p. 30.
10. Garcie Riera, Emilio. *Historia Docu-*

mental del Cine Mexicano: 1974–1976. Jalisco, Mexico, Universidad de Guadalajara, 1992.
  11. Thomas, Kevin. "TV Review: 3 'Stories of Love' in Traditional Style." *The Los Angeles Times*, 2 May 1974, p. 97.
  12. Sullivan, Kaye. *Films for, by and About Women.* Scarecrow Press, 1985.
  13. *A Storm of Strangers: The Irish.* Directed by Chris Jenkyns. Macmillan Films, 1974.
  14. *Black Christmas Revisited.* Directed by Carl Brundtland. Critical Mass Productions, Inc., 2002.
  15. *Black Christmas Revisited.* Directed by Carl Brundtland. Critical Mass Productions, Inc., 2002.
  16. "Black Christmas (1974)." *TCM,* http://www.tcm.com/this-month/article/382629%7C410638/Black-Christmas.html.
  17. Kilday, Gregg. "Frankenheimer's 'Iceman' Another Chance for U.S." *The Los Angeles Times,* 21 Oct. 1973, p. 439.
  18. *Variety* quoted in Halliwell, Leslie. *Halliwell's Film Guide.* Guild Publishing Ltd, 1983.
  19. O'Brien, Bridget. "The Big Night Dad Brought Home an Oscar." *The Los Angeles Times,* 10 April 1988, p. 699.
  20. "Newsmakers: Hard Hat Earns Pin Money with New Skill." *The Los Angeles Times,* 17 Dec. 1975, p. 56.
  21. Lamparski, Richard. *Whatever Became of...? All New Ninth Series.* Crown Publishing, 1985.
  22. "Oscar Winning Actor O'Brien Dying of Alzheimer's Disease." *Arizona Daily Star,* 20 Nov. 1983, p. 12.
  23. Princess Yasmin Ali Khan. "We Didn't Know Then What We Know Now." *The Shriver Report: A Study by Maria Shriver and the Alzheimer's Association,* https://www.alz.org/shriverreport/khan.html.
  24. Spears, Gregory. "Children of Alzheimer's victims Plead for Help." *Boca Raton News,* 22 May 1985, p. 7.
  25. "Actor Wages Futile Fight." *The Victoria Advocate,* 17 Nov. 1983, p. 10a.
  26. Gindick, Tia. "Relatives Share Concerns About Alzheimer's Disease." *The Telegraph,* 23 Dec. 1983, p. 32.
  27. "Relatives of Alzheimer's Victims Plead for Funding." *Chillicothe Gazette,* 22 May 1985, p. 1.
  28. "Medicine in the News: Alzheimer's Hearings Launched" *Journal of the Arkansas Medical Society,* Vol. 82. 1, June 1985, 64.
  29. Kronholm, William. "Relatives Recall the Horror of Alzheimer's Disease." *The Times-News,* 22 May 1985, p. 25.
  30. "Alzheimer's Research Fund Sought by Kin of Victims." *Fort Lauderdale News,* 22 May 1985, p. 4.

Epilogue

  1. "Edmond O'Brien, Dolph Sweet Die." *The Sumter Daily Item,* 9 May 1985, p. 35.
  2. "The Case of O'Brien vs. O'Brien." *TV Guide,* 27 Oct. 1962, p. 16.
  3. "The Case of O'Brien Vs O'Brien." *TV Guide,* 27 Oct. 1962, p. 15.
  4. O'Brien, Bridget. "The Big Night Dad Brought Home an Oscar." *The Los Angeles Times,* 10 April 1988, p. 699.
  5. Anderson, Nancy. "Yesterday's Stars Today: O'Brien Brilliant in Conversation." *Lodi News-Sentinel,* 20 Oct. 1972, p. 7.

Appendix

  1. Sullivan, Kaye. *Films for, by and About Women.* Scarecrow Press, 1985.
  2. Anderson, Nancy. "Yesterday's Stars Today: O'Brien Brilliant in Conversation." *Lodi News-Sentinel,* 20 Oct. 1972, p. 7.
  3. Shaeffer, Lew. "Concerning the Activities of Amateur and Professional Groups: The Little Theaters." *The Brooklyn Daily Eagle,* 14 April 1935, p. E9.
  4. Gardiner, Goodsir. "Legitimate Theater Returns, Acclaimed by Large Audience." *The Herald Statesman,* 16 June 1936, p. 9.
  5. "In Leading Role: Herbert Duffy to Play Lead in Mystery Drama 'The Bat' Next Week." *The Herald Statesman,* 23 June 1936, p. 9.
  6. Oakley, Anne. "County Residents Featured in Shows at Summer Theaters." *The Herald Statesman,* 26 June 1936, p. 20.
  7. "Best Years' Domestic Drama, Presented by Urban Playhouse." *The Herald Statesman,* 7 July 1936, p. 9.
  8. "'Busman's Honeymoon' Coming to Mount Kisco." *The Brewster Standard,* 9 July 1937, p. 2.
  9. "Westchester Playhouse." *The Brewster Standard,* 23 June 1938, p. 8.
  10. "What I'd Like to Listen to Tonight." *Quad-City Times,* 1 April 1938, p. 18.
  11. "Today's Radio Broadcasts: Today's Features." *The Chicago Tribune,* 15 April 1938, p. 27.
  12. "Radio Programs." *The Brooklyn Daily Eagle,* 3 Dec. 1939, p. 44.
  13. "That's Right on Broadway." *Motion Picture Herald,* 9 Dec. 1939, p. 17.
  14. "News of the Studios." *The New York Sun,* 23 Dec. 1939, p. 22.
  15. "Radio Programs." *The Brooklyn Daily Eagle,* 10 Feb. 1940, p. 18. "Radio: Two Programs Based on Life of Lincoln to Be Broadcast Tonight on NBC and CBS." *The Central New Jersey Home News,* 10 Feb. 1940, p. 3.

16. "Contact." *The Miami News*, 17 March 1943, p. 16.
17. "Soldier Show." *The Miami News*, 7 April 1943, p. 8.
18. "Ambitious Radio Show." *The Miami News*, 25 March 1943, p. 18.
19. "Edmond O'Brien on 'War Town' Broadcast." *The Plain Speaker*, 13 July 1944, p. 6.
20. "Program High Lights." *The Indianapolis Star*, 16 July 1944, p. 45.
21. "Tonight's Radio Programs." *The Cincinnati Enquirer*, 10 June 1945, p. 34.
22. "Your Programs." *The Des Moines Register*, 1 March 1947, p. 5.
23. "TV Radio: Video-Radio Briefs: Eden Talks on Eve of Visit to the U.S." *The Los Angeles Times*, 18 Jan. 1956, p. 67.
24. "Edmond O'Brien Stars in New Show." *The Deseret News*, 13 Oct. 1949, p. F-2.
25. Bowers, Lynn. "What Hollywood Itself Is Talking About!" *Screenland*, Sept. 1951, p. 11.
26. "Ginger Rogers in KSD: Billed Tuesday Night in Martin-Lewis Show." *St Louis Post-Dispatch*, 14 Dec. 1952, p. 102.
27. "Features on Television and Radio: Radio." *Star Tribune*, 3 Nov. 1954, p. 39.
28. "Radio." *The Los Angeles Times*, 16 May 1958, p. 34.
29. "Radio Highlights." *The Los Angeles Times*, 14 May 1955, p. 17.
30. "Andy Devine and Edmond O'Brien Guest on 'Music Hall.'" *The Times*, 29 May 1955, p. 53.
31. "Navy Program Stars Film Actor." *Honolulu Star-Bulletin*, 7 Jan. 1958, p. 18.
32. "Television." *The Brooklyn Daily Eagle*, 17 July 1950, p. 19.
33. Bowers, Lynn. "What Hollywood Itself Is Talking About!" *Screenland*, Sept. 1951, p. 11.
34. "Television." *Fort Lauderdale News*, 20 Aug. 1954, p. 24.
35. Crosby, John. "Radio & Television: Offbeat." *The Montgomery Advertiser*, 27 Feb. 1956, p. 9.
36. "TV Highlights." *The Los Angeles Times*, 22 Jan. 1955, p. 27.
37. "TV Highlights." *The Los Angeles Times*, 13 Sept. 1955, p. 29.
38. "Mysteries of Zodiac." *The Post-Standard*, 11 Sept. 1955, p. 92.
39. "TV." *The Los Angeles Times*, 16 May 1958, p. 34.
40. "Special." *Independent Press-Telegram*, 19 July 1964, p. 145.

Bibliography

Armstrong, Stephen B. *Pictures About Extremes: The Films of John Frankenheimer* (Jefferson, NC: McFarland, 2007).
Bergan, Ronald. *The United Artists Story* (New York: Octopus Books, 1986).
Bishop, Jim. *The Mark Hellinger Story: A Biography of Broadway and Hollywood* (New York: Appleton-Century-Crofts, 1952).
Blottner, Gene. *Columbia Noir: A Complete Filmography 1940–1962* (Jefferson, NC: McFarland, 2015).
Blumberg, Joel, and Sandra Grabman. *Lloyd Nolan: An Actor's Life with Meaning* (Albany, Ga: BearManor Media, 2010).
Bordman, Gerald. *American Theater: A Chronicle of Comedy & Drama, 1930–69* (New York: Oxford University Press, 1996).
Borgnine, Ernest. *Ernie: The Autobiography* (New York: Citadel, 2008).
Brownlow, Kevin. *The Parade's Gone By* (Berkeley, CA: University of California Press, 1968).
Cesari, Ernesto. *Mario Lanza: An American Tragedy* (Fort Worth, TX: Baskerville Publishing, 2004).
Church, Roy A., and Andrew Godley. *The Emergence of Modern Marketing* (London: Frank Cass & Co, Ltd., 2003).
Cohen, Karl F. *Forbidden Animation: Censored Cartoons and Blacklisted Animators in America* (Jefferson, NC: McFarland, 2004).
Connellan, Owen. (Translator) *The Annals of Ireland Translated from the original Irish of the Four Masters* (Dublin: Bryan Geraghty, 1846).
Cowans, Jon. *Empire Films and the Crisis of Colonialism 1946–59* (Baltimore, MD: Johns Hopkins University Press, 2015).
Cox, Jim. *American Radio Networks: A History* (Jefferson, NC: McFarland, 2009).
Curtis, Tony, and Barry Parris. *The Autobiography* (New York: William Morrow & Co, 1993).
Dauth, Brian. *Joseph L. Mankiewicz: Interviews* (Jackson: University of Mississippi Press, 2008).
Dawson, Jim. *Nervous Man Nervous: Jim McNeely and the Rise of the Honking Tenor Sax* (Milford, New Haven: Big Nickel Publications, 1994).
Dewey, Donald. *James Stewart: A Biography* (Atlanta, GA: Turner Publishing, Inc., 1996).
Dimendberg, Edward. *Film Noir and the Spaces of Modernity* (Cambridge, MA: Harvard University Press, 2004).
Donati, William. *Ida Lupino: A Biography* (Lexington: University of Kentucky Press, 1996).
Eames, John Douglas. *The MGM Story* (New York: Octopus Books, 1979).
_____. *The Paramount Story* (New York: Octopus Books, 1985).

Erickson, Hal. *Encyclopedia of Television Law Shows: Factual and Fictional Series About Judges, Lawyers and the Courtroom, 1948–2008* (Jefferson, NC: McFarland, 2009).
Everitt, David. *King of the Half Hour: Nat Hiken and the Golden Age of TV Comedy* (Syracuse, NY: Syracuse University Press, 2001).
Fishgall, Larry. *Against Type: The Biography of Burt Lancaster* (New York: Simon & Schuster, 1995).
Gardner, Ava, with Peter Evans. *Ava Gardner: The Secret Conversations* (New York: Simon & Schuster, 2014).
Garner, James, with Jon Winokur. *The Garner Files: A Memoir* (New York: Simon & Schuster, 2012).
Garrett, Betty. *Betty Garrett & Other Songs: A Life on Stage and Screen* (Lanham, MD: Madison Books, 1999).
Garrett, Eddie. *I Saw Stars ... in the 40s and 50s* (Victoria, British Columbia, Canada: Trafford Publishing Ltd., 2005).
Gifford, Barry. *Out of the Past: Adventures in Film Noir* (Jackson: University of Mississippi Press, 2001).
Goble, Alan. *The Complete Index to Literary Sources in Film* (East Grinstead, West Sussex, England: Bauker Saur, 1999).
Graver, Gary, with Andrew J. Rausch. *Making Films with Orson Welles: A Memoir* (Lanham, MD: Scarecrow Press, 2011).
Green, Paul. *Jeffrey Hunter: The Film, Television, Radio and Stage Performances* (Jefferson, NC: McFarland, 2014).
Grisham, Therese, and Julie Grossman. *Ida Lupino, Director: Her Art and Resilience in Times of Transition* (New Brunswick, NJ: Rutgers University Press, 2017).
Halliwell, Leslie. *Halliwell's Film Guide* (London: Guild Publishing Ltd, 1983).
Hardy, Phil. *Encyclopedia of Westerns* (New York: Octopus Books, 1985).
Hare, William. *L. A. Noir: Nine Dark Visions of the City of Angels* (Jefferson, NC: McFarland, 2004).
Haskin, Byron. *Director's Guild of America* (Berkeley: The University of California Press, 1984).
Hastie, Amelie. *BFI Classics: The Bigamist* (New York: Palgrave Macmillan, 2009).
Henriksen, Margot A. *Dr. Strangelove's America: Society and Culture in the Atomic Age* (Berkeley: University of California Press, 1997).
Henry, Marilyn, and Ron Desourdis. *The Films of Alan Ladd* (New York: Citadel Press, 1983).
Hirsch, Foster. *The Dark Side of the Screen: Film Noir* (Cambridge, Mass: Da Capo Press, 1981).
Hirschorn, Clive. *The Columbia Story* (New York: Hamlyn, 1988).
_____. *The Universal Story* (New York: Octopus Books, 1983).
_____. *The Warner Brothers Story* (New York: Octopus Books, 1979).
Jarlet, Franklin. *Robert Ryan: A Biography & Critical Biography* (Jefferson, NC: McFarland & Co, Inc., 1997).
Jewell, Richard B., and Vernon Harbin. *The RKO Story* (New York: Octopus Books, 1983).
Kabatchnik, Amnon. *Blood on the Stage, 1925–1950: Milestone Plays of Crime, Mystery & Detection: An Annotated Repertoire* (Lanham, MD: Scarecrow Press, 2010).
Karp, Joseph. *Orson Welles's Last Movie: The Making of The Other Side of the World* (New York: St. Martin's Press, 2015).
Krutnik, Frank. *In A Lonely Street: Film Noir, Genre, Masculinity* (Oxford, England: Routledge, 1991).
Lansman, Larry. *A Guide to American Crime Films of the Forties and Fifties* (Santa Barbara, CA: Greenwood Press, 1995).
Lee, Peggy. *Miss. Peggy Lee: An Autobiography* (New York: Donald I. Fine Publishing, 1989).
Linet, Beverly. *Ladd: A Hollywood Tragedy* (New York: A Berkley Book, 1980).

Lower, Cheryl Bray. *Joseph L. Mankiewicz: Critical Essays with an Annotated Bibliography and a Filmography* (Jefferson, NC: McFarland, 2014).
McBride, Joseph. *Searching for John Ford: A Life* (New York: St Martin's Press, 2001).
____. *Whatever Happened to Orson Welles? A Portrait of an Independent Career* (Lexington: The University Press of Kentucky, 2006).
McCaffrey, Donald W. *Three Classic Silent Screen Comedies Starring Harold Lloyd* (Madison, New Jersey: Fairleigh Dickinson University Press, 1976).
Mangan, Richard. *Gielgud's Letters* (London: Weidenfeld & Nicholson, 2004).
Mannering, Derek. *Mario Lanza: Singing to the Gods* (Jackson: University of Mississippi Press, 2005).
Manso, Peter. *Brando: The Biography* (New York: Hyperion, 1994).
Marschall, Rick. *The Golden Age of Television* (New York: Smithmark, 1995).
Mason, James. *Before I Forget* (London: Hamish Hamilton, 1981).
Mayer, Geoff. *Historical Dictionary of Crime Films* (Lanham, MD: Scarecrow Press, 2012).
Meil, Eila. *Casting Might-Have-Beens: A Film by Film Directory of Roles Given to Others* (Jefferson, NC: McFarland, 2005).
Monk, Philip. *Double-Cross: The Hollywood Films of Douglas Gordon* (Toronto: Art Gallery of York University, 2003).
Morley, Sheridan. *John Gielgud: The Official Biography* (New York: Simon & Schuster, 2010).
Moyer, Daniel, and Eugene Alvarez. *Just the Facts, Ma'am: The Authorized Biography of Jack Webb* (Santa Ana, CA: Seven Locks Press, 2001).
Oderman, Stuart. *Lillian Gish: A Life on Stage & Screen* (Jefferson, NC: McFarland, 2000).
O'Hara, Maureen.*'Tis Herself: An Autobiography* (New York: Simon & Schuster, 2005).
Osteen, Mark. *Nightmare Alley: Film Noir and the American Dream* (Baltimore, MD: Johns Hopkins University Press, 2013).
Ottoson, Robert. *A Reference Guide to the American Film Noir, 1940–1958* (Lanham, MD: Scarecrow Press, 1981).
Park, William. *What is Film Noir?* (Lewisburg, PA: Bucknell University Press, 2011).
Pike, Andrew, and Ross Cooper. *Australian Film 1900–77: A Guide to Feature Film Production* (Melbourne: Oxford University Press, 1998).
Pomerance, Murray, and Barton R. Palmer. *A Little Solitaire: John Frankenheimer and American Film* (New Brunswick, NJ: Rutgers University Press, 2011).
Quirk, Lawrence J. *The Films of Fredric March* (New York: Citadel Press, 1971).
____.*The Films of Ronald Colman* (New York: Citadel Press, 1979).
____. *The Films of William Holden* (New York: Citadel Press, 1973).
Renoir, Jean. *Renoir on Renoir: Interviews, Essays and Remarks* (Cambridge: Cambridge University Press, 1989).
Richmond, Peter. *Fever: The Life and Music of Miss Peggy Lee* (London: Picador, 2007).
Rubin, Martin. *Thrillers: Genres in American Cinema* (Cambridge: Cambridge University Press, 1999).
Ruppli, Michel. *The Mercury Labels* (Westport: Greenwood, 1993).
Schwartz, Ronald. *House of Noir: Dark Visions from Thirteen Film Studies* (Jefferson, NC: McFarland, 2013).
Server, Lee. *Ava Gardner: Love is Nothing* (New York: St. Martin's Griffin, 2006).
Seydor, Paul. *Peckinpah, The Western Films: A Reconsideration* (Urbana: University of Illinois Press, 1999).
Shadolan, Jack. *Dreams and Dead Ends: The American Gangster Film* (New York: Oxford University Press, 2001).
Sherman, Vincent. *Studio Affairs: My Life as a Film Director* (Lexington: The University Press of Kentucky, 1996).
Silver, Alain, and Elizabeth Ward. *Film Noir* (London: Secker and Warburg, 1979).
Somerset-Ward, Richard. *An American Theater: The Story of Westport County Playhouse, 1931–2005* (New York: Yale University Press, 2005).

Stack, Robert, and Mark Evans. *Straight Shooting* (New York: Macmillan Publishing Company, 1980).
Sterling, Christopher H. *Encyclopedia of Radio* (Lanham, MD: Routledge, 2004).
Stewart, Lucy Ann Liggett. *Ida Lupino as Film Director, 1949–1953: An Auteur Approach* (New York: Arno Press, 1980).
Strachan, Alan. *Secret Dreams: A Biography of Michael Redgrave* (London: Weidenfeld & Nicholson, 2004).
Taylor, Russell, et al. *Hollywood: 50 Great Years* (London: Colour Library Books, 1991).
Terrace, Vincent. *The Encyclopedia of Television Pilots, 1937–2012* (Jefferson, NC: McFarland, 2013).
Thomas, Bob. *Golden Boy: The Untold Story of William Holden* (London: Weidenfeld & Nicolson, 1983).
Thomas, Tony, and Aubrey Soloman. *The Films of Twentieth Century Fox* (The Citadel Press, New Jersey, 1979).
Tonguette, Peter Prescott. *Orson Welles Remembered: Interviews with His Actors, Editors, Cinematographers and Magicians* (Jefferson, NC: McFarland, 2007).
Torme, Mel. *It Wasn't All Velvet: An Autobiography* (London: Robson, 1988).
Tranberg, Charles. *Fredric March: A Consummate Actor* (Albany, GA: BearManor Media, 2013).
Tranberg, Charles. *Robert Taylor: A Biography* (Albany, GA: BearManor Media, 2011).
Troyan, Michael. *A Rose for Mrs. Miniver: The Life of Greer Garson* (Lexington: The University of Press of Kentucky, 2010).
Truffaut, Francois. *The Films in My Life* (New York: Touchstone: Simon & Schuster, 1978).
Turner, Adrian. *The Making of David Lean's Lawrence of Arabia* (Limpsfield: Dragon's World, 1994).
Vieira, Mark. *Into the Dark: The Hidden World of Film Noir* (Philadelphia: Running Press, 2016).
Vickers, Hugo. *Vivien Leigh* (London: Hamish Hamilton, 1988).
Vinson, James, et al. *The International Dictionary of Films and Filmmakers: Actors and Actresses* (London: St. James Press, 1986).
Warren, Bill, and Bill Thomas. *Keep Watching the Skies: American Science Fiction Movies of the Fifties* (Jefferson, NC: McFarland, 2010).
Wayne, Jane Ellen. *Ava's Men: The Private Life of Ava Gardner* (London: Robson Books, 1990).
Weddle, David. *If They Move—Kill Em: The Life and Times of Sam Peckinpah* (New York: Grove Press, 1994).
Ziegler, Philip. *Olivier* (London: MacLehose Press, 2013).

Index

Abbott, John 39
Academy Awards 1, 50, 112, 114, 124, 148, 151, 164, 174
"Act of Contrition" 33
An Act of Murder 39, 47–49
Act of Violence 48
"Actor's Blood" 10
Adams, Gerald Drayson 67
Adams, Nick 137
Addy, Wesley 11
Adler, Luther 57
The Admirable Crichton 6
The Admiral Was a Lady 63–64
Agar, John 104
Airline Pilots Association 145
Airport 145
Akins, Claude 166
Alda, Alan 171
All About Eve 54
All My Sons 38
Allbritton, Louise 26
Allegret, Yves 138
Allied Artists 79–80, 135
Allyson, June 170
Always Tomorrow 113
The Amazing Mrs. Holiday 22–23, 24, 36, 44
The Ambitious One 138
L'Amitieuse 137–38
Anderson, Maxwell 9
Anderson, Michael 129, 131
Andrews, Lois 26
Angel Face 102
Anna Christie 113
Annie Get Your Gun 166
Another Part of the Forest 39, 42–44
Anthony, Ray 135
Araiza, Raul 172
Arbeid, Gerry 173
Arden, Eve 21
Around the World in Eighty Days 131
As You Like It 83
Aschler, Irving 73

Asner, Ed 144, 145
Atkinson, Brooks 85

Backfire 50–52
Bailey, Bob 32
Baker, Carroll 162
The Balding Affair 169
Baldwin, Agnes Bridget (mother) 3–4, 25–26
Baldwin, Elizabeth (aunt) 4
Baldwin, Dr. Francis W. (uncle) 4
Baldwin, Mary (aunt) 4
Baldwin, Mary Anne (née Tobin) 3
Baldwin, Michael (grandfather) 3–4
Ball, Lucille 16–17, 18, 21, 54, 117
Banks, Pulan 21
The Barber of Seville 45
The Barefoot Contessa 1, 92, 109–14, 119, 146
"Barn Burning" 146
Barrie, J.M. 6
Basehart, Richard 138
The Bat 8
Batanides, Arthur 141
"Batter Up" 118
"Battle Hymn of the Republic" 33
Battle Zone 100
The Beautiful Blonde from Bashful Bend 47
Beckett, Samuel 96
Beery, Noah 81
Beery, Wallace 137
Begley, Ed 31, 50, 86
Behind Locked Doors 67
A Bell for Adano 124
Bendix, William 38, 135
Bergen, Polly 71
Bergman, Ingrid 113
Bernardo O'Higgins 62
The Best of the Bard 92
The Best Things in Life Are Free 54
Best Years 8
Bettger, Lyle 77

227

228　Index

Between Midnight and Dawn 65–67, 104
Beyond the Sunset 73
The Bible 164
The Big Combo 105
The Big Frame 106
The Big Heat 100, 104
Big House, U.S.A. 106
The Big Land 67, 80–81, 82, 133
The Big Steal 67
The Bigamist 97–100
Billboard 34
Birdman of Alcatraz 158
Bixby, Bill 172
Black Bart 42
Black Christmas 172–73
The Black Sword 113
Blind Alley 32
The Blind Mirror 102
"The Blind Spot" 30
Blood on the Moon 95
"The Blue Men" 125
Blyth, Ann 43, 54
Bodeen, DeWitt 138
Bogart, Humphrey 30, 100, 109, 110, 111, 113, 137, 146
Bombardier 18
Bonanza 81
Boone, Richard 162
Booth, John Wilkes 30
Borgnine, Ernest 165, 166
Born Yesterday 40
Boru, Brian 3
Boulder Dam 59, 60
Bowers, William 38
Boxoffice 157
Boyd, Stephen 165
Boys Clubs of America 42
Brand, Neville 56, 158
Brando, Jocelyn 100
Brando, Marlon 89, 91
Brandt, Malcolm 164
Brazzi, Rossano 109, 110, 111
Breaking Point 143
Bredell, Ellwood 36
Breen, Joseph 98
Brennan, Walter 30, 166
Britton, Pamela 54
Broad, Jay 169
Brooke, Rupert 34
Brooklyn Daily Eagle 25
Brooks, Geraldine 47, 48, 48–49
Brown, Jim 161
Brown, John Mason 11
Browning, Elizabeth Barrett 34
Bruce, Carol 24
Buchanan, Edgar 76
Buffalo Grass 80
Buka, Donald 67
Burr, Raymond 31, 133
Burton, Richard 163
Bury the Dead 10

Busman's Honeymoon 9
Buttons, Red 162

Cabaret 14
Caesar and Cleopatra 138
Cagney, James 52, 53, 54
Calhern, Louis 89, 90, 91
Campbell, Beverly (alias Garland) 56
Cannes Film Festival 48
Cantro, Sydney 73
Cape Fear 153
Cardenas, Ruby 62
Cardiff, Jack 109
Carey, Harry 18
Carey, Harry, Jr. 72
Carlson, Richard 18
Carmichael, Hoagy 116
Carnera, Primo 101
Carradine, John 156
Carroll, Joan 21
Carroll, Madeleine 83
Carter, Helena 46
Cassavetes, John 154
"Castro vs. Batista" 145
Caulfield, Joan 46
Cavalcade 107
CBS Radio 29
CBS Television 32, 122, 123
Chandler, Raymond 125
Chaney, Lon, Jr. 124
"Charlie C Company" 124
Chatterton, Ruth 13–14
Chertok, Jack 140
Chicago Fair 1950 62
The Child Buyer 162
China Venture 100
Chock Full o' Nuts 6
Christian, Linda 102
Clark, Bob 173
Clark, Dane 50
Clarke, Charles G. 136
Climax 124
The Climbers 138
Clooney, Rosemary 131
Clyde, Andy 166
Cobb, Lee J. 25, 166
Coburn, Charles 21
Cochran, Eddie 135
Cochran, Steve 100
Cohen, Harold V. 10, 35, 132, 151
Collinge, Patricia 84
Collins, Joan 136
Collins, Ray 45
Collins, Russell 9
Colman, Ronald 39, 40, 40–41
Columbia Laboratory Players 6
Columbia Pictures 89, 135
"The Comedian" 125
Comingore, Nancy 21
"Coney Island Winter" 126
Confessions of a Scoundrel 114

Connolly, Shirley 42
Connors, Chuck 163
Conrad, William 36
Conte, Richard 6, 105, 164
Cook, Billy 93
Cook, Elisha, Jr. 115
Cooper, Gary 45
Coriolanus 163
Cornfield, Hubert 149–51
Cortes, Hernan 172
The Count of Monte Cristo 22
The Country of the Blind 32
Cow Country 79–80, 100
Coward, Noel 83, 107
Craig, James 21
Crain, Jeanne 135
Crane, Stephen 34
Crawford, Broderick 106
Crawford, Joan 100
"Crazy Town" 30
Crolla, Henri 138
Crowther, Bosley 53, 113, 165
Cry Copper 106
A Cry in the Night 81, 132–33
Cukor, George 14, 28, 40
Culp, Robert 143
Cummings, Irving, Jr. 19
Curse of the Cat People 95
Curtis, Tony 151, 154
Custer, Gen. Armstrong 70
Cyrano de Bergerac 63

D-Day the Sixth of June 132
Dailey, Dan 135
The Dam Busters 131
The Damned Don't Cry 52
Damone, Vic 116
Dandalos, Nick 113
A Dangerous Profession 81
Daniels, Marc 146
"Danny Boy" 26
Darin, Bobby 154
Dark of the Sun 149
"The Dark Stranger" 125
Darrieux, Daniele 54
da Silva, Howard 81
Daughters of Atreus 8
Davenport, Harry 22, 45
Davis, Bette 21, 43, 173
Davis, Maxwell 56
Davis, Owen 124
Day, Doris 39, 165
Day, Laraine 115, 149
Day of Triumph 133
Dead Reckoning 67
de Carlo, Yvonne 38, *76*
Decca Records 33
de Corsia, Ted 31, 89
Dederich, Chuck 163
The Deep Six 135
The Defenders 142

de Laurentiis, Dino 113, 164
De Mille, Cecil B. 89
Denver and Rio Grande 77–79, 82
Design for Living 83
Desmond, Johnny 37
The Devil and Daniel Webster 87
Devine, Andy 128
The Diamond Orchid 164
The Dick Powell Theater 144
Dieterle, William 12, 13, 86, 87
The Difference 93
Dillinger, Nat 69
Dillman, Bradford 173
Disney, Walt 154–55
The Dispossessed 138
Dix, Richard 33
D.O.A. 1, 54–58, 65, 123
Domergue, Faith 102, 113
Domino, Fats 135
Domino Parlor 36
Donlevy, Brian 81, 133
Donner, Richard 142
The Doomsday Flight 144–45
Dortort, David 81
A Double Life 39–41, 89
"Double of Nothing" 141
Doud, Gil 32
Douglas, Gordon 66
Douglas, Kirk 154, 159
Dragon, Carmen 33
Dream No Evil 170–71
Dru, Joanne 59, *60*
Drums Along the Mohawk 75
Duel in the Sun 75
Duff, Howard 142
Duke, Doris 26
Durbin, Deanna 20, *20*, 22–3, 44, 45, 68
Duryea, Dan 43
Duse, Eleonora 113
Duvivier, Julien 21

Eckhart, Eileen 125
The Ed Sullivan Show 123
Edward II 30
Eire Bureau of Tourism 69
Eldridge, Florence *43*, 47, 48
Ellery Queen's Mystery Magazine 124
Elmer Gantry 151
Empire Theater, NY 9
English, Marla 104–05
"Epipac" 172
Erhlich, Jake 120, 142
Erickson, Leif 81
"An Error in Chemistry" 124, 146
Erskine, Chester 102
Escape 32
Ethel Barrymore Theater, NY 84
Evans, Betsy 33
Evans, Maurice 11, 165
Evans, Vince 46
"Everybody's Playing Polo" 142

Index

Ewell, Tom 134
The Executioners 153

The Fake 100
Family Portrait 10
Family Rosary Crusade 33
Fantastic Voyage 164–65
The Farmer's Other Daughter 170
Father Takes a Wife 18
Faulkner, William 124, 146
FBI 106, 155
Fenton, Leslie 73
Ferguson, Frank 107
Fernandel 138
Fernandez-Santos, Angel 112
Ferrer, Jose 63
A Few Flowers for Shiner 102
Fiesta 119
"Figaro" 45
Fight for Freedom 30
Fighter Squadron 45
Film Bulletin 77, 96, 168
filmmakers 123
First National Bank 6
Fitzgerald, Barry 22, 76
Fitzgerald, Ella 128
Fitzgerald, F. Scott 83
Five Star Final 124
Fix, Paul 77
Fleming, Rhonda 73, 74
Flesh and Blood 144
Flesh Peddler 54
Fonda, Henry 158
Fontaine, Joan 38, *97*, 98, 99, 100
Fontaine, Lillian 99
Fontana of Rome 110
Fontane Sisters 62
Fool's Hill 10
For the Love of Mary 44–45
Ford, Constance 125
Ford, Glenn 73, *74*, 133
Ford, John 117, 155–58
Ford, Wallace 72
Fordham University 5, 6
Foreign Correspondent 99
44th Street Theater, NY 8
The Four-Poster 85
Fowler, Gene 54
Franciosa, Anthony 162
Francis, Anne 133
Frankenheimer, John 125, 158–60, 173
Fredericks, Ellsworth 159
Freeman, Mona 137
Fregonese, Hugo 113
Friel, Brian 168
From Here to Eternity 69, 100
"The Further Adventures of Gallagher" 144

Gabel, Martin 29
Gable, Clark 99

Gaddis, Martha 158
Gaddis, Thomas E. 158
Galileo, Galileo 172
Gardner, Ava 36, 37, 47, 109, *110*, 112
Garner, James 139, 170
Garrett, Betty 6, 26
Garson, Greer 91
Gaslight 40
Gassmann, Vittorio 112
Gauguin, Paul 138
Geary Theater, San Francisco 14
George, Gladys 76
Georges, Francois 133
Gielgud, John 1, 6, 8, 91
Gilberto, Astrud 143
Gillespie, "Dizzy" 56
A Girl, a Guy and a Gob 16–18, 67
The Girl Can't Help It 133–35, 137
"The Girl from Ipanema" 143
Girl on the Spanish Steps 110
Gish, Lillian 9
The Glass Bottom Boat 165
Glassberg, Irving 39
Gleason, Jackie 143
Godard, Jean-Luc 150
Goddard, Paulette 102
Godfrey, Arthur 102
Goff, Ivan 52
Golden Boy 135
Golden Gate Theater 18
Golden Globe Awards 159
Goldsmith, Jerry 159
"La Golondrinha" 168
Gomez, Robert 143
Gone with the Wind 14, 162
Goodbye My Fancy 83
Gordon, Gordon 106
Gordon, Michael 39
Gordon, Mildred 106
Gordon, Ruth 40, 171, 174
Gotham Productions 69
Grable, Betty 47
Grafton, Samuel 84
Grahame, Gloria 106, 142
Grant, James Edward 68
Grant, Marshall 36
"Grant vs. Lee" 145
Granville, Bonita 26
The Great Imposter 154
The Great Lie 21
The Great Missouri Raid 71
The Greatest Show on Earth 89
The Greatest Show on Earth (TV) 147
Greeley, Horace 156
Greene, Clarence 56
Greene, Lorne 6
Greenspun, Hank 113
Greer, Jane 63
Griggs, Loyal 153
Gruber, Frank 80
Guffey, Burnett 69

Index

The Gun 81
Guns of the Timberland 81
Guthrie, Carl 139
Gwenn, Edmund 97, 99

Hagen, Uta 10
Hail, America! 33
Hale, Barbara 65
Halloran, John 53
Hamilton, Patrick 30
Hamlet 6, 8–9, 49, 92, 112, 120, 131, 177
The Hamlet 146
The Hanged Man 143
Hanna, David 111
Hanley, William 144
The Happy Time 102
Hardwicke, Sir Cedric 13
Harlow 162
Harlow, Jean 128
Harris, Dick 98
Harris, Jed 10
Harris, Richard 173
Harrison, Joan 38
Hart, Moss 24, 25, 26
Harte, Brett 169
Haskin, Byron 70–71, 75, 77, 79
Hasso, Signe 41
Hatcher, Mary 117
Hawks, Howard 81
Hayden, Sterling 77, 78, 106
Hayes, Gabby 168
Hayes, John 170
Hayes, Peter Lind 83
Hayworth, Rita 154, 175
Healy, Mary 83
"Hear the Mellow Wedding Bells" 142
"The Heart Is a Forgotten Hotel" 126
Hecht, Ben 10
Heflin, Van 104
Hefti, Neal 163
Hell on Frisco Bay 104
Hellinger, Mark 36, 37
Heming, Violet 5
Hemingway, Ernest 36, 37
Hendrix, Wanda 63
Henreid, Paul 142
Henry, Shifty 55
Henry IV, Part 1 11
Henry V 155
Hepburn, Katharine 83
Here's Love 163
Hervey, Irene 133
Hester Street 69
The High Chaparral 147
High Vermilion 75
Hiken, Nat 168
His Majesty O'Keefe 71
"The History of Henry Esmond, Esq." 33
"Hit and Run" 123
The Hitch-Hiker 1, 93–96
Hitchcock, Alfred 30, 105

Hitler, Adolf 9, 30, 60
"Hitler vs. Chamberlain" 145
Hobo News 96
Hodiak, John 101
Hogan, Darlene 73
Holden, William 86, 87, 116, 136, 166, 167
A Hole in the Head 126
Holiday 123
Holt, Nat 70, 71
Homeier, Skip 125
Hoodlum Empire 86
Hoover, J. Edgar 106
Hope, Bob 55
The Hope Diamond Jinx 154
Horner, Harry 138
Houdini, Harry 5
Houseman, John 91
How Green Was My Valley 102
How Santa Claus Came to Simpson's Bar 169
Howard, "Hot Licks" 56
Hudson, Rock 45
Hughes, Dorothy B. 143
Hughes, Howard 112
Hugo, Victor 13
The Hunchback of Notre Dame 12–13, 86
Hunter, Jeffrey 151–53, 152
Huston, John 164
Hutton, Betty 24
The Hyde Side 69

I Am a Camera 14
"I Am an American" 33
"I Leaned on a Man" 81
I Remember Mama 14
"I Speak for Democracy" 33
I Walk Alone 70
"Icebound" 124
Ice Station Zebra 165
Île de France 149
"I'll Take You Home, Kathleen" 45
"Immortal Gentleman" 30
In a Lonely Place 69, 143
The Inner Light 11
The Intruders 145
"The Invisible Government" 144
"The Iron Captain" 126
Isn't It Shocking 171
It Happened Yesterday 131
I've Got a Secret 124
I've Got Sixpence 84–85, 92
Ivo, Tommy 124
Ivy 38

Jaeckel, Richard 107
Jagger, Dean 72, 77, 78
Jailbait Babysitter 170
Janssen, David 151, 152
Jason, Rick 68
Jessel, George 32
Jigsaw 170

Johnny Dollar (TV pilot) 32
Johnny Eager 69
Johnny Midnight 140–42
Johnson, Ben *167*
Johnson, Erskine 62
Jones, Carolyn 104
Jordan, Louis 62
Jourdan, Louis 165
Journey to the Center of the Earth 69
El Juicio de Socrates 172
Julius Caesar 9–10, 35
Julius Caesar (film) 89–92, 98, 111

Kael, Pauline 165
Kamen, Clifford 123
Kanin, Fay 83
Kanin, Garson 40, 134
The Kansas City Story 62
Kefauver, Sen. Estes 60, 86
Kelley, Barry 59, 107
Kelly, Gene 154
Kelly, Nancy 18–21, *19*, 117
Kennedy, Arthur 154
Kennedy, Pres. John F. 158
Kerr, Deborah 91, 100, 113
The Keystone Cops 96
The Killer Wore a Badge 106
The Killers 30, 36–37, 112
King Lear 92
The Kiss 170
Kiss Tomorrow Goodbye 66
Kitt, Eartha 138, 163
Kitty Foyle 18
The Knave of Diamonds 38
Knotts, Don 168
Knox, Alexander 68
Knudsen, Peggy 46
Kohn, Edmond 118
Kossoff, David 130
Kotcher, Leo 67
Kraft Television Theater 137
Krasner, Milton 40
Kruger, Otto 59, *60*

Ladd, Alan 79, *80*, 81, 116
Lady Godiva 5
Lady Windermere's Fan 6
Lancaster, Burt 36, 37, 38, 100, 103, 116, 158, 159
Landers, Lew 89
Lane, Abbe 133
Lang, Fritz 100
Langner, Laurence 5
Lanza, Mario 25–26, 135
La Rue, Ray 56
The Last Case of Mr. Moto 136
The Last Tycoon 83
The Last Voyage 148–49
"The Late Throw" 118
La Torre, Charles *61*
Laughton, Charles 13, 21

The Law Strikes Back 122
Lawless Territory 79
Lawrence, Marc 170
Lawrence of Arabia 154
Lean, David 154
Leave Her to Heaven 13, 84
Lee, Peggy 128
Lee, Rowland V. 22
Leigh, Vivien 14
Lerner, Alan Jay 84
Leslie, Aleen 69
Levin, Henry 69
Levine, Sam 36
Lewis, Mike 79
Lewis, Sammy 135
Lichtenstein, Roy 173
Liebovitz, Matthew 34
Life 69
The Life of Nick the Greek 113
Liliom 10
Lindfors, Viveca 50, *51*, 84
Ling, Eugene 67
The Little Foxes 43
Little Richard 135
Llewellyn, Richard 102
Lloyd, Frank 107
Lloyd, Harold 16–17, 18
Lloyds of London 59
Lockridge, Richard 11
Lockwood, Vice Adm. Charles A. 139
London, Jack 54
London, Julie 149, *150*
"Lonesome Road" 126
The Long, Hot Summer 140, 146–47
"The Long Shot" 124
The Longest Day 158
Lord, Jack 144
Loren, Sophia 164
The Los Angeles Times 13
The Lost Weekend 59
Lothar, Ernst 48
The Love God? 168
Lovejoy, Frank 32, 93, *94*
Lucky Luciano 171–72
Lugosi, Bela 117
"Lullaby of Broadway" 140
Lund, John 32
Lupino, Ida 33, 93–100, *98*, 103, 120, 123, 142
The Lux Family Theater 32
Lux Playhouse 126
Lux Video Theater 122
Lynn, Jeffrey 42

MacArthur, Gen. Douglas 42
Macbeth 49
MacDonald, John D. 153
MacGinnis, Niall 166
MacLane, Barton 79
MacLean, Alistair 165
MacMillan & Wife 147

Index

MacMurray, Fred 106
MacRae, Gordon 50
Macris, Marie 24
Mainwaring, Daniel 93
Malden, Karl 25, 147
The Male Principle 154
Malone, Dorothy 148, 149
The Maltese Falcon 102
Man in the Dark 87–89
Man in the Middle 164
Man-trap 151–53
The Man Who Lived Twice 87
The Man Who Shot Liberty Valance 155–58
The Manchurian Candidate 158
Mandel, Johnny 149
Manett, Claire 24
Manganese 138
Manhattan College 5
Mankiewicz, Joseph L. 1, 54, 89, 90, 91, 109–13
Der Mann, der seinen Morder Sucht 56
Manners, Dorothy 95
Manning, Bruce 22
Mansfield, Jayne 134, 135
March, Fredric 43, 44, 47, 159
The March of Time 29
Marcus, Larry 98
"Maria's Theme" 109
Marks, Percy 38
Marlowe, Christopher 30
Marquand, John P. 136
Marshall, E.G. 144
Marshall, Herbert 38
Marshall, William 24
Martin, Dean 81
Marvin, Lee 128, 155
Mason, James 84, 89, 91, 111
Masquers Club 120
Mate, Rudolph 56, 57, 106
Mathews, Kerwin 165
"A Matter of Life" 123
Mauree, Mike 46
Mayo, Virginia 53, 81
The Mazda Mines 83
McCambridge, Mercedes 54, 169
McCarthy, Sen. Joseph 39
McClintic, Guthrie 8
McCoy, Horace 86
McDowall, Roddy 170
McGavin, Darren 145
McGivern, William P. 104
McGowan, Tom 69
McGraw, Charles 36
McIntire, John 137
McLaglen, Victor 22
McNally, Stephen 144
McQueen, Steve 151
Meet the Wife 8
Meisner, Sandy 6
Men in Crisis 145–46
Mendelssohn, Eleonora 8

Mercury Theater 9, 10
Mercury Theater of the Air 29
Meredith, Burgess 9
Merrill, Gary 25, 54, 169
Metro Goldwyn Mayer 11, 89, 111, 170, 177
Metronome 54
Metropolitan Opera 5
Meyer, Emile 104, 126
Meyer, Johnny 112
Michaels, Beverly 56
Michealis, Adrian 33
Middleton, Robert 126
Miele, Elizabeth 8
"Mighty Lak a Rose" 22
Miles, Vera 142, 143
Miller, Ann 24
Miller, Arthur 38
Miller, Marvin 106
Millhauser, Bertram 38
The Mills of God 48
Minotis, Alexis 131
Mintor, Allen 131
Miracle on 34th Street 99, 163
Les Miracles N'ont Lieu qu'une Fois 138
Miranda, Carmen 47
Mission: Impossible 147
Mr. and Mrs. Smith 18
Mr. Skeffington 52
Mitchum, Robert 102, 164
Moliere 138
Molnar, Ferenc 10, 21
The Money Man 104
Monogram Pictures 100
Montgomery, Robert 143
Moon Pilot 154–55
Moore, Michael 76
Moore, Terry 68, 69
Morgan, Michele 24
Morrow, Vic 166
"The Most Tragic Brutus" 30
Motion Picture Daily 16, 40, 151
Motion Picture Herald 42
Move Over Darling 39
"Muddy Track" 30
The Mummy's Hand 36
The Munday Scheme 168
The Murder 102
Murder in the Tate Gallery 100
Murphy, George 16, *17*
Murray, Don 145
Musuraca, Nicholas 95
Mutiny on the Bounty 107
The Mutual Family Theater 32–33
My Beloved 33–34
"My Gypsy Heart" 110
My Six Convicts 122
"Mysteries of the Zodiac" 117

Naish, J. Carroll 77, *78*
Naismith, Laurence 163
Naked Alibi 106

Index

Nascimbene, Mario 110
NAXOS 34
NBC University Theater 33
Nefertiti 173
Neighborhood Playhouse School of the Theater 6
Nelson, Barry 25
Nero, Emperor 135
"The Net Draws Tight" 125
Netcher, Molly 46
Neubach, Ernst 56
Neuman, E. Jack 142
New York Giants 118
The New York Sun 11
The New Yorker 90
Newman, Alfred 13
Newman, Paul 133
Niesen, Gertrude 24
Nigh, Jane 26
Night Beat 32
1984 1, 129–31
99 and 44/100% Dead 173–74
Niven, David 154
No, No, Nanette 18
Noiret, Phillipe 154
Nolan, Lloyd 33, 54, 171
"Not Even the Gulls Should Weep" 142
Noticias de la Historia 172

Oates, Warren *167*
Obliging Young Lady 21–22
Oboler, Arch 30
O'Brien, Agnes Mary 4
O'Brien, Brendan J. (son) 119
O'Brien, Bridget E. (daughter) 114, 119, 166, 174, 176–77
O'Brien, James (grandfather) 3
O'Brien, James Alfred (father) 3
O'Brien, James F. (brother) 4
O'Brien, Kathleen Marjorie (sister) 4, 5
O'Brien, Liam F. (brother) 4–5, 46, 68, 83, 102, 106, 113, 118, 120–21, 126, 131, 132, 140, 154, 164, 169, 172
O'Brien, Maria M. (daughter) 119, 142, 166, 174, 175
O'Brien, Pat 54, 170
O'Brien, Winifred C. 4
Odds Against Tomorrow 104
O'Driscoll, Martha 24
O'Dwyer, Mayor Bill 54
Oedipus Rex 131
O'Hara, Maureen *12*
O'Herlihy, Dan 146
O'Keefe, Dennis 100
Olivier, Laurence 1, 14, 92, 131, 172
"On Moonlight Bay" 45
On the Waterfront 114
One Touch of Venus 47
O'Neill, Eugene 113
Operation 16-Z 100
Orlando, Guido 114

The Orloff Whip 104
Orwell, George 1, 129, 130
Ostow, Stuart 162
Othello 6
The Other Side of the Wind 169–70
Ottawa After Dark 138–39
Ouspenskaya, Maria 8
Out of the Sky 84
The Outsider 145
Overell, Beulah 102
Oyama, Reiko 136

Pachuco 54
Paint Your Wagon 84, 119
El Pais 112
Palance, Jack 106
Palmer, Lilli 169
Parachute Battalion 18, 19, 24
Paramount Pictures 47, 79, 153
Parisy, Andrea 138
Parker, Col. Tom 137
Parks, Larry 65
Parnell 10
Parry, Harvey 76
Party Girl 67
Pass, Joe 163
Paxinou, Katina 131
Peck, Gregory 54
Peckinpah, Sam 126, 161, 166–68
Pendergast, Tom 62
Penn, Arthur 144
Penthouse 63
Pepper, Art 163
Pepsi Cola 118
Peron, Evita 164
Peron, Juan 164
Perry Mason 142
Pete Kelly's Blues 128, 134
Petticoat Larceny 22
The Phoniest Game on Broadway 113
Picco, Millo 5
Picture Show 105
Pidgeon, Walter 133
Pilate, Pontius 164
Pinter, Harold 36
Pinza, Ezio 42
Pirandello, Luigi 164
Pitts, ZaSu 77
Planet of the Apes 165
Playhouse 90 125
The Play's the Thing 21
Pleasence, Donald 130, 165
Plunder Road 150
Poe, Edgar Allan 34
Ponthier, Francois 138
Ponti, Carlo 113
Popkin, Harry 54
Popkin, Leo C. 56, 57
Poppaea 135
Porter, Don *60*
Portrait in Black 113

Index

Portrait of Jennie 87, 125
Ports of Call 123
Powder Town 22, 30
Powell, Dick 30, 134
Preminger, Otto 102
The President's Lady 69
Presley, Elvis 67, 135, 137
Preston, Robert 18
Price, Vincent 38, 113, 170
Prince, William 63
Private Hell 36 100
Production Code Administration 98
Prowl Car 65
The Prowler 104
Pushover 106

The Quiller Memorandum 131
Quine, Richard 163–64
Quinn, Anthony 113
Quinn, William M. 47
Quirino, Pres. Elpidio 46

Race Street 81
The Rack 133
Rackin, Martin 81, 120
Rafferty, Chips 138
Raines, Ella 38
Rains, Claude 142
Ranieri, Katyna 110
Rathvon, Peter 131
RCA School Broadcast 33
Rear Window 105
The Red Badge of Courage 34
Red Carpet 69
Redgrave, Michael *129*, 130, 131
The Redhead and the Cowboy 73–74
Redwing, Rodd 73
Reed, Alan 141
Reed, Walter 22, 45
Reeves, George 25
The Remarkable Mr. Pennypacker 69, 131
"Rendezvous in Japan" 136
Rennahan, Ray 71, 75, 79
Renoir, Jean 22–23
The Restless and the Damned 138
Rex Harrison's Stories of Love 172
Rheingold Beer 118
Ride the Pink Horse 143
Riff Raff 81
Riggs, Lynn 36
The Right of Way 164
Right You Are Mr. Moto 136
Rio Bravo 81
Rio Conchos 161–62
Ritter, Thelma 158
River of Mystery 166
RKO 11–12, 16, 21, 29
Roberts, Ben 52
Roberts, Jane 46
Robin Hood 33
Robinson, Edward G. 30, 126

Robinson, Karl 123
Robinson Crusoe on Mars 71
"Rock Around the Rockpile" 135
Rogell, Albert S. 81
Rogers, Ginger 21
Rogers, Kasey *78*
Rogue's Regiment 42
Roman, Ruth 106, *107*, 108, 146
Romeo and Juliet 14–15, 16, 49
Romero, Cesar 117
Rooney, Mickey 125
Roosevelt, Pres. Franklin D. 158
Roosevelt, Teddy 158
Rope 30
Roseman, Leonard 165
Rosi, Francesco 171
Rossellini, Roberto 113
Rosson, Harold 128
Roszla, Miklos 40
Rouse, Richard 56
Rubinstein, Serge 62
"Run Softly, Oh Softly" 142
Russell, Charles 30
Rust, Richard 142
Rutherford, Ann 170
Ryan, Robert 166

Sabinson, Lee 84
Sailor on Horseback 54
St. James' Theater, NY 11
St. Patrick's Cathedral, NY 11
St. Thomas Parochial School, NY 5
St. Vincent's Hospital, NY 4
Salkind, Alexander 114
Sam Benedict 120, 140, 142–43, 162
San Juan 115
Sanders, George 148–49
Sands, Tommy 137
San Juan, Olga M. 32, 46–47, 54, 62, 84,
  100, 112, 115–20, 131, 135, 142, 149, 166,
  174
Saturday Evening Post 75, 106, 136
Saval, Dany 155
Sawtell, Paul 72, 75
Saxon, John 173
Sayers, Dorothy L. 9
Scandal Sheet 67
Schallert, Edwin 13
Schary, Dore 89
Scheier, Paul 162
Schenk, Nicholas 111
Schifrin, Lalo 145
Schlitz Playhouse 126
School of Dramatic Art, NY 8
Schor, Lou 98
Scorsese, Martin 172
Scott, Ken 136
Scott, Lizabeth 67, 68, 69
Scott, Randolph 18
Screen Director's Playhouse 126
Sebastian, Ed 116

The Secret of Convict Lake 39
Seltzer, Frank 60, 61, 62
Selznick, David O. 14
Serling, Rod 133, 144, 145, 159
Seven Days in May 158–60
711 Ocean Drive 30, 59–62, 65, 70
Seven Hills of Rome 135
"Seventeen Gypsies and a Sinner Named Charlie"
The Seventh Victim 95
The Shadow 29
Shakedown 69
Shakespeare, William 1, 6, 9, 39, 47, 49, 62, 86, 89–90, 91–2, 120, 122, 141, 142, 152, 163, 177
The Shanghai Story 106–08
Sharif, Omar 154
Shaw, George Bernard 138
Shaw, Glenn Byam 131
Shaw, Irwin 10
Sheaffer, Louis 85
Shelton, Anne 110
Sheppard, William 120
Sheridan, Ann 24, 36, 118
Sheridan, Richard B. 6
Sherman, Vincent 52
Shield for Murder 2, 102–106, 151
Shimoda, Yuki 141
Shirley, Anne 24
Shulman, Irving 54
Siegel, Bugsy 59
Siegel, Don 100, 143
Silver City 75–77, 79, 82
Silvers, Phil 168
Simmons, Jean 102
Sinatra, Frank 126
Sing, Boy, Sing 137
"The Singing Idol" 137
Siodmak, Robert 36, 56
Six Characters in Search of an Author 164
Slaughter Trail 81
Sloane, Everett 174
Smith, Alexis 86
Smith, Kent 83
Socrates 172
Soft Touch 153
Somewhere in the City 50
Son of Frankenstein 22
"The Song of the Barefoot Contessa" 110
Sothern, Ann 162
Sounds of Synanon 163
Spiegel, Sam 154
Spotlight Theater 125
Spotted Horses 146
Stack, Robert 45, 136, 149
The Standard Hour 33
Stanislavsky, Konstantin 152
Stanley, Kim 125, 144
The Star 33
The Star and the Story 125
"The Star-Spangled Banner" 33

The Star Wagon 9
Steiger, Rod 172
Steinbeck, John 135
Steiner, Max 45
Sterling, Jan 129, 130
Stevens, Leith 152
Stevens, Mark 65, 66, 67
Stevens, Stella 151, 153
Stewart, James 155, 157, *157*, 176
Stewart, Paul 169
Stone, Andrew 149
Stone, Virginia 149
Stopover Tokyo 135–37
"Stopwatch Finale" 33
Storm, Gale 65, 67
Storm in the City 86
A Storm of Strangers: The Irish 172
The Story of Louis Pasteur 87
"Stranger in the House" 144
Stranger on the Third Floor 95
Straus, Richard 54
A Streetcar Named Desire 83
Streeter, James 55
The Streets of San Francisco 147
Stripe Playhouse 141
Strode, Woody 148, 149
Sturges, John 45
Sudden Danger 150
"Sugar and Spice and Everything..." 142
Sullivan, Barry 100
Sunset Boulevard 33
Susannah and the Elders 10
Suspense 30
"The Swallow" 168
Sylvia 162
Synanon 163–64
Syracuse University Drama School 166

Talman, William 93, *94*, 95
Tantagos, Alexandros 133
Tarantino, Quentin 167
Target: The Corrupters 144
Tartuffe 138
Tashlin, Frank 135
Task Force 45
Taylor, Don 25, *44*
Taylor, Robert 132
Temper the Wind 54
The Tempest 6
The Ten Commandments 113
Thackeray, William Makepeace 33
Thank Your Lucky Stars 117
Them! 67
There Goes Lona Henry 21
These Many Years 45–46
They Only Kill Their Masters 170
Thinnes, Roy 146
The Third Voice 149–51
Thomas, Lowell 154
Thorne, Chief Hoskie 73
Through the Thin Wall 21

Three Rogues 21
Three Smart Girls 22
Thunderbolt! 45
"A Ticket for Thaddeus" 126–27, 133
"Tide of Darkness" 144
Time 53
The Times (London) 90, 155
Tiomkin, Dimitri 55
To Catch a Thief 147
To Commit a Murder 165
To Have and Have Not 124
To Slay a White Horse 164
Tobias Is an Angel 138
Tobin, the Rev. Dr. Richard H. 4
Todd, Richard 132
Tone, Franchot 17–18
Too Late Blues 154
Too Late for Tears 70
Topkapi 159
Torme, Mel 116, 125
Torvay, Jose 96
Totter, Audrey 46
Tower of London 22
Tower Room 14-A 125
"The Town That Slept with the Lights On" 126
Tracy, Spencer 91
Treacher, Arthur 22
Treasure Island 71
The Treasure of Sierra Madre 96
The Treasure of Sierra Madre (radio) 30
Trevor, Claire 24, 30
A Trip to Scarborough 6
The Tropics 138
Truffaut, François 113, 150
Truman, Pres. Harry S 62
Tryon, Tom 155
Tucker, Forrest 71, 72
Turney, Robert 8
The Turning Point 86–87
Twelve O' Clock High 54
20th Century-Fox 26, 27, 135. 146
Two Loves Have I 98
Two of a Kind 67–69
Tycoon 115

UCLA 85
Une Si Jolie Petite Plage 138
Unexpected Uncle 21
Union Station 56
United Artists 56
U.S. State Dept. 69
Universal Studios 13, 35, 83, 166
The Unsuspected 36
Up Periscope 139
Uprising 133
Urban Playhouse, Yonkers, NY 8
Ustinov, Peter 159

Vaccaro, Brenda 170
Vallee, Rudy 63
Vallve, Rev Arturo 20
Van Druten, John 13–14, 84–85
Van Heusen 118
Variety 64, 108, 164, 173–74
Veiller, Anthony 36
Verne, Jules 69
Videla, Pres. Gabriel G. 62
Vincent, Gene 135
The Virginian 147
The Viscount 165–66
"Voice of the Dummy" 141
Volonte, Gian Maria 172
Volpone 33
Vonnegut, Kurt 172
Voodoo Woman 105

Wagner, Robert 135, 136, 147
Wagner, Trudy 142
Wake Me When It's Over 151
Walker, Doak 42
Wallis, Hal 69
Walsh, Raoul 45
Walsh, Thomas 106
"War of the Worlds" 29
The War of the Worlds 71
War Town 25, 30
Warden, Jack 125
Warner, Jack 52
Warner Bros. 46, 50, 52, 83, 143
Warpath 70–73, 82
Warrick, Ruth 21
Waterfront 131
Waterloo Bridge 132
Waxman, Philip 106
Wayne, John 81, 103, 115, 155, 157
The Wayward Bus 135
The Web 38–39
Webb, Jack 128
Webster, Margaret 6
Welch, Raquel 165
Welcome Danger 17
The Well 56
Welles, Orson 9–10, 13, 29, 35, 146, 169–70
Wells, H.G. 32
West, Adam 141
Westchester Playhouse 5, 9, 10
Westport, Connecticut 5
What's a Nice Girl Like You...? 170
When Worlds Collide 56
White Heat 52–54, 65, 83
Whitman, Stuart 161
Whitty, Dame May 14
Wichard, Al "Cake" 56
Wicked Woman 56
The Wild Bunch 126, 166–68, 173
Wilde, Cornel 14, 105
Wilde, Oscar 6
Wilder, Alan 117
Wilder, Billy 56
Wiley, Sen. Alexander 60

Williams, Tennessee 83, 146
Williford, Ray 122
Wilson, Donald Powell 123
Wilson, Meredith 163
Winged Victory 24–28, 35, 147
Wingreen, Jason 146
The Winston Affair 164
Winters, Shelley 39
The Wizard of Oz 128
WKAT (Miami) 30
A Woman's Face 40
The Wonderful World of Disney 144
Wood, Natalie 132, 133
Woodward, Joanne 125
"The Word" 30

The World Was His Jury 137
Wycherly, Margaret 53
Wyler, William 45, 117
Wynn, Keenan 164
Wynter, Dana 132, 154

"You Forgot to Remember" 171
Young, Collier 123
Young Women's League of America 42
Yours Truly, Johnny Dollar 30–32, 34, 65, 86, 122

Zane Grey Theater 126
Zazie dans le Metro 154

www.ingramcontent.com/pod-product-compliance
Lightning Source LLC
Chambersburg PA
CBHW051219300426

44116CB00006B/639